Self-evaluation in the Global Classroom

Self-evaluation is going global. This book describes what happened when teams of school students from across the world embarked on the trip of a lifetime to explore the school lives of their international contemporaries.

The students involved in *The Learning School* project used a variety of tools to evaluate the learning, motivation and self-evaluation abilities of school students in the UK, Sweden, Japan, Germany, the Czech Republic, South Africa and South Korea. From the easy freedom of the Swedish school to the highly structured day in the Czech Republic, this study shows that success and effectiveness in education really is in the eye of the beholder.

The results of this study have significant implications for school leaders and managers, policy-makers and academics, and all those concerned with school improvement. This lively and accessible book makes intriguing and important reading, raising fundamental questions about how we judge quality and effectiveness in teaching and learning.

John MacBeath is a Professor at the Faculty of Education, University of Cambridge. **Hidenori Sugimine** is a Professor at Nara Women's University, Japan.

Self-evaluation in the Global Classroom

John MacBeath and Hidenori Sugimine

With Gregor Sutherland, Miki Nishimura and the students of The Learning School

RoutledgeFalmer
Taylor & Francis Group

LONDON AND NEW YORK

First published 2003 by RoutledgeFalmer
11 New Fetter Lane, London EC4P 4EE

Simultaneously published in the USA and Canada
by RoutledgeFalmer
29 West 35th Street, New York, NY 10001

RoutledgeFalmer is an imprint of the Taylor & Francis Group

© 2003 John MacBeath and Hidenori Sugimine

Typeset in 10/12pt Goudy by Graphicraft Limited, Hong Kong
Printed and bound in Great Britain by MPG Books Ltd, Bodmin

British Library Cataloguing in Publication Data
A catalogue record for this book is available from the British Library

Library of Congress Cataloging in Publication Data
MacBeath, John E. C.
    Self-evaluation in the global classroom / John MacBeath and
    Hidenori Sugimine ; with Gregor Sutherland, Miki Nishimura, and
    the students of the Learning School.
        p. cm.
    Includes bibliographical references and index.
    1. Educational evaluation—Cross-cultural studies.   2. School
    improvement programs—Cross-cultural studies.   I. Sugimine,
    Hidenori.   II. Title.
    LB2822.75 .M336 2002
    379.1′58—dc21   2002031665

ISBN 0-415-25825-1 (hbk)
ISBN 0-415-25826-X (pbk)

Contents

List of figures

List of tables

Introduction

This book is about a ground-breaking initiative, difficult to capture in linear text, a unique experiment in self-evaluation on a global scale. Known as the Learning School it is a story in which school students take centre stage, as chroniclers of their own learning and of the schools who learned with, and from them. In their own words students describe their change in role from passive recipients in the classroom to active evaluators, creating knowledge for teachers to 'consume'. Each successive chapter expands our knowledge not only of how school learning 'works' but also of how we can get closer to understanding its internal dynamic.

'I have probably learnt as much in these 10 months as I did in 13 years of school,' writes one of the Scottish students while a Swedish student describes opening an intellectual door that had remained closed during her school years:

> One thing that the Learning School did for me and probably for everyone else who has done a similar thing is that it has opened the doors in my mind, and I now believe that I can do anything. The question we all have to ask ourselves is, are we brave enough to jump out there into the unknown not knowing what we might find or would we rather stay on safe ground?

It is a book of its time, written in a period when researchers are turning more and more to the student voice as a source of school improvement. It comes at a time when teachers are ready to listen more closely to what their students have to say. More than at any other time in history teachers are willing to learn from their students, not only in obvious areas such as ICT, where a 7 year old can often be more skilled and knowledgeable than her teacher, but in respect of learning itself. With a proliferating literature on the brain, multiple intelligences and metacognition, teachers have become increasingly aware of how much they still have to learn and what a rich resource their pupils can be in making the learning journey together.

It gives the lie to the recent words of the ex-Chief Inspector of Schools who wrote: 'Teachers teach and children learn. It is as simple as that' (Woodhead, 2002). As anyone close to school practice knows, it is far from that simple.

There is a growing literature on schools as learning organisations and a widening acceptance by practitioners that schools are places in which teachers and headteachers can learn and can model the process of learning. The Newham headteacher whose notepaper describes herself as Cauther Tooley Head Learner sends an important signal about the role of leadership in the twenty-first century.

For the schools in the eight countries visited by the Learning School students – Germany, the Czech Republic, Japan, Hong Kong, Korea, South Africa, Scotland, Sweden – it was not always a comfortable experience to be open to scrutiny by school students and not all teachers viewed the initiative with unbridled enthusiasm. But it is to the schools' credit that they opened their doors, literally and metaphorically, to the students of the Learning School and welcomed them back again for a second or third visit.

It is to them that this book owes a debt of thanks as it was their courage, foresight and hospitality that made this venture possible. And thanks to the students they agreed to release for a sabbatical year, to others of the students who, having left school, availed themselves of a gap year, but a gap only in the sense of time not in terms of their education.

Many people played a part in making this initiative a success – host families in each of the countries who gave so much but also gained much in return. The Learning School students' gratitude to them is warmly acknowledged in Chapter 4. To Hidenori Sugimine who has supported the project throughout its life and to whom all LS students acknowledge a large debt of gratitude for his wisdom and guidance.

A heartfelt personal thank you to Gregor Sutherland and Miki Nishimura who not only guided LS2 so skilfully through its turbulent life but invested many hours in pulling together the data for this book.

Thank you also to the RoutledgeFalmer team, Anna Clarkson, Louise Mellor and copy editor Susan Dunsmore.

Special thanks to the staff and leadership team of Anderson High School for their risk-taking and unconditional support of the project. To Ian Spence, a most unusually adventurous headteacher and to Stewart Hay, a tireless advocate, enthusiast, mediator, trouble-shooter, counsellor, critic and inventor without whom the Learning School would have been but a fantasy too far.

John MacBeath

Part I
The Learning School

1   The story begins

John MacBeath and Stewart Hay

The Learning School

- Teams of school students from five (year 1) to eight (year 3) countries
- Visiting schools in each of those countries
- Spending up to 6 weeks in each school
- Living with host families
- Using tools to evaluate learning, motivation, self-evaluation
- Feeding back results to the teachers and management
- Presenting findings to policy-makers, academics, international conferences
- Three successive cohorts (LS1, LS2, LS3) revisiting schools with new research themes, new challenges

---

Stories come in different shapes. There are stories told objectively by authors, omniscient people who perch above the narrative and give themselves licence to intrude into every private space, even into their character's deepest thoughts and feelings, admitting no ambiguity because they have assumed an unquestioned authority as to what actually happened. Then there are those more modest authors who tell their story from a singular point of view. They can only guess at what is happening in other people's lives and how the narrative will unfold. Then there are books recounted from multiple perspectives, perhaps the most stunning in the genre André Brink's *A Chain of Voices*, in every chapter ambushing the reader into another version of reality, reminding us that every story, every history depends on the narrator.

In David Edmond and John Eidinow's (2001) wonderful account of the historic Cambridge meeting between Wittgenstein and Popper, Wittgenstein's threat to Popper with a poker is pieced together from those who were there – eminent scholars, all of whose testimony to the events is different in significant detail. Perhaps it was the emotionally charged nature of the event that brought so many disparate recollections but the authors leave us not knowing what actually happened or even who was there and who was not.

So it is with the evaluation of schools. How we judge our schools, how we describe events within them depends entirely on who tells the story. Some inspectors may lay claim to an objective truth but, as we know, there are many truths and many different ways of seeing the same event. School self-evaluation at its richest and most profound explores that dangerous territory, seeking out the anomalies and contradictions. As we see in this book, a good lesson, a good teacher, a good learning experience is not some objective entity but dependent on where you sit, what you bring to that judgement, how you frame or construct the situation. So we read accounts of two students in the same class with the same teacher – one engaged, one bored, one seeing the teacher as a source of inspiration, one pursuing her own learning path in spite of the teacher. The freedom of the Swedish school is relished by some while others struggle with the lack of structure and direction around them. In the highly structured Czech school some find their own direction while others are stifled by the lack of opportunity for individual expression.

The Learning School students too, as itinerant evaluators, bring their own histories, cultures, linguistic conventions to their observations in classrooms and in post-lesson interviews. (See pp. 15–26 for a full description of the Learning School Project.) What they see is determined by habits and ways of seeing. What they elicit in interviews is dependent on the questions they ask, their understanding of the answers and their translation of these ideas into their own linguistic register – even when speaking the same language. But their great asset is time – time to go back and verify what they have understood. Their great strength is the dialogue that takes place within the group over time, revisiting and refining their individual and joint learning. And their primary advantage is their status (or lack of it). They are themselves schools students, shadowing other school students, so they are able to get close to the real and very different experiences of life in school.

But they leave us with as many questions as answers. They never lay claim to objectivity or definitive truth. But their own accounts and the accounts of students they observe have a special authenticity because they resonate with our own experiences as students or teachers and with a rich vein of ethnographic literature.

The Learning School has, over three years of its life, constantly re-invented itself and is known within its own restricted code as LS1, LS2, LS3, for its three successive incarnations. Each new group of students, recruited from the participating schools, is able to build on what has gone before so that the Learning School is indeed a learning community with a distributed intelligence and an organisational memory. But year on year those who join have to experience for themselves the immense challenges not only of the research task but of living and working together as a team.

It is almost impossible for a book to capture the vitality and excitement of the Learning School. It is impossible for words to contain the intense frustrations and anxieties that are integral to real and powerful experiences of learning. This is such a unique experiment in school improvement, a story is so rich in all its facets, that we struggle in a book like this to find a beginning. Arundhati Roy tells us that all beginnings are contained in their endings so you might like to start with the personal accounts of students written at the end of their learning journey (Chapter 4). Or begin with the accounts from teachers as to the impact on their schools (Chapter 5). Or the impressions of people who were at presentations by the learning school students – some eminent researchers in their own right, some policy-makers and some teachers (Chapter 6). Or, if you choose to start at the chronological beginning then it is Chapter 2 which describes what the students did on their global itinerary while Chapter 3 describes the range of tools used by the Learning School group to probe beneath the surface of overt behaviour and explore the inner life of learning and motivation. Perhaps we will gather some data on how people do read this book and we will further our understanding of that much abused notion of learning styles.

Part II (Chapter 7 onwards) sets out some of the findings. To provide them all would require an encyclopaedia, so voluminous were the data collected by each successive cohort of students. So, in the editing of these chapters we are only offered glimpses into the lives of school students in six countries but these short extracts are very telling in what they reveal and in what is often concealed from teachers and parents. We learn something of the rhythm of the school day and the rhythms of learning. We see evidence of engagement and disengagement, interest and boredom, anticipation and dread, anxiety and frustration. We are offered insights into rising and diminishing confidence, growth, diminution and fluctuations in self-esteem. We begin to make connections between what teachers do and what students do but discover that the causal relations are not as reciprocal as we might assume. We read of young people living out their own lives in classrooms in which sometimes teachers and peers are a distraction from their learning. We follow them into their home and family lives and discover an equally tenuous relationships between parents and their children. Parental guidance and help are often interpreted by young people as intrusive and irritating. And we discover a corollary too. Some parents see themselves as having little influence because they apparently do nothing but their children testify to a powerful underpinning sense of support. And so it is with teachers who convey implicit messages to their students and which students read with an acute emotional intelligence.

There is so much here that reflects and reinforces studies by researchers who have penetrated the underlife of classrooms, but in these chapters it comes from first-hand accounts of young people who have not yet read those books but may now come to them with a deepened understanding. There are further insights too because this has an international dimension and reminds us how similar and how different school life is the world over. It causes us to question again what school is and what it does. It poses a whole new raft of questions about school effectiveness and the meagreness of the measures we have often brought to that line of inquiry.

It is set in the context of a growing comparative database from the Organisation for Economic Co-operation and Development (OECD), the European Commission and TIMSS (the Third International Mathematics and Science Study) in which countries are ranked in terms of their impact on student learning. A comparison with the recent PISA study (OECD, 2001) is revealing. These students have covered some of the same ground as PISA, in some cases arriving at quite similar conclusions, in others being able to probe deeper beneath the statistical surface of data which, presented in raw form in the PISA tables is difficult to make sense of. Korea is a case in point. It comes out well in PISA's comparative performance rankings but accompanied by some quite baffling data. Why, for example is it one of the countries in which students say they are least in control of their own learning? Why does it do worst of all countries on co-operative learning? Why are Korean students below the international norm on interest in mathematics and reading? Why is Korea so low in its ranking (well below the international norm) on time spent on homework? Why, equally remarkably, is Japan the country with least time on homework of all OECD countries? PISA does not provide us with the answers to these enigmas but we do get much clearer insights from the students of the Learning School who also collected data on homework but went further to observe young people doing their homework, questioning them on their approach and attitude both in the home and classroom context (see Chapter 19 for PISA data on homework).

While the Learning School only visited one school in each country (including Korea) we begin to see things through a different lens, classrooms refracted from the inside, in which the quality of learning is put to a stern test. No claim is made that these schools constitute a representative sample, but nonetheless each does reflect its surrounding culture. In all cases the classroom is but one source of learning and the differences in cultural settings from Japan to Sweden are arresting. In his own testimony, given at the International Congress in Copenhagen, a student from Korea described how, for the first time in his ten years of schooling, he had begun to ask questions, to think, to discuss, to find new frames of reference. By coincidence and happy accident, on the same day a Korean researcher presented a paper on the Korean educational system. Questioning its high standing in the recent PISA 'league table', he argued that it was not the school that added the value to student scores but the extra tuition that students got outside school in a society obsessed with high achievement. He finds that students are often too tired from their extra-curricular efforts to pay attention in class and he produces a statistic which has such clear resonance with the methodology and findings of the Learning School students that it is worth reproducing here. It asks teachers and students the same question. What proportion of students during a typical lesson are paying attention to what is being taught? (see Table 1.1). Teachers and students tend to agree that this is clearly a problematic concern but the differences in their respective judgements parallel closely the findings that appear in this book.

These Korean students, like many identified in the Learning School studies, are highly efficient motivated learners and hence do well in exams, planning and studying and with well developed strategic approaches to achievement but they appear to meet only two of Zimmerman's three criteria of self-regulation: 'Self-regulation refers to the degree that individuals are meta-cognitively,

Table 1.1 The degree of student's attention in classes

Teachers NH(%)	Almost all students devote their attention to the class	About half students devote their attention to the class	A few students devote their attention to the class	No student devotes his attention to the class	Total
	122 (18.3)	321 (48.2)	213 (32.0)	10 (1.5)	666 (100.0)
Students NH(%)	Almost all students devote their attention to the class	Two-thirds of students devote their attention to the class	One-third of students devote their attention to the class	No student devotes his attention to the class	
	97 (8.3)	313 (26.6)	537 (45.7)	228 (19.4)	1175 (100.0)

Source: Yi, Jong-Tae *et al.* (2000, p. 66)

motivationally, and behaviourally active participants in their own learning' (Zimmerman *et al.*, 1994).

As the LS3 researchers found, the meta-cognitive aspect was least well developed and often even virtually absent among secondary school students. Many students, as Chapter 18 tells us, were weak in self-evaluation, too busy learning to consider how they were learning. This was not peculiar to Asian-Pacific countries but true in all schools, even those where teachers expressed a concern for learning how to learn.

While there is, throughout the chapters of this book, a consistently high level of praise for good teachers and good teaching, students are less fulsome when it comes to the quality, pace or exuberance of their learning. In Chapter 4 Learning School students from all participating countries testify to failures of a regime which did not move them beyond their intellectual comfort zones or extend their horizons. All participants write about the skills and understandings that they never acquired in school and some describe in detail the skills they gained working as a team and the accountability that went with it: social, moral and intellectual accountability – to one another, to host families, to schools and to the project on which they had, with some trepidation, embarked. These are some of the skills described:

- challenging your own values and assumptions;
- learning to see things from different perspectives;
- working as a member of a team;
- exercising leadership;
- learning to compromise;
- observing with discrimination;
- working to deadlines;
- taking difficult decisions;

- learning to deal with conflict;
- making presentations to large, and critical, audiences;
- exercising initiative;
- writing for different audiences;
- increasing self-knowledge.

We cannot help being struck by the contrast between how these young people now talk about their learning and the comments made by those whom they interviewed. For the school students, learning is typically described in terms of volumes of notes taken, efficiency in preparation for exams, success in tests. The student researchers, on the other hand, describe months of struggling to get to grips with what motivation and learning really mean and they describe how long it took to come to a new and critical understand of their own learning.

> Before I joined Learning School, motivation was something I never thought of and suddenly I had to find out what made other students want to learn before I knew what made me learn. I spent some time reflecting on myself and today I can say that I came up with things I never thought influenced me at all because I always thought I did things for myself and not for any other reason. Now I am looking forward to going back to school and seeing how much I will reflect on myself in the classroom as well as the teachers and my peers. I hope that now I have enough knowledge about motivation and I am able to motivate myself in all subjects.
>
> (Karolina)

It has been said that fish were the last to discover water and that, sadly, school students are often the last to discover learning. So, in examining data on students' accounts of learning we have always to return to this question of definition and awareness. One of the tantalising paradoxes is that the most satisfied students may be the least aware and least negative in their appraisal while those who have learned most about the nature of their learning may be the most critical. We are still in the foothills of our understanding of learning says Harvard's David Perkins and perhaps the more we ascend, the less sure we are of our foothold. In Guy Claxton's terms – a developing confidence in uncertainty:

> Learning starts from the joint acknowledgement of inadequacy and ignorance . . . There is no other place for learning to start. An effective learner, or learning culture, is one that is not afraid to admit this perception, and also possesses some confidence in its ability to grow in understanding and expertise, so that perplexity is transformed into mastery.
>
> (Claxton, 2000)

The following extract from Colin Bragg's account captures something of the nature of learning, 'a winding and sometimes misty path'. Not at all like the clear objective, the plan and the smooth linear path to its fulfilment.

To think that in at the very beginning of this project we as a group were looking through textbooks in an attempt to understand the word 'Motivation' and now a year down the line a report on the subject of motivation in all of the schools we visited exists. Somehow in amongst the arguments and lengthy debates our determined co-ordinators led us on a winding path, that even they will admit became a little misty, in achieving our objective.

(Colin)

How it came about

The background to and origins of the Learning School, an international year of living and learning together for small groups of students from seven partner schools, are a mixture of serendipity, chaos and planning. The story actually begins in the late 1980s with a project known as the Global Classroom.

During the period 1988–96 seven schools gradually developed a formal global partnership, known as the Global Classroom. There are four European schools in the partnership. They are Anderson High School (AHS) in the Shetland Isles, Bobergsskolan in central Sweden, Graf Friedrich Schule in Diepholz, Germany, and Gymnásium Zlín in the Czech Republic. There are two schools in Asia – Nara Women's University Secondary School in Japan and Shin Ill High School in South Korea and one in Cape Town, South Africa, Harold Cressy High School.

The schools partnership operates in four interconnected ways. First, small groups of senior students agree annually on themes about which they will exchange information, ideas and materials using ICT. A partner school hosts an annual conference attended by all participating students. Second, senior students have the opportunity to take part in extended exchange programmes spending anything from a term to a school year in a partner school, ideally hosted by a family on a reciprocal basis. Third, schools within the partnership share curricula, for example, Anderson High School and Harold Cressy High School teach a common South African History course and Gymnásium Zlín and Anderson High School share curricula for language teaching.

ICT enables regular and constant contact between and among the partnership of schools. During the build-up to the millennium in each of the partner schools there was discussion of ways of marking the millennium within the Global Classroom partnership. An idea that emerged in Anderson High School was to invite students from each of the partner schools to form an International Studies class that would spend the year travelling among all partner schools. Quite what and how the group would study was never fully worked out. The idea of an international student group living and learning together did, however, capture the imagination and interest of all the partner schools.

In each of the schools, students, staff and some parents discussed how within the partnership it might be possible to enable an international group of students to live and learn together for up to a year. E-mails, phone calls, faxes and letters were exchanged. Ideas flowed across the wires thick and fast – most people were enthusiastic and keen while a few were uncertain and dubious about the concept.

Also going on in each of the schools was the continual and constant debate about standards of education and school accountability. In Scotland every school had a large and daunting file entitled 'How Good is Your School?' containing a set of criteria to be measured using Performance Indicators. Connecting this weighty tome and the idea of a small group of students from the partnership of schools learning together was a series of chance coincidences and ideas that caught the creative minds of a few key players in the development of the idea of the Learning School.

Among the first was an Anderson High School student, Jeremy Barnett. A participant in the Global Classroom from its inception in 1997 and one of the students keenly involved in the discussions about establishing an international class, Jeremy asked when leafing through 'How Good is Your School?', how students' views would contribute to answering the question. The answer at the time – autumn 1998 – was certainly hesitant but it prompted much thought and subsequent discussion in Anderson High and in partner schools. The wires were once again hot and a 'virtual conference' took place on possible roles for students in the process of school evaluation.

One key and vital figure in the early discussions on the development of an international education strategy was Mrs Hope Johnston of the then Scottish Office Education Department and the now Scottish Executive. In February 1999 Mrs Johnston hosted a major conference as part of the European Year of Learning at the Scottish Executive's Victoria Quay offices. An invitation was extended to Anderson High, enabling a team of extended exchange students from three of the partner schools in the Czech Republic, Japan and South Africa along with students from AHS to present the Global Classroom. In preparation for this event the team of students from AHS – Jeremy Barnett, Mathew Greenhalgh and Joe Williamson along with Robert Janícek from Zlin in the Czech Republic, Saeko Yoshida from Nara, Japan, and from Cape Town, Warren Reid – all discussed how both as students of schools and also as visitors to partner schools they had ideas, thoughts and contributions to offer about life and learning in schools.

Robert Janícek, a visiting Czech extended exchange student from Gymnásium Zlín to Anderson High School in winter 1999, to a frequently asked question as to why he was attending Anderson High, gave the answer 'I'm learning to learn'. Such an answer of course prompted – after a sigh of 'What?', the inevitable follow-up question. It was a comment that was to spark much interest and was of course to be fed into the ongoing 'virtual debate and conference' among the partner schools on the role of students in the process of school evaluation.

The headteacher of Anderson High School, Ian Spence, and Staff Co-ordinator of the Global Classroom project in Bobergsskolan, Sweden, were the two key figures to pick up on and develop Robert's 'learning to learn' comment. Both saw that the comment went to the heart of what goes on in schools and that much potential could lie in a study in their respective schools of students examining how and how best they learn to learn.

The Principal of Nara Women's University Secondary School, the Japanese partner school, Professor Hidenori Sugimine, from the formation of the Global Classroom partnership, always saw potential for co-operation in educational research between the schools. He found the idea of student contribution to school development and evaluation attractive and the idea of a small team of students from each of the partner schools working together to look at aspects of learning in each of the schools was novel, interesting and with considerable potential. He suggested the possibility of a joint UK/Japanese educational research project on an aspect of learning.

The search for a UK educational researcher likely to be interested in the idea of supporting a UK/Japanese international student research project was the last part in the mixture of serendipity, chaos and planning that was to lead to the Learning School. Also in Scottish schools in the winter of 1999 was the Learning File – an excellent tool for use in examining learning in and out of classrooms. This was the work of a Glasgow-based teacher and researcher Matthew Boyle, and he was someone contacted at the outset in the search for a possible UK educational researcher to join Professor Sugimine in supporting an as yet vaguely defined international student research project of aspects of learning. To the good and grateful luck of all past, present and future participants of what has become the Learning School. Matthew Boyle showed real interest in the idea and, in addition, agreed to discuss the idea with Professor John MacBeath, then Director of the Quality in Education Centre at the University of Strathclyde in Glasgow.

A meeting was arranged with Professor MacBeath, Matthew Boyle and Duane Henry (former student of Anderson High and undergraduate at Stirling University). In the inauspicious setting of a service station near Stirling the possibilities of a team of students who had recently completed their studies in each of the partner schools undertaking a study of aspects of learning was formally discussed. Agreement was reached to meet again within a month, this time with Ian Spence, Headteacher of Anderson High, present.

Some two years ago almost to the day – early March 1999 – a second meeting formulated the structure of an international student research project. With a UK and a Japanese graduate student co-ordinator and a small team of students from each partner school together with support, direction and guidance from both professors, the Learning School project evolved from idea to possibility.

From possibility to reality was to take a further six months. This was a time of searching for funding in each school to support the cost of student travel and insurance. It was also the time of agreeing between and among schools on suitable, appropriate and acceptable times for student research to be undertaken. A time also of agreeing research strategies and procedures and finding time in the summer prior to the beginning of the research for participants to meet and begin 'learning to learn' individually and together.

This process was to continue throughout the year of living and learning together for the members of the first Learning School who began their research at Anderson High in August 1999 and finished with presentation and submission of their findings in a voluminous and detailed report in Nara, Japan, in June 2000. The process continues for members of the second Learning School currently researching in Harold Cressy High School in Cape Town, South Africa.

Teaching and learning in schools all over the globe can be challenging, demanding and taxing. It requires much of educators and learners alike but it offers a great deal to both in return. To educators there is the unique and invaluable opportunity to teach and learn with the people who will shape and form tomorrow's world. For learners there are infinite possibilities to learn with educators within their respective schools and beyond.

Schools have always been dynamic places – the clash of minds, of generations of attitudes and of ideas. Out of the various clashes can come chaos and, in turn, out of chaos can come order. The chaos theory perhaps best explains how a small international group of students have come to travel to seven partner schools studying aspects of learning.

But as Arundhati Roy tells us, all beginnings are contained in their endings and so we will begin with one ending, with the accounts of young people who were in the Learning School, indeed, who *were* the Learning School.

2   What we did

Gregor Sutherland

I hear and I forget. I see and I remember. I do and I understand.

(Confucius)

Where the Learning School began is not easy to pinpoint because it grew out of existing networks and there was no obvious beginning. Most of those who joined had been involved with the global classroom, had attended conferences or been involved in international exchanges and visits. They had the taste for international education and wanted more. Our own involvement with the Learning School began in Nara, Japan, in June 2000 at a Global Classroom Conference where, having been presented with the finding of Learning School 1 we enlisted, with enthusiasm, as co-ordinators of Learning School 2. This is not always how it begins but each year builds on the momentum of the last and by the time Learning School 3 came about, there was no shortage of volunteers.

The very first thing that happens usually with the Learning School, its real beginning, is when groups of students begin to come together from different points around the globe, assembling in Anderson High School in the dog end days of summer.

Forming groups

Some of the first thoughts which go into each Learning School project are about the members who will make up the team. One or two senior or former students are chosen by each of the participant schools to become Learning School researchers for the period of ten months. Each school has its own selection system and criteria for applicants to meet. Some schools pick their representatives on the basis of academic and linguistic ability. Other schools have very few criteria and choose students who are keen. Sometimes the criteria also includes social and personal skills. Will they be a good team player? Are they responsible enough?

Once chosen, the members are invited to make contact with each other. E-mail addresses are shared and soon the members who are going to spend so long together are getting to know each other. Sometimes, the members already know each other as they may have met while taking part in an exchange, or at one of the annual Global Classroom conferences.

For most, the first time they meet their new colleagues face to face is in August when each Learning School project begins. In the first two years of the project there was only one group, but as the project grew and more schools wanted to participate, two groups had to be created. Nevertheless, the first meetings are an interesting and exciting, but also apprehensive, time. Imagine how it must feel for them: beginning in a perhaps strange and foreign country and with people who are almost entirely unknown and also strange. It can be a difficult time which is not always full of pleasure as the members struggle to adjust to new cultures, come to terms with homesickness and having to talk in a different language virtually all of the time. It can take some time for members to feel comfortable and happy in their new social and professional surroundings.

Learning how to communicate and work as a group which is so diverse is a major challenge that each Learning School project must try to overcome. Over time, perhaps as long as the life of the project, the participant students must learn cultural and personal respect.

Planning and research design

According to logic, planning should one of the first things to be done. However, planning the detail of the project and the research design is largely left until after the members have met and formed some kind of comfortable group-ness. While the Learning School project pursues quality in the research which it conducts, input from outsiders and supervising academics is kept to a modest and directive minimum. It is the intention that the LS project be understood by the members and that they develop the research in the ways they think best and most appropriate. Of course, they are advised and supported when needed. The only aspect which is cast in stone before the researchers come together is the topic which will be investigated. There is no real reason why the topic should be fixed beforehand, it might be equally as beneficial to allow the members themselves to decide on what is worthy of examination. Nevertheless, that is the way it has been done so far.

So what do the groups plan and design? Well . . . after getting to know each other a little, the next task is to get to grips with the actual research they will do. The most immediate priority is to try to understand the nature of the issue to be investigated. What are the research aims or specific questions? Does every-one understand them? Do they mean the same for each member? A long time and a lot of effort have to go into ensuring that the group have some kind of working understanding of their goals in the research and become familiar with any concepts or terms which are integral to the project. This can take a long time and, as we have seen in successive LS projects, may not occur until the end of the year.

Brainstorming was one of our favourite strategies for coming up with ideas and possible avenues for investigation. Sometimes we became completely carried away and would spend ages in front of the blackboard in room C3.1 letting our ideas flow. We always thought they were great and that those times were so creative and beneficial, but, a couple of hours later, when we had all come down a bit, we would realise there was another way we could have thought about things, or that some of the ideas we had come up with were a bit flawed. So, back to the blackboard to modify or develop the ideas we had earlier thought were so good. The development of strategies to conceptualise and understand the themes we were asked to explore and research, and the creation of tools for gathering data was often done in this cyclical and evolutionary way. It could be very exciting and organic, but when the ideas just kept coming but not crystallising, we would become a bit frustrated that there was not enough research being done, and that too much time was being spent on thinking and discussing.

This was particularly the opinion of the teacher who was the liaison link with the school. He was anxious that there was not enough action and that we were wasting valuable research time by engaging in so much thinking and brainstorming. I suppose he felt that the members needed to be seen getting on with things and using their positive inquiring presence to better effect in carrying forward their research in the school. But for us it was difficult without being clear about our understandings of the theme and how to go about gathering good quality data in a way that was acceptable for teachers, students and parents.

Although a lot of ideas came from within the group, and from their own individual understandings and interpretation of issues, other sources were referred to. Sometimes a member would spend an hour or two looking for useful information on the Internet, or in books and journals. If all else failed, a phone call or an e-mail to one of the academic advisors was always very helpful and inspiring. We always tried to do it by ourselves first though. If you don't do that, the quality of the experience changes completely; a sense of ownership is lost and motivation can be compromised.

For a full description of the tools which successive Learning School projects have used over the past three years, see Chapter 3.

Getting to know the schools

While we were planning the tools we would use and how our programmes of investigation would unfold, we were forced to think about and accommodate the differences between schools and what could be possible and what might cause difficulties or simply be impossible to realise.

We were already getting to know the Scottish school. I had studied there myself, as had the two Scottish researchers in the group. Furthermore, one of the Czech members of the group had spent the last school year on extended exchange to the school in Scotland. Most of us were quite familiar with the field already. The rest of our group had to learn about the school so we took them on guided tours at first. We took them through all the buildings which housed various departments joined by corridors. We also had to explain each year group in the six year school was designated a corridor or an area in the school, and that we had to become familiar with the fifth year area where our 16-year-old research objects could be found, lost and hopefully rediscovered.

During those early days in the Scottish school we began to plan our research and to think of the subject areas we could focus on and perhaps compare. The Scottish school offered a complete spectrum of subjects, but not all were compulsory. Only English and Maths were required, but even then, they could be taken at various levels.

The discussions that took place in the group during these introductory tours fed into our planning, beginning to highlight some of the differences we were going to have to deal with, some of the rethinking we would have to do in different contexts, and gradually revealing more and more about the schools we were about to visit in the coming year.

Karolina from Sweden told us about her school system and how we would have to adapt some things and take into consideration certain factors and features of the school and the community we would all too soon be joining. She spoke of how small the school was, and how it was made up of three year groups. For some of us, the notion of a three year senior high school was unfamiliar. Where in the Scottish school the 16 year olds we were focusing on were among the oldest members of the school, their contemporaries in Sweden were the youngest in their school.

Karolina went on to explain how the Swedish school system worked. Karolina's early attempts to familiarise us with the Swedish education system were bolstered by one of the teachers in Sweden. On our first day at school, a teacher took the Learning School team aside to be educated about Swedish education. Both Karolina and the teacher did very well. They explained that students could select certain programmes according to their interests, so they developed quite individualised academic profiles. They also pointed out some programmes were more technical and vocational in their content while others were more traditionally academic but with biases to social sciences or natural sciences. Some people who didn't think they could fit into any of these programmes were allowed to select courses and modules to build their own tailor-made profile. From those early descriptions of the Swedish school, we were already struck by how flexible, and innovative the Swedish system was, and the extent to which responsibility was devolved to the student.

The next school we would visit would be quite different again. The Czech school was an altogether much more traditional school, a highly academic *Gymnasium*. Where the previous schools were comprehensive, the Czech school was selective and entry to the school was by academic performance and ability. A full range of academic subjects was offered, but very little in the way of the technical and vocational curriculum that the Scottish and Swedish schools included. Stepan and Honza told us about the entrance examinations they had taken to get into the school. Some of us who were unfamiliar with the Czech school were quite amazed when they told us that many students take entrance exams at the age of ten. Others joined the school at the age of fourteen. We wondered, were they more prepared for the rigour of the academic *Gymnasium* at that age, or were those who came into the setting earlier at advantage? This led us to think that we might compare the results of those two intakes. We also got some information about the school from the research and reports that Learning School 1 had conducted and produced. We were looking forward to the possibility of interesting results and comparisons between the comprehensive and selective school systems.

The German school was similar. We were told by our German colleague how her school was also a *Gymnasium* and that like the Czech school the curriculum was academic and a large percentage of the graduands would go on to higher education. Even at an early stage we were quite excited about what the results would show, and we wondered about how the importance of motivational factors might correspond to these differences in system and educational culture.

The next school on our agenda was the South African one. Hemispheric seasonal inversion meant that our South African member only joined the group in the early stages of our research in Sweden. This was about two months after the rest of the group had met and begun the project. Hyden was duly inducted into the research and was soon making important contributions and giving us valuable insights into the South African experience of education. Unfortunately we had to prepare ourselves for a few problems as we began to realise that the programme of research we had developed might not be easy to replicate in South Africa. We had chosen to look at motivation in a range of subject areas, and many of them were not represented in his former school.

Our final research field was Japan. Most of Learning School 2 had attended the Global Classroom conference that had been hosted by the Japanese school the previous year, so we were quite familiar with the school and the system. The Japanese member school is an interesting and experimental school which is attached to a local university. Kazuyo had been a recent student at the school, and she explained how it was a six-year, combined junior and senior high school, that it was quite prestigious and that getting a place at the school could be very competitive. Our research in Japan was hosted by the university rather than the school itself. We therefore had to hope that the plans we were making would be acceptable to the school.

Although we shared a lot of information about the schools we would visit from an early stage, and incorporated this into our research design and planning, we were not quite prepared for some of their features and the challenges they would present us with. We were just settling into the starting time of 8.55 a.m. in Scotland when we had to adjust to getting up at what seemed like the middle of the night to be at school for before 8.00 a.m. in Sweden. The situation worsened when we arrived in the Czech Republic where a whole lesson would be taught and finished by that time in the morning. This was the tip of the vast iceberg of different experiences we had in schools.

Going about our business

Once tools were established, and we were reasonably happy about their trans-ferability across the partnership of schools, the process of actually going about gathering information began. We went from the challenge and excitement of creating the tools to apprehensively using them. Before any tool could be used, however, we had to discuss our intentions with staff and negotiate the kind of access we would require. The kind of access and intrusion caused by our research depended on the type of tool we were using.

Sometimes we had to ask for 20 minutes of class attention for the pupils to complete questionnaires. These were the most overt intrusions into classes and relied on the good-will of many teachers. Other types of data gathering methods, by their nature, were obtrusive in a very different way. By shadowing or observing classes, we did not seek to interrupt, but to try to capture information through watching or experiencing classes which were as 'normal' as possible.

How did the presence of researchers affect the classes they went into? Some teachers said they had never taught so badly, and even missed out sections of the curriculum because they were so nervous during an observed lesson. Other teachers were much less affected, and invited the researchers back to observe at any time. No teachers were forced to accept us into their classes, but that is not to say that we were welcomed by all teachers. A small minority of teachers did not allow Learning School access to their classrooms.

I think the experience was quite different for the students who were in the classes which LS researchers sat in on. The LS researchers were of a similar age to those they were watching, and shadowing. They were not threatening; they were peers and shared similar interests and perspectives despite differences of nationality and language. Formal inspection is generally dreaded by schools, teachers and perhaps even students, but LS researchers do not cause that kind of intimidation. Perhaps this is because they are not 'experts', in the professional sense, and their findings and work may not be trusted anyway. Maybe it is because there is a sense that Learning School research can be controlled, that it isn't 'high stakes', and produces no report available for public scrutiny.

Writing up

Gathering data tends to be the fairly straightforward process. It is relatively easy to collect and generate huge amounts of information, especially from teams so large and eyes and ears so perceptive and sharp. How to transform all that information into a document or report has always been a challenging issue for the Learning School members, and will remain so, as long as the participants are inexperienced researchers. It is also during the process of analysing data and writing up research that new questions arise, weaknesses can be seen and areas for improvement are identified. Sometimes, in the midst of a week intended for writing up a final report for a school, members find themselves around the table thrashing out new ideas about how to gather better information more effectively and how to analyse it more usefully and efficiently.

Presentations

Presentations serve two purposes. First, and mainly for schools, they are a vehicle for feeding back the results of the research into the participating schools. Second, presentations are also a means of promoting, sharing and informing others about the philosophy and goals of the Learning School.

School presentations are typically an hour in length and are held just before the departure of the Learning School group and are not exclusively for staff. Parents and students are also invited to attend. Learning School groups have also given presentations to universities (Nara Women's University, the University of Cambridge, the University of Cape Town and UMEA in Sweden); government departments (the Scottish Executive Education Department, the Hong Kong Department of Education) and at international conferences (International Congress for School Effectiveness and Improvement 2002). Some presentations which the Learning School have given have been to mixed audiences, for example, school staff, local and regional government staff and interested academics. This was the case in South Africa in 2001.

For almost all Learning School projects the essential ingredients of a presentation remain the same and generally adhere to a traditional reporting framework. Each presentation usually begins with an introduction, which may include some background information about the project, the current topic being researched, and the research aims. Following this, there is usually a presentation of the methodology and the tools for gathering data. Finally, the actual findings are presented and any conclusions drawn.

Some audiences are more interested in the details of the findings and not the overall concept or the background to the project. These audiences are typically the teachers in the Global Classroom partnership: they are already familiar with the concept and have perhaps been involved in the project by contributing ideas or in the data gathering process. Their interests lie in what has been discovered – the specifics, in detail. For many others who come along to a Learning School presentation, the exact findings are only important in that they illustrate the effectiveness of the concept. For those (typically academics and civil servants), the whole project is under scrutiny. Learning School members have tried to appreciate the different perspectives which various audiences can have, and try to achieve a desirable balance between conceptual and methodological information, and results.

Going between countries: the travel

Being an international project, there is a lot of ground to cover between countries and schools. For financial reasons, the year of research is split into European and global components. All research is completed in Europe before the groups head off to the far-flung corners of the globe. Learning School groups 1 and 2 had similar travel itineraries, but because of the enlargement of the project in its third year, Learning School 3 did things a bit differently.

Learning School Travelogues

LS1

We began research in the Scottish school in August 1999. Our second school was in Sweden. We arrived there in October, just as things were beginning to get cold. The journey was by plane. After Sweden we went on to the final European school in our research – the Czech school. That trip was done by plane and train. We went back to Scotland to do some catch-up research and to prepare for a presentation at the Scottish Executive in Edinburgh. Straight after that, we went to South Africa. After our research there we had a break and spent a few weeks on our Easter break. We made our way to the next school (in Japan) by air, touching down and enjoying visits in Australia, New Zealand and even Fiji. After Japan and the Global Classroom Conference 2000, we all flew back to the UK where we said goodbye to each other.

LS2

We started our research like LS1, in Scotland in August. We then went on to the Swedish school, followed by the Czech School and the new European participant school in Germany. We spent a bit longer in the Scottish school while we planned and devised our research. We were there for about seven weeks, while we spent about four or five weeks in the rest of the schools. In LS2 we squeezed another school into the itinerary, Germany, which meant that we were just settling in at each school and family when we had to move on again. That made the year very exciting but at times quite tiring.

Like LS1 we had to go back to Scotland in February to do some additional research, but this coincided with another presentation at the Scottish Executive and our departure to South Africa. After our busy schedule of visiting four European schools and one African school we were really glad to have a break from the research and have the opportunity to spend time in Australia and New Zealand on the way to Japan over Easter. After Japan, we went to Korea, to visit a prospective Asian partner school. On the way back to the UK we stopped in Hong Kong and gave a presentation to the Education Department. We gravitated back to Scotland and spent time there writing up our findings before heading back to Germany to participate in the 2001 Global Classroom conference. After Germany we gave a presentation at Cambridge University. Then it was time to say goodbye to those who were heading off to their home countries far away but we spent a couple of days in London together before the final and eventual split. It was an emotional time.

LS3 – *ongoing* . . .

We are divided into two groups because there are more schools to visit this year. One group began researching in Scotland while the other started in the Czech Republic. We moved on to Sweden and Germany respectively, then gave our presentation to the Scottish Executive in early February as a whole project. After spending a few days together as a huge group in Edinburgh we split again and headed off for warmer climes. The group that had been in Scotland and Sweden went on to South Africa while the other group has gone to Hong Kong. Soon we will meet up in New Zealand to enjoy the break in our research schedule together. When we are suitably relaxed and re-energised we will get back to the research and the Hong Kong group will go to South Korea while the other group heads for Japan. We are all going to meet up again soon after, as we are scheduled to spend some time together in Japan to analyse our findings collectively and with the help of local professors. When all that is done, it will be June and time to make final presentations of our work before we all head off to our respective home countries after ten months of living and learning together internationally.

Life in a suitcase

People are at their worst when they are carrying a suitcase that is too heavy for them. Several members, from all Learning School groups will know what I am talking about. There is nothing worse than having to struggle with luggage while trying to get from A to B, perhaps catching a bus or a busy train. We all had far too much luggage. It was as simple as that. We had huge suitcases, backpacks and cases protecting our laptops and it was just too much. Sometimes luggage was lost, never to be seen again. On other journeys our luggage was damaged or delayed, but at least we got it back. Sometimes, the damage was our own fault. As we rushed on and off buses and trains and dragged our cases through airports, stations and cities all around the world it was inevitable that they would begin to disintegrate.

I think the strain of coping with all that luggage was only part of the reason those times of travelling could be so trying and bring out the worst in people. Every time we were travelling we were leaving a country, a family and new friends that we had grown very fond of and close to. Of course we would be more upset and irritable than usual for a while, until we began to settle in at our next port of call. Add to that, the 30 kg suitcase and a flight of stairs at a bus station and it was no wonder the tears began to well.

I always found that the times when travelling became pleasant and enjoyable were when we were all aboard, whether it be train, plane, bus or ferry (yes we used them all, several times). When everyone is in their seat and safe in the knowledge that their luggage is stowed somewhere and is coming along too, then the relaxation can begin. We became a group again, just us and all around us strangers. Those were the times we bonded and shared a real sense of being part of a special group.

Host families

In each country visited, the members of the Learning School team are hosted by the families of students who attend the school being visited. Sometimes the host students no longer attend the school, but have perhaps been involved in exchanges before and would like to get involved again. Without the support of numerous families in this way, the Learning School project would not have even begun. Thankfully hosting is a reciprocal pleasure. The Learning School members who are hosted obviously have an incredible experience of home life in the country they are visiting. Such an insightful and privileged experience creates treasured memories and a first-hand experience and understanding of daily family life in the country and culture. The benefits are not all one-sided though, as the host families can have a valuable experience from interacting with the member they host. They may learn about the culture of their guest, or practise using another language.

Members have grown to actually feel like a part of the family they are staying with. In some cases, they have become so familiar and at home that their hosts treat them as anything but a guest. When a Japanese student had to leave her hosts in South Africa, there were floods of tears despite the fact that this was at last the 'graduation of the tea-slave'. Another member, staying with a Swedish host family was lovingly referred to as 'the butler'. Of course LS members can never feel like a real son or daughter, but it is certainly the case that very special and meaningful relationships have been built up through hosting experiences.

Hosting is not always an easy experience, for either party. Sometimes cultural and linguistic differences are hard to overcome. Hosts are keen to treat their guests very well and put a lot of effort into making their stay comfortable. LS members also have to adapt to their new families and their daily customs and perhaps cultural and religious traditions. Even if things are tricky for a while, and lots of egg shells are being trod on, the whole hosting experience is generally an enjoyable one for everyone concerned.

Extra curriculum

It will come as no surprise to you that there are plenty of additional experiences that go hand in hand with the Learning School adventure. No year of living and learning internationally could be anything less than exciting, stimulating and full of challenges and opportunities. While conducting research, the members of the group went about their work and tasks with considerable professionalism. Of course, we spent lots of time together outside the realm of research, although it is hard to tell where research ended and social and personal lives began. The two were often inextricably entwined. Having said that, there were a few occasions when the research agenda was almost entirely set aside to devote time to holidays. At those times, the group were no longer a team of diverse professionals working on a project, they became purely friends as they spent days and nights revelling in the activities and fun the holiday times afforded. So what did the groups and their members get up to on those brief breaks away from the research?

The groups certainly embraced their new-found travelling spirit and often took off on adventures at weekends and between visiting countries. If there was a spare weekend in Sweden all would board a train and spend it in Stockholm, or when in Germany, a weekend excursion to Berlin. Perhaps by staying with friends, or in a youth hostel, the group could spend a few days at modest cost in some of the most exciting cities of the world.

Members have taken advantage of already being on the road and spent holiday times in different or unusual places. Learning School 1 and 2 members took the decision to spend the New Year celebrations in Prague, with fantastic sightseeing, concerts, fireworks and night life. Learning School 3 members took a different approach to marking the occasion by holing themselves up with host families and friends in chilly rural Sweden. These 'different' New Year arrangements are partly brought about by necessity (because some members are thousands of miles from home) and partly because of the freedom which members now feel to break away from the traditional ways of spending a Christmas or New Year holiday.

There has usually been a break in the research itinerary in late March/early April. In Learning School 1 and 2 this has coincided with the journey onward from South Africa to Japan. Needless to say, members took the opportunity to plan the stop over destinations which their round-the-world tickets permitted, with some care. Sometimes plans were altered, just to be modified as another Australasian Pacific adventure opportunity became apparent. These three-week breaks were planned with a real spirit of 'the world's my oyster'.

For the record, Learning School 1 members spent time in Sydney, then split to go on to New Zealand to tour the South Island or to take in the Fijian Islands. Of course, some had appetites that were entirely insatiable, and did all three, before arriving at Osaka's Kansai Airport to begin their final round of research. In similar style, Learning School 2 spent time in Sydney before hopping across the Tasman Sea to take in the sights, sounds and adventures of New Zealand's South Island. The South Island has been a hit with both Learning School groups as it seems to perfectly accommodate the adventurous spirit which the members have accrued during the months of LS life. A considerable 'bungee' tally is accumulating. Quite what Learning School 3 will get up to in this slot in the itinerary remains uncertain, but I expect it will be no less daring.

What didn't we do?

Some have asked that question. The answer is not much really. There was certainly little extra that could have possibly been squeezed into those months. The year was so packed with experiences and doing – and learning. It was a challenging year, and perhaps not everyone is suited to this kind of adventure, it might take an especially adventurous and outgoing kind of young person to embark on a year with the Learning School. The challenges of living in different countries, cultures and with different families are significant enough without the added and considerable task of conducting an ambitious research project at the same time. However, for those who have done it, I am sure they do not regret it. In Chapter 4, they speak for themselves.

3 Tools for schools

Gregor Sutherland and Miki Nishimura

Introduction

The Learning School project now has at its disposal a number of tools which have been tried, tested, modified and re-tried for the purpose of gathering the rich and informative data upon which the findings of its research are founded. Broadly speaking, the kit contains two types of tool: those which are more often used to find out how much or to what extent something happens, and those which are used to try to understand *how* something happens. More technically, these two types of instrument can be thought of as quantitative and qualitative respectfully. The Learning School students, coming fresh to research, were not on familiar terms with the great dilemmas of educational research, with the ontological and epistemological questions which academics worry over, but that is not to say that successive groups ignored such issues. Lots of time went into discussions of the appropriateness of certain tools for different purposes, gathering information about certain events or phenomena, and what the nature of those might be in the first place.

This chapter serves as an overview of the tool kit. Each Learning School project has a rummage around in the bag at the start of the year, pulls out a few interesting things, to wonder how they might be useful and consider how they could be modified to help in their own research. Sometimes the rummage is a stimulus for creating a new tool which is then a hybrid of a couple of others. Great fun can be had hauling out old questionnaires, evaluating their strengths and weaknesses, or even criticising them for their want of insightful interrogatory questions or their simple lack of visual appeal or user friendliness. While it might be really enjoyable and exciting to plan for the incorporation of, for example, sophisticated video footage of classes and online questionnaires into a piece of research, groups have all the time to bear in mind the *fitness for purpose* of tools, and the practical implications that the use of certain tools can present.

Learning School groups, just like professional researchers rarely get it right first time. Inevitably, there is a process of reflecting on the tools it has created after their initial use. Sometimes questionnaires are modified or even scrapped, or new observation schedules are drawn up to consider and record data previously not thought of as important to the research. Drastic changes are made early in the research, but minor modifications occur throughout as the researchers continually reflect on the use of tools, so that over time, they are well developed and are used by researchers with skill and precision.

The kit

What follows is a description of the tools the Learning School has used in the past three years of research. We will not explain every tool as used in each project as that would be time-consuming and tedious. Instead, we hope you will get a general feel for the tools and, where they are interesting, the more specific uses they have had.

Questionnaires

We have chosen to describe questionnaires first. Do not read too much into that. Perhaps this decision is chronologically inspired; questionnaires are perhaps the oldest tool in our kit bag, and, certainly in our experience, it was the first tool we grasped and began to fashion to our own requirements. The research group we were involved with also used the questionnaire as a general scene-setter and introduction aid. When the business of research was over, we always presented the results from our questionnaires before that of any other tool. The rationale for that was to move from the general to the specific. Thus, it seems entirely appropriate that we continue to put questionnaires first for no other good reason than those mentioned above.

To date, all Learning School projects have elected to use one or more questionnaires in their research, and with the exception of one questionnaire, they have been used to gather quantitative data. Although not particularly inspired, questionnaires are useful and important tools for the Learning School for several reasons. First, they can be translated in advance and e-mailed to the next school on the itinerary in plenty of time for the school to give it the once over, approve it (no school has rejected a questionnaire as yet), and make copies. Added to this, questionnaires can be quickly administered and returned, provided that a few teachers are willing to devote the necessary time for their completion during classes. Second, as we have mentioned, questionnaires have mainly been used in such a way that they generate statistical data, which are intended to transcend language differences, although in an international context translation presents a major challenge. However dull it might seem, for some, a few hours at a computer inputting and manipulating numbers can be a welcome respite from the intensive listening and communicating in second or even third languages. The beauty of numbers is that there is no reason for anyone to be excluded, or at least disadvantaged, on the grounds of linguistic ability, which much of the rest of the Learning School's research does rely on.

Each questionnaire has to be very carefully translated into the native language of those who are being asked to complete it. This goes some way to ensure that in every country and school, students have the same opportunity to respond fully, honestly, naturally and confidently. Although most students who fill out Learning School questionnaires are fairly competent users of the English language (and perhaps others), by giving it to them in their native language we hope this gives all students the chance to understand the questions more fully and completely and to respond more accurately and confidently. The more we can find a common technical language, the more reliability is increased.

It is worth stressing how important the quality of the translation actually is. We often faced the problem of not being able to literally translate our words from English into Japanese, for example. Sometimes there just isn't a comparable word in another language for an important term like 'motivation', for example. We tried to overcome this difficulty by turning to our own research members, who, with increasing insight into the themes and issues being explored, and their inside understanding of the research and the issues we wanted to gather data about, could cleverly translate without distorting the meaning. Although we could not be certain, we did suspect that had translations been done by those outside the group, ambiguities and distortion could have crept in.

While we have argued that questionnaires are quick and easy to administer and collect, the process of translating the answers to any open response questions back into English can be very time-consuming. Nevertheless, it has to be done with the same attention to detail that we have described above. Where there was any ambiguity about a person's response and what the translation should be, we either tried to track down the respondent to ask them about their answer, or to discuss the response with a few collected helpers with good language skills. To this day we remain fairly confident about the reliability of our translations. Of course, there are ways of avoiding this scenario entirely: don't ask open-ended questions or at least those to which the answer may be ambiguous!

As we have said, we were always given permission to use class time to distribute our questionnaires and for students to complete them. This went a long way to ensuring that we had a good response rate. It was also a good opportunity to introduce ourselves as school-invaders to the students we wanted to make friends with and gain so much insight and information from. By being present, but not threateningly or intimidatingly, we hope the students felt that the questionnaires were a bit more real and that if they did have some questions about it, we were on hand to explain, or allay their fears about confidentiality or the prospect of their information falling into the hands of teachers.

The research of each Learning School project is always focused on a specific year group. Questionnaires are therefore given to every member of that year. As some schools are bigger than others, the number of students in any year varies, typically from around 80 in the smaller schools to about 200 in the larger ones. These sample sizes are obviously quite different and restrict the comparability. However, in order to be able to compare data across the range of schools, samples of the same size were extracted at random from each school's complete data set. Those results and comparisons can be found in subsequent chapters in Part II.

One Learning School group employed a qualitative questionnaire in order to find out about how parents influenced their children's learning and motivation. Conducting semi-structured interviews may have been more appropriate, but for reasons to do with time and convenience semi-structured questionnaires were sent out to a small sample of parents, whose sons and daughters were participating in case study aspects of the research. We were very pleased with the response we had to those questionnaires, given that they required more thought, or at the very least, more writing than 'tick box' questionnaires. Of course, the same rules and procedures regarding translation mentioned above applied here as well, perhaps even more strictly, given the complex nature of the qualitative responses we sought and received and the likelihood that parents were less linguistically capable than their sons and daughters.

Interviews

It is impossible to stress too highly just how important interviews have been to the research process of the Learning School. We can watch classes, shadow students and send out questionnaires, but there is little as powerful and insightful as getting at the feelings and understandings that students have about their learning.

Not all interviews are the same. They range from those where the researcher has specific questions to ask and wants certain answers, to the kind of completely informal interview which in actual fact is more like a conversation between friends. Some of the more structured interviews are informed by certain events and issues that the researcher has seen, perhaps during a period of observation or shadowing. They make take an hour or so at the end of the day for the researcher to ask about all the things he or she noted down throughout the day which sparked his or her curiosity.

If a student is being shadowed by a researcher for a longer period of time, a relationship builds up between them and the free time they have between lessons can be useful to quickly ask a few questions about the lesson, the way they feel, or how they think they did in that class, or what they got from the lesson, or what could have been better for them? Sometimes, we even asked what made them act in the way they did in a particular lesson. The reasons they gave were often very illuminating and there is no doubt that using the time they had together and the peer-like relationship they had were effective ways of getting information and finding out about learning.

One of our members developed a style of interviewing which was particularly suited to the topic she was investigating. The researcher had to find out about the things that made you do things. In other words – motivation, or the lack of it. As you can imagine, this kind of psychological investigation was not easy. Many students had never even thought about the factors that influenced what they did – they just happened and were occurred unconsciously. So for many, our research was the first time they had been asked to consider these issues, so getting information and forming understandings were exceptionally difficult, especially when the researchers themselves were relatively new to the idea as well. Therefore, our researcher developed a very subtle and inquiring style during her conversational interviews and discussions throughout the shadowing process. If the student she was following couldn't come up with explanations, she didn't simply leave an empty space in her note book, she just thought of other ways, alternative avenues, to get to that blank spot and fill it up. She was persistent, but not overtly or in a way that the pupil being researched felt uncomfortable.

Interviews were also used to gain information from teachers, headteachers and other members of the community such as representatives from business and further education.

Interviews were usually conducted in one-on-one situations, and typically at the end of a day. For several reasons, interviews were not recorded. First, there were not always tape recorders available to use. With a team of up to eight researchers interviewing at the same time, we would have required several recorders and lots of batteries and tapes. While this may have been an ideal situation we were by no means stuck. We tried to note the important points during the interviews, and when they were over, write them up more fully perhaps incorporating the information into a report about the whole day or the whole week spent with a particular student.

We had to pay particular attention once more to language in our interviews. Perhaps the language problem was not quite as crucial for the interviews as it was for the questionnaires, because of the opportunity to rephrase or reword questions and explain the meaning and intention behind questions during interviews. However, in some countries where there was a particular language barrier we found it advantageous to find and use translators. This made the interview process more difficult and time-consuming but we accepted the necessity for translation if our data were going to be reliable.

Observation

Observation has been used in two of the three projects to date. This tool is all about the using the eyes. It is not unusual for people to join classes and to sit in on the learning experience, but what is a bit different is for these people to be students, the peers of those they are watching. Usually those who come to observe classes are line managers, department or faculty heads, or local or national inspectors. Being observed by the latter group can be quite uncomfortable and a disconcerting experience for teachers and perhaps the pupils too. Pupil observers can be a different matter. The class is usually full of young people anyway, another one or two doesn't really hurt, or that is the theory. Their focus, their reason for being there is slightly different to those they sit among. They are not trying to understand the subject and the topics that are being explored, taught and learned. Their focus is to observe specific aspects of that process.

Observation can be carried out in different ways. One Learning School group observed classes in general, while another group homed in on individuals, seeking to explore their very unique experience of the lesson. The choice of style depends entirely on the nature of the issue being investigated and whether the aims of the research are best realised through whole class or individual observation.

Learning School researchers are often asked 'How can you get any meaningful understanding of lessons when you cannot understand the language and what is being said?' It is surprising just how much can be understood from just using the eyes. Their power is sharpened and enhanced by being unable to picking up oral messages and signals. Furthermore, perhaps the use of the eyes alone gives a purer and more understandable picture. Do the visual and oral messages and signals mutually reinforce or conflict? Is there too much going on in a classroom for an observer to be able to absorb and make some sense of both visual and oral signals? By only using the eyes, and concentrating on harnessing their power, the researcher becomes quite skilled at picking up on the physical behaviour or body language of the individual or group he or she is observing, or perhaps the different types and frequencies of interactions and changes of task.

From time to time, it is useful to find out the nature of a particular conversation, but that can be done by asking about it at the end of the lesson. The pupils that are being researched are usually quite happy to explain any of the details of content that the researcher cannot pick up on. They do so honestly as well. If a conversation they were having with their neighbour was about TV or what they will do at the weekend, they will usually say so. Because the Learning School members are young people themselves, non-threatening and without the power or authority (or role for that matter) of teachers, there is no fear of admitting they do certain things that are inappropriate or that their teachers might not approve of.

To assist observers in their task they are normally simply equipped with an observation schedule and a pencil. While observation schedules can look entirely different because of the nature of the issue that is being explored, Learning School has used fairly similar pro formas. The types of information we have sought to gather have been about teaching and learning styles, and we code them to make them easier to note down as they occur and change during a lesson. We have also noted the behaviour of certain individuals chosen and asked if they would like to be involved in the research project. Sometimes we have tried to understand the ways in which whole classes behave and respond to certain conditions and events and things that the teacher does. In the observation schedule these notes are broken down into thematic constituent parts and completed chronologically. After the lesson, the observer might grab just enough time to ask the pupil being watched a few questions, then the researcher can return to base camp to write up the information in a short report on that particular observation which includes the significant features and particular pieces of evidence that were gathered.

For some, the observation process is daunting. More often than not, the students are more comfortable with the experience than their teachers. After a few minutes of glancing over at their friendly *rapporteur* at the start of the lesson, to check and see if they are actually writing anything down about them, they begin to settle into back into their lessons and what is going on around them. Within minutes, the observer has just become another member of the class.

It can be quite a different matter for teachers. Some teachers really don't mind having a new face among the learners, even with that different purpose for being there. Many teachers have gone as far as to thank the observer and to invite them back at any time they want to do more observation. Other teachers are more nervous about letting someone sit in on their classes. We are not sure why, not being teachers, but perhaps there is a sort of fear, maybe even several types of fear. Some teachers might just be the type to become a little nervous just knowing that someone has the lesson under a different type of surveillance. Other teachers might lack confidence in their teaching ability and be quite unhappy about having it exposed by those who are not supposed to know best. Others, still, might be perfectly good teachers and have nothing to fear from the observation and eventual report, but they just have no interest in or time for the notion that pupils can be observers and make useful comments about learning and how it occurs for those who experience it. Increasingly though, those teachers are quite few and far between.

Shadowing

Shadowing has things in common with observation, but they are nonetheless quite distinctive tools. Where observation allows information to be captured about a moment in time – a specific lesson, shadowing has a longer-term perspective. Shadowing means just that – to become the shadow of a student and to follow them, be near them and to feel and experience their range of daily interactions. A shadow might follow their informant for a day, or two days or perhaps even a week to build up information, insight and crucially a sense of understanding that particular case. Shadowing really allows the student researcher to become close to those they follow. They become privileged insiders and get as close as possible to the real experience of learning as their shadowee knows and understands it.

Just as in other parts of the research, the participants are invited to come forward and volunteer for shadowing. We have wondered whether it is more useful and interesting to pick those whom we want to shadow and learn about and from. Shadowing is an intimate process though, and its success relies considerably on a good relationship between the shadow and the shadowee. The willingness of the latter to participate is therefore quite crucial to facilitate the kind of communication and inside access that is sought and valued and allows the rich descriptive accounts of their learning to emerge.

Shadowing does not stand alone as a method or tool, it is more holistic and therefore combines several types of tool or instrument. As mentioned under interviews, the shadowing process, by its nature, lends itself to a relaxed and less formal type of interview which is more like a discussion, or two friends talking about their learning, why they respond to certain things the way they do, how they feel about other things, how they interpret certain events or phenomena. These are fairly in-depth and personal questions, that are best asked and answered through a process like shadowing.

Shadowers have various ways of conducting their work and making notes about the case they are following and investigating. Because shadowing is more discreet, more natural and less inspectorial, the need for a clipboard and coded schedule is less. They seem quite inappropriate for the type of tool shadowing is. In any case, precoding and scheduling themes and answers might marginalise the important information that comes from the informant. We want to understand them, their learning and their experience in their own terms – not our predefined ones. We want to know how they conceive, construct, interpret and make sense of themselves and their learning.

Spot checks

These are like the little gold nuggets in the kit. They give fantastic information that is so interesting to gather, process, view and interpret. The spot check is like a mini-questionnaire which captures point in time information about certain things – perhaps the feelings of a student or their levels of concentration or learning. They are passed out to students at regular intervals and completed over a long period of time. Some spot checks have been designed for whole classes to complete every 20 minutes or so. For other research questions and aims, it was more appropriate to give these spot checks to individuals at regular intervals.

One Learning School group gave the spot check to whole classes during general observation of lessons. Other groups chose to combine the spot-check tool with individual shadowing and interviews, so that a rich description emerged that was built upon a triangulation of information from three tools.

Spot checks can be completed very quickly. At most they only include four or five questions and the response to each can usually be indicated by ticking a box or circling a number that corresponds to the level of the particular thing they are asked to evaluate at that moment in time. The results of spot checks are therefore graphs that depict various changes occurring in motivation, for example, over the length of a day. In the case reports that accompany them, the researcher can draw on and include the vast information they have gathered during shadowing that complements and explains the features and trends in the spot-check graphs.

Conclusion

The kit bag is full and ready to be delved into. Every August the members make themselves familiar with the contents and use these tools in various adapted versions to gather information that will answer the questions they have been given or have devised. The tools are quite strong, they are used carefully and considerable attention is paid to making sure they work well and are generating the right kind of information, and information that is a healthy balance of the valid and the reliable. It does go wrong from time to time, though. I am sure this happens even in professional research. There is a tape recorder that doesn't work, a class that has been cancelled or has switched rooms. One pair of re-searchers who had been shadowing a pupil together came back to the work room to write up their reports after a lesson, but their notes only contained and documented the horrified written conversation they had 5 minutes into the lesson when they realised that the pupil they had been shadowing all day was nowhere to be seen and that they had gone to the wrong class. They felt too embarrassed to get up and leave the room to find the girl they were supposed to be glued to. Sometimes it can all go wrong because the researcher is invited to participate in the lesson in some way. Like in the music classes where researchers were asked to sing a song in their native language for the class to listen to, learn from and enjoy. Fun and interesting for the class may be, but not beneficial for the research process, and certainly confusing for the researcher. Therefore the lesson has been – be prepared for when things inevitably do not go according to plan, but always try to be as rigorous as possible. And remember, the tools must reflect the issue that is being investigated and their use must be fit for that purpose.

4 A lifetime of learning (in one year)

The students of the Learning School (1 and 2)

This chapter is rich and powerful testimony to the impact of the Learning School on those who made it and lived it. It is not just a collection of personal stories, moving as many of them are, but it raises far-reaching questions about the very nature of learning and the place of schooling in the lives of students. As many of these student researchers testify, the most significant benefit of all is to make you reflect on your own learning and prepare you for further or higher education, or for life long and life-wide learning.

> When I today look back on the past year I can both laugh and cry but mostly I just smile. It seems now like a faraway dream and not something I have done. It was a year of adventure in many ways and nothing one can imagine.
>
> It was difficult to come home again and try to be 'normal' but maybe I will never be 'normal' ever again and the big question is now if I want to. It is like standing on the edge of something unknown just like it was one year ago when I was sitting on the pier in Bergen looking out at the sea and waiting for the ferry that would take me to the Shetland Islands. I am now at the same point as I was one year ago but now I do not have a big sea in front of me but my future and that feels more scary.
>
> One thing that the Learning School did for me and probably for everyone else who has done a similar thing is that it has opened the doors in my mind, and I now believe that I can do anything. The question we all have to ask ourselves is, are we brave enough to jump out there into the unknown not knowing what we might find or would we rather stay on safe ground? One last word is, jump! It is only you who are holding yourself back. If you do not take the step out you might regret it for the rest of your life but if you do, you can always come back to safety again.
>
> (Karolina)

This year has been a massive education to us all, an almost vertical learning curve. I often worried that I was not using this opportunity to learn as much as I could but now after having stepped back indefinitely from this particular journey I can see how by watching and feeling another culture from within you cannot help but learn infinite amounts. It is the greatest educational tool ever to have at one's disposal. Teaching things schools will never be able to teach, through first-hand experience, feeding a desire to understand the world in which we live. This year has given me a real thirst to continue to test myself academically and to become more aware of different societies, cultures and people, as I am sure it has to everyone who was a part of Learning School 2.

(Colin Bragg)

My year in the Learning School is a time I appreciate and will forever treasure. It is one of the best times I have had in my nearly two decades of existence and absolutely the time with most happening. It is a time where I personally have developed, met new friends, broadened my horizons and became more aware of life outside the borders of Sweden.

I will never regret my participation in the Learning School. It has been so good and I have personally gained so much that the word regret would never cross my mind. It was only in the beginning when everything was a mess that I thought about whether or not I had made the right decision. The lack of instruction and guidelines at the beginning of the project made me, as well as the rest of the group, uncertain where this year would end.

Now, when the end is near and the journey is soon at its final port, I'm glad there wasn't much prepared for us. Before I almost cursed it but now I praise it instead. Inexperienced as we were, guidelines would have been very useful but there were almost none. So it was up to us to make the best of the year, and that I feel we did. The feeling of achievement is now greater because it was us that accomplished it. With some help from the universities and the schools, the end result is above my first expectations. We could also look at aspects we found more interesting because our hands were not tied by instructions.

(Jimmy Kartunnen)

I have gained so many things from this project. But I could say that the most precious thing was I could admit and adopt the different way of thinking or behaviour, and environment, which came from the various cultural differences. In the beginning of Learning School 2 I tended to determine and evaluate things based on my view, which had grown up for a long time in Japan. In Japan it was kind of natural that to be different from others meant being more negative than positive. Therefore I was getting confused because there were too many things to refute and I had no idea how to interpret them, which did not fit my view at all. However, in the process of discussing and just chatting with members in the daily round, I realised that what was natural and the right thing for me was not always the case with them and vice versa, and this difference must be really natural. Gradually I learned not to see things just from my view and to try to think from different aspects, what we call positively. It was also at the same time that I started to doubt what I took for granted in Japan and gained a better opinion of Japan at the same time.

(Kazuyo)

This year has allowed me to see things from a different angle and to realise that sometimes we place limitations on ourselves and that there is so much more that we can do. I have been researching and observing students learning but also learning myself. As I saw learning in five different schools and many classrooms, I also saw what I would have been like in those situations and would have loved to have been able to evaluate my own preferred style of learning. It has also made me appreciate that only so much is down to other people and that if you really want to succeed, you need to put in the effort yourself and in the end you're the one who will benefit. This has been said to students in the Anderson High School so often but after a year immersed in others' learning I could really recognise the truth of that statement. With this recognition I will be able to move forward and work hard utilising the rich experiences of the Learning School so as to make the most of future opportunities. . . .

I have probably learnt as much in these ten months as I did in thirteen years of school. I have enjoyed the good times and survived the bad times and learnt a lesson from the problems. It has been a great year and I am glad to have been a part of it, so, thank you, LS2. It has been a privilege to have travelled, researched and grown with you. My last thank you goes to the man who started this project, because if it were not for him, none of us would just have had one of the best years of our lives. So thanks, Stewart, for your guidance and your friendship.

(Jolene)

Travel

Many people travel around the world but so many get a distorted view of the most incredible places from their hotel room or tour bus windows. The chance to understand real life and culture away from manufactured tourist attractions. The chance to see culture that is not made of plastic and cheap glazed ceramic ornaments but culture through the lives of real people who have led incredible lives. It is humbling when I think that so many people have allowed me to share their most precious memories and, in doing so, a fraction of their lives.

(Colin Bragg)

Travelling around for almost a year was from time to time very frustrating. The travel itself was always fun and exciting but living out of a suitcase for ten months was both frustrating and made me realise that I had packed far too much and that I was not all that great at packing after all. There were times like in Hong Kong when I was so close to just leaving my suitcase on the pavement and walking away. So this is a piece of advice to all of you out there who are planning to do a 'round the world trip'. Buy a suitcase and pack it but before you go, throw away half of the things you have just packed because you will never use them!

(Karolina)

I am still extremely grateful to Learning School for all the travelling experience I got during the last year. If I take it just practically, I have been to many airports either directly facing or just passively taking part in many problematic situations beginning with lost luggage and ending with lost tickets. It might be useful at some point in the future to know what to do when things go wrong. It was during this year when I started using the Internet to book flights or hotels. For the first time in my life I took part in hiring a car. I really appreciate all the hard times as well. For instance, trying to save a few Korean *won* pulling our luggage through half of Pusan and then finding out that we had saved approximately a pound each. It was great to try it all in practical life and probably more importantly in unknown environments and to learn (hopefully) from them when we face similar situations again.

(Honza)

A funny moment was the three hours taxi ride from Aberdeen to Edinburgh. Miki and I volunteered to give up our the seat on the plane by taking another later flight. However, we could not get it and the air-hostess at Aberdeen Airport recommended we should go to Edinburgh Airport by taxi and take an earlier flight. So we enjoyed three hours in a taxi, which British Airways paid for and we finally missed the flight. I remember the meter of the taxi showed £160 and we sympathised with BA, which was not rewarded indeed. We arrived in Heathrow much later on. However, the next day, we got to fly business class to San Francisco. We got the royal treatment and I felt I was in heaven both in height and service. However, it was a great pity that I got serious diarrhoea and did not remember the trip fully. It was only great joy for me that the toilet was always vacant and easy to go to repeatedly.

(Kazuyo)

I was taking an earlier bus back to Fränsta, where I was staying and I managed to get on the wrong bus. So being a bit panicked I got off the bus in Erikslund. I asked for directions in a shop and the assistant drew me a small map. She told me that once I got to the motorway, it was only 2–3 SWEDISH miles to Fränsta. I knew I had about an hour and a half to get home before anything looked suspicious. So I started walking. I got to the motorway, which had already been about 2–3 BRITISH miles and started walking down the motorway. Walking and walking and walking! Still no signs for Fränsta! Two kind ladies gave me a lift home in their van. I realised that it was more than three miles home. I got home at the exact same time as if I had come with my normal bus. I told my host family about two weeks later what I had done. My host father could not stop laughing. Eventually he stopped laughing and said, 'One Swedish mile is about 6 British miles!' Let that be a lesson to anyone going to Sweden.

(Jolene)

Another positive fact about this practical part of travelling is that you get to know the people you travel with. You see very quickly through them when you travel because you face many challenges on such travels and everybody reacts differently to those. I admit that I did judge people according to how they behaved in these extreme situations that we went through and I believe that people show the hidden parts of their character when they struggle.

(Honza)

Teamwork

The more I have learnt about other people this year, the more I have learnt about myself.

(Jolene)

I sometimes wonder how a group can come together, almost complete strangers, coming from such contrasting cultures and become so close and intimate with one another. Then I think to myself, maybe this is the way things should be.

Take someone out of his or her familiar surroundings and place them somewhere that is totally new, they can become a completely different person. They do not need to worry about the barriers they usually put up; they can be totally at ease with themselves and others alike and suddenly their self-confidence rockets. What better way to start a relationship, with total confidence and trust in one another.

As you would expect with a group of 16 to 18-year-old students, spending the best part of a year working and socialising together, the relationships at times were a little tense. Spending so much time together has many pros and cons. You are given the opportunity to really get to know the people that are so close to you. To know how they respond, react and feel towards many things.

Although this is the case, living so close together can also take its toll on the group. Spending time in unfamiliar places, people naturally reach out for things that they are used to and familiar with, and for us, that was each other. Spending so much time working as one sometimes proved difficult for the group. You would sometimes tire with the monotony of days, doing the same things with the same people over and over again; tension would sometimes be unbearable between us.

Looking back though, I wouldn't change a thing. Even the really rough times we have been through, those times where nothing ever seemed to go right. All these experiences we have had, we have experienced together. This year has benefited me beyond all comprehension

(Jeremy Barnett)

I had never thought how to get on well with people before I joined the Learning School but I learned much about how human relations work in real life through the year of being together with particular members. It has been just like a sitcom drama in which people struggle to live better with neighbours and friends. Wherever I went, I was not alone all the time and I had never had people too close to me before apart from my family. The experiences of being in the group will remain with me for rest of my life as such an unusual and unique memory. . . .

The relationship between me and the other members of the group was quite often complicated because of cultural differences and sometimes I felt the way we were brought up made it more difficult because it was so different from person to person. The way I feel for the group is a mixture of love and hate in the same way as one thinks of their family because these people had been my family and closest to me for almost a year. The work was very difficult at times but it was nothing compared to the human relations both inside and outside the group. It was sometimes hard to first work together the whole day and then meet up again in the evening in our spare time. Sometimes it was quite important to have people around me that were not interested in the project and with whom I could talk about other things.

(Karolina)

I believe that living with different people from different cultures has given me much as a person. Getting to know the Learning School 2 group has been something wonderful but also something challenging. I know that I will always treasure in my heart the memory of the month I spent with the group.

For ten months we were to live as a group so how to turn eleven individuals into one group? Instruction for co-ordinators, simultaneously take into account the personality traits of all the people you have just met and cross-reference this with culture, family background and all other data you have at your disposal, allowing you to quite simply form a perfectly balanced group which will be easily maintained for the entirety of the project. If only things were as simple as that, instead we see an introduction to a problem faced by Learning School 2. We were in fact working with humans not machines and no matter what anyone says, people are complex and totally unpredictable.

We were not totally naïve, we had accepted that not everyone will get on with the rest all of the time but we soon found out that in a high pressure often claustrophobic atmosphere, tolerance, consideration, communication and compromise were to make up the glue holding the group together.

I can remember days when it all seemed too much, everyone sitting in a silent room with looks of defeat etched on faces but then something would happen and everyone would rally round more determined than ever to see the year out to a meaningful conclusion.

Personally I felt like walking away from the project at times but I was held back from doing so by a feeling of responsibility to everyone. The phrase 'I feel like I'm running blind' was not a welcome one six months into the project but a vital one; without it the enthusiasm and optimism with which the project had started could have all but disappeared. It acted to focus the group and sparked the exceptionally long debate mapping out our route to the finish. The group bond lasted until the end and a shared sense of achievement was so satisfying for me.

(Colin Bragg)

Stepan has taught me to laugh at myself. He believes that life is never so serious that you can't find something funny to laugh at.

Colin has taught me that even if things don't go your way, then moaning about it solves nothing.

Hyden has taught me to take things as they come. Enjoy today and worry about tomorrow, tomorrow.

Miki has taught me that to make other people happy, you sometimes have to sacrifice something of yourself.

Honza has taught me to speak my mind. If there is a problem then you should get it out in the open, argue about it and then just get over it.

Karolina has taught me a lot about learning to accept myself. It is not about changing the way you are but liking the way that you are.

I find it hard to put into words what Gregor has taught me. Maybe what Gregor has taught me is that sometimes you have to adapt to certain situations in order to keep the peace. Sometimes saying nothing is the best way of saying something.

Han Woong was not with the group long enough to get to know him as well as I would have liked. I missed him quite a lot after he left. When he was in the group, it always felt like we had someone watching over us. He was always concerned about the members of the group.

(Jolene)

What I leaned from members was not to give up understanding and try to make it. I think that this group was a manufactured group for me and, honestly speaking, most of the group were people with whom I would never have spoken or communicated with if they were in the same class at school, for instance. In school, I could avoid working with them if I felt that I could not get along with them. However, here in Learning School 2 I could not help facing the problem because we were sharing most of the time together, both research and in private. Therefore, I was sometimes stressed and tired that I had to work with them even when I did not want to. I really wanted to give up making the effort of getting along with them and just run away somewhere. However, other members always tried to make things better and to understand the others and I learned especially from co-ordinators and members from the Czech Republic. I really learned to respect their attitudes.

(Kazuyo)

Families

In all the countries we visited to conduct our research we lived with host families and this was a very good way to learn more about their culture and society. The hosts became very important to me. I needed a good family because of the stress in schools. I had to be able to relax when I came home. The most important thing is to be treated as one of the family members. I felt uncomfortable when I stayed with a family where I was seen as a guest for the time I was staying there.

I got along best with those families where I could do what I wanted but also they allowed me to help around the house. I also enjoyed being left alone to some extent. It was fun to have a family member of my own age in the house and I often became very attached to them because they were the only friends I had outside the group and I needed sometimes to be with people who did not talk about the research but just normal things. I am glad today every time I receive e-mail from any of my previous hosts, just telling me how they are.

(Karolina)

The saddest moment in the Learning School 2 experience I could say was definitely the day that we left Cape Town in March. It was painful both for my host family and me. They called me 'Tea slave' as a joke and I made their tea every time they had a cup. The last night in Cape Town, I gave them a thank you card and wrote 'The graduation of the tea slave'. They were almost crying. The next morning that I left, the breakfast was prepared on the table. The moment that I saw it, I was almost crying too because there were four cups of coffee, which I had never seen on the breakfast table. I understood their feeling, that they did not want to show me they were making tea, nor could they ask me to make tea once I had written the graduation on the card. Everyone was totally quiet and it was the first time that they were so quiet.

(Kazuyo)

When I came back home from London I spent about ten days there meeting my whole family and all my friends that I had not seen for a long time. They of course started asking me a lot of questions but two of them were the most frequent. Firstly, they asked me where all I have been to and, secondly, where did I like it most. When I was asked for the first time I think that I said Sweden and Japan but later on when I was asked again I started thinking why they were the places I favoured most. I realised quite quickly that I had a great relationship with the people that I lived with in these countries. Sweden and Japan are both completely different cultures and also the families were very different but their attitude towards me or my attitude towards them appear to me a little special. It is quite peculiar that both these families were families of other LS members but I am not sure how significant this fact was. And because both these families are of other LS members I am pretty sure that they will read this essay too and I would like to thank them again for all that they did for me and tell them how important they were to me.

(Honza)

Friendships

Often debate was fiery but friendships were never in question, as we knew we would need to help each other further down the road. I think it is fair to say that in this environment we all matured and developed people skills very quickly and became mature enough to make sure petty differences were never allowed to ruin relationships.

(Colin Bragg)

Presenting findings

Of course, during LS2 I have learnt a lot from our research. I am much more confident at talking in front of large audiences. I have learnt general skills from the work: research methods, how to write reports, how to prepare presentations, that sort of thing. However, even after all the presentations we've done, there are still a few that made me really nervous: The Scottish Executive, Hong Kong and Cambridge. I worried a lot about the Cambridge presentation. I was convinced that I was going to look like a fool in front of all those academics and while Professor MacBeath was there. I did not want to show up the project while his colleagues were there. Thankfully it never happened and the presentation was a success.

(Jolene)

I would like to mention the presentations, as all of them were very significant for me. I do not know how many presentations we had done but they were always special for me. I am not sure why but I always looked forward to them. Presentation was always a moment for me when I could stand up and tell everybody about our project and what we all found out. I also liked the atmosphere of it, the moment when I was presenting our results to teachers, professors or even ministerial advisers. This is something that I am really grateful to the Learning School for; the opportunity to be pre-senting at so many institutions, some of which had at least really big names. This means to me a great life experience and a big step forward. I have tried it and if a similar opportunity comes in future, I will not worry about it but go towards it.

It was the Hong Kong presentation which I felt was the most rewarding moment. Actually it was the second time that we presented in front of the policy-makers but the first time since the Scottish Executive, I got confused and did not recognise what was I doing. The problems of language also gave me the difficulty of understanding what they were asking us. In the Hong Kong presentation, I was very excited. We focused not only on the findings from the research but on the method both in general and what we used in the research. It was a very creative presentation and I was very satisfied with the result. I felt that audiences were very interested in the project and I was very proud of myself that I was in this project at that moment. The preparation was conducted in the extremely tight schedule. I will never forget the night, when we were packed in the hotel and moved room to room with the scripts that we had just written to submit to Gregor and Miki.

(Honza)

Culture shock

South Africa and Japan are the cultures, that are most different from my own, and I struggled to understand them. In South Africa, the whole soci-ety was different and difficult to live in. Most of the time I felt safe but it is only now when I look back on my time there do I realise that I was very protected by my hosts and never did anything on my own. The people amazed me because they were always happy and nice to me but somehow I felt for the first time in my life different and white. I had never before thought about my colour in that way and here the colour seemed to be such an important issue.

Before going to South Africa I read a bit about their history but to read in a book and actually be there in the middle of it and experience it is a whole different thing. Cape Town is the most beautiful city I have been to but in the same way the most dangerous and with a lot of issues to clear up before it will be a good environment to bring up children. Cape Town is very divided as far as religion, culture and money are concerned, in a way I had never experienced before and it sometimes scared me.

Religion played a big role in the lives of the people in South Africa. I stayed with a Muslim family during my six weeks there. This was very interesting coming from a family where religion does not play an important role and now living with a family whose religion I did not know all that much about. Islam was a religion I regarded as something bad because of the Middle East and the problems they have there with people practising their religion and hiding their human rights crimes behind religion. My hosts were lovely people and not very religious but I had the chance to spend Eid with them, which is one of the Muslim Christmases.

(Karolina)

Tackling the task

To think that at the very beginning of this project we as a group were looking through textbooks in an attempt to understand the word 'Motivation' and now a year down the line, a report on the subject of motivation in all of the schools we visited exists. Somehow in amongst the arguments and lengthy debates our determined co-ordinators led us on a winding path, that even they will admit became a little misty, in achieving our objective.

(Colin Bragg)

What I want to say is that only when we started thinking properly about the research and took it as our own project and responsibility did we start discussing it, speaking about it and all trying to improve it. It took us at least the whole first half a year to grasp and understand the aims of the research and our tasks. However great a loss of time it might seem to be, I would never say that this time was wasted by our unprofessional approach. I feel that right during this period the biggest challenges came. Challenges that had to come and which one person did not manage to handle and all the others were greatly affected by. I think I will never forget the evenings at Miki and Gregor's flat in Ange discussing the ways forward and who was to take which part of the project. Nor will I forget the day when Hyden asked us in Germany: What are we actually working on here? The third event to remember will be probably the big row in Shetland about the research, five days before the presentation at the Scottish Executive. These are only the highlights of the events that happened during that time and that challenged us all. There were definitely other occasions as well when I wondered where to go from here and what am I actually supposed to do now, but I am grateful for all of them, and I believe that they only helped me to be little bit stronger and hopefully also wiser.

(Honza)

Classroom observation not only helped the project and me but helped the observed students as well. I found I developed a very supportive relationship with them as I was interested in their learning and personal aspects and, vice versa, they showed they were interested in knowing about aspects of me. I was very fortunate with the observed teachers as well. Both of them were fully supportive of the research and we had many debates about the class and its problems, allowing all parties, teachers and students, to improve on what they were doing. The teachers had shown, for me, an extraordinary interest in the students. They were entirely available for the students and would be willing to help with anything. This entirely redefined my perspective of the teacher's role.

Sweden helped me a lot to be comfortable with observation since there were so many things to look for but it gave me the opportunity to practise my styles of observing in many different situations and environments. The variety of experiences helped me to create a stable base for further observing and I also gained confidence in my ability to analyse and write a report about observed aspects. Although the Swedish report is the first academic style that I have ever written in, I personally consider it my best one.

(Matthew Greenhalgh)

Learning

Before I joined the Learning School, motivation was something I never thought of and suddenly I had to find out what made other students want to learn before I knew what made me learn. I spent some time reflecting on myself and today I can say that I came up with things I never thought influenced me at all because I always thought I did things for myself and not for any other reason. Now I am looking forward to going back to school and seeing how much I will reflect on myself in the classroom as well as the teachers and my peers. I hope that now I have enough knowledge about motivation and I am able to motivate myself in all subjects.

(Karolina)

Skills that I have picked up during my time on the Learning School:

- Discussion skills – Not only did we have many, many discussions but these usually turned into heated debates. The one skill that can never get you wrong in a debate is diplomacy, one has to list others' views and respect them even if you really disagree. Hopefully I have acquired just a little of this skill at least, because these situations need to be approached carefully and ideally with objectivity. Frustration will not lead to solution but communication just might.
- Writing ability – With all the reports and presentations which needed to be written.
- How to present myself – Besides meeting many important people during the course of the Learning School, we also did many presentations. These were usually very formal and required us to be professional and well prepared. These presentations always made me really nervous, like my life depended on them, but the more and more I did, the less nervous I felt.
- Common sense and clear thinking skills – Being put in so many new situations and figuring how to approach them appropriately.
- Project/teamwork – This was of course the most vital skill necessary when travelling with other people for six months. People cannot

co-exist for such a long time without having problems with each other and we certainly did have our share. These kinds of situations will definitely be part of life at university, in the workplace and just generally in the 'real world', as I so often refer to it. When we want something to be successful and also to have everybody relatively content, one needs to compromise. If anything, I hope to learn the skill of compromise as a tool of co-existence in this world.

- Problem-solving skill can be associated with almost every aspect of being a traveller researcher for six months. As a group, we had to solve many types of problems, regarding the presentations, interviews, authority and working as a group. Individually, I had to solve problems both regarding the group and also personal ones.

(Joe Williamson)

I personally realised many things which I was unable to see before. The long time I spent abroad sharpened my critical awareness and it helped me to adopt a critical approach which made me understand. It seems that although this school teaches such a broadly focused range as well as in-depth knowledge, it is no longer enough. Simply because I feel that my personal approach to study and my opinions of it would not be supported but repressed. I also realised what I already thought that might have been truth before. One of the most distinct features of the Czech nation is envy. As soon as one does more than the others, any kind of positive recognition can be forgotten. However, from the observation point of view, it was productive. In particular the English Department took the research and its findings very seriously. Furthermore, some changes in those researched classes have been made following our suggestions.

(Robert Janícek)

My eyes are now more opened to the world I live in and a better under-standing for other cultures has been achieved. My confidence as a person has grown due to many reasons. Just to have been honoured with the opportunity to experience this year is one. Appreciation for our work from the schools and communities we have lived in is another. My confidence in English has also grown. To speak English has become a part of my daily communication and is no longer a problem. The bigger presentations to the Scottish Office and BP have been great challenges and how well the performances went has indeed increased my confidence. The year of the Learning School has made me a better person, at least I hope so.

(Jimmy Kartunnen)

In summary

Working and socialising, living and learning in a small group situation have been a vitally important aspect of life of the Learning School. Of course there have been difficult times, there have been tensions and tears, frustrations and anger from everyone. To admit these feelings is more difficult than to keep them pent up, and to work them through as a group is yet more difficult. But often that is how things have been with this group. To have to work with the same set of colleagues every day, to have to socialise with them, relax with them, travel with them, to have them knowing how you feel, how you have changed and are changing – we have experienced all these things over a long period and to still be laughing, socialising and working well with them at the end of it all is not an achievement to be dismissed.

To work in this kind of close group is a situation that many never have the opportunity to experience. Perhaps only after distancing themselves from it will the group be able to see all the qualities which they have developed: patience, tolerance of others, accepting other people's opinions, sharing ideas, relying on others and so on. Now, in the closing days of the project, I think it is difficult to see these clearly. From a slightly different perspective we, the co-ordinators, have been able to watch all these develop over the months in individuals and in the group as a whole and that has been rewarding.

The group who began this project in August of last year are not the group who are now finishing it. Ten months away from one's native country is in itself an experience which broadens minds and develops confidence and independence. Add to this the research aspect of the Learning School and the responsibility which each member of the group has had and the results certainly cannot be summed up in a few pages, indeed, they cannot be summarised on paper. Suffice to say if everyone launches themselves into their future with the enthusiasm that has gone into the Learning School, all members will deserve their ensuing success.

(Debbie Moncrieff and Kotoro Naraia, co-ordinators of LS1)

5   The impact on the schools

In this chapter teachers and headteachers discuss the impact of the project on their schools. Differences of emphasis emerge, revealing something about the culture and receptivity of these schools as well as about the teams of young researchers. Running through all accounts, though, is a positive stream of praise for their insight and positive contribution. Most clearly of all LS students have brought a challenge and a new perspective which is the lifeblood of schools in the midst of global change.

Learning School in Ange, Bobergsskolan (Sweden)
Nils-Olov Hagman

Bobergsskolan in Ange is one of the smallest upper secondary schools in Sweden. Ange itself is situated in an area which is sparsely populated. Like many small communities we are fighting a battle against depopulation. One of the most important features in this battle is to develop our high school.

Since 1997 we have been involved in the Global Classroom Partnership. The GCP has given our students many opportunities of global interaction with their peers in the partner schools. In 1999 it was decided to make welcome the Learning School students to give us the first of three profiles of our school.

Staff and students were somewhat confused when the Learning School I came to our school and started their research. However, it was quite clear from the very start that the young researchers and their co-ordinators had a professional approach and they were universally supported by our head teacher, our staff and our students. To have a large international research group in our school for six weeks underscored our international ambitions.

The results of the research of LS1 gave us further food for discussion and important points were made both in the written report and in their oral presentation to the entire staff.

LS2 was warmly welcomed in our school. The good work of LS1 was not forgotten and both staff and students had high expectations of LS2. The theme of the year 'Motivation' was extremely interesting since it is something we often discuss. LS2 helped us gain insight into what factors motivate or demotivate our students. Certain weak points in our organisation were pointed out and, as a result of the findings of LS2, we have taken steps and measures to rectify these weak points. Again, our international profile was highlighted during the weeks we had the pleasure of hosting LS2 in our community and at our school.

Needless to say, the advent of LS3 was eagerly awaited. The theme of the year, 'Student self-evaluation', is as interesting as the theme 'Motivation'; and again our expectations were high, although we realised that research in this field might be more difficult. The results of the research gave us ideas and inspiration on how to improve our school. We are going to use the results of the research in future in-service training days for the staff.

Many members of the staff have stressed that, apart from the research, the members of the LS teams are very good role models for our students. They give our students the opportunity to discuss and compare different cultures and life-styles. This aspect is invaluable for a small rapidly depopulating rural community as ours.

We are constantly contacted by other Swedish high schools that want information about LS. Finally, GCP and LS have inspired both staff and students to bring the international perspective into the classroom. We now have several international projects under way and more to come.

Nara Women's University Secondary School (Japan)
Kenji Hirata

The aim of this section is to provide a brief sketch of the impacts of the Learning School Project on our school, Nara Women's University Secondary School (NWUSS). The year 2000, the last year of the twentieth century and of the second millennium, was a very busy but richly productive and memorable year both for our school and Learning School Project 1. In that year we hosted the fourth Global Classroom Annual Conference, where the Learning School 1, which had started their activities the previous year, made their first formal presentation here, the last stop of their one-year tour.

NWUSS is one of the three state-owned 'secondary schools', a new category of schools established for the first time in 2000 by the Ministry of Education, Culture, Sports, Science and Technology as one of the radical education reforms still in progress at various stages in Japan and we are expected to conduct experimental research into improving teaching methods in secondary education. We are proud in taking the initiative in the reforms as an experimental school. In fact we have been positive about anything progressive and the Learning School Project was no exception. In 1999 we had decided to involve ourselves in this project. That is because we found this project promising and worthwhile in terms of a catalyst for the school reform. We were also very lucky to receive continued guidance and support from Nara Women's University.

One of the most impressive elements was the workshop the Learning School 1 organised as one of the programmes of the Global Classroom 2000 in Nara. They represented six different types of class where the participants of the conference played the role of students and the Learning School researchers and co-ordinators played the role of teachers. One of the students who took part in the workshop said that they had never realised the existence of so many different teaching styles and that the teaching styles affect their own learning so much. After that they discussed the ideal school in groups. They also published a small report book here in Nara thanks to the support from our vice-principal.

The Learning School has raised a lot of interesting issues in our school, which offered us a good opportunity and some helpful methods to reflect on what is happening and going on at school. In the Education Reform Plan for the twenty-first century called the Rainbow Plan, our Ministry of Education emphasises the need to implement the school evaluation system including the establishment of the self-evaluation system, which requires us to obtain a true picture of the many-sided complex situation consisting of inseparable and interactive factors and to look at them in perspective. The Learning School Project has given some helpful insights in order to access what is going on in the classroom from inside, not from outside.

Through our reform we have been making every effort to be more student-centred at various levels, which we think is necessary in order to develop good learners who are ready to be responsible for their learning. To be student-centred is what the Learning School is for and what they are doing in fact. The Learning School Project provides us with a lot of data and their own analysis of them. It is important to take into consideration the cultural variables when they analyse the raw data. The research presupposes the idea that everything that happens in the classroom is time-bound, context-bound and culture-bound. To analyse the data they need enough understanding of the respective culture and their sense of values. If we jump to sweeping generalisations, we might end up making mistakes. It is important to build up a cumulative knowledge of the respective cultures and have a balanced view of them.

What should be kept in mind, however, is that the Learning School Project is not a panacea. If all we do is just see them passing before our nose, we can get little benefit from this project. It depends on the students and the teachers at school to make active use of the results of their research. Access to the information offered by the project is very important to get full benefit. But we have to say that not all our students and teachers are good enough at understanding the report written in English. We think that we should make the report more accessible to all involved, both the observer and the observed.

Lastly, we would like to add that their report and presentation are not all they offered us, and that we learned a lot directly and indirectly through their teamwork beyond their cultural differences, their exchange with the host families and the local people and especially the young people's aspiration to better future education.

Anderson High School (UK)
Ian Spence

A school must offer and provide quality teaching and learning. How this can be done exercises the minds of all teachers. Managing the process and developments required to deliver this depends on the good-will, perseverance and dedication of staff and students.

Enabling two universities in conjunction with a team of international students to look at research and report on learning in Anderson High School presented both a challenge and an opportunity. It was an opportunity to build the school's commitment to encourage teachers and students to think about, discuss, consider and review teaching and learning as part of a continuous reflective process of school self evaluation. It was a challenge to see if the belief that encouraging teacher and student autonomy in decision-making about learning and teaching would result in greater teacher satisfaction and promote student achievement.

The launch of the Learning School in September 1999 saw a round of staff meetings, Heads of Department meetings, departmental and inter-departmental meetings as the school prepared to open classes to a team of international student researchers backed by two university education departments. 'Life and learning goes on as normal' was the approach taken to deal with this step into the relative unknown.

Having a former student of Anderson High School as one of the two graduate co-ordinators of the group (the second co-ordinator is always from Japan) offers familiarity for staff and the research team. All was not entirely familiar. The term Learning School both fascinated and confused the Head School Janitor who on more than one occasion asked 'Learning School – surely a school is a place where you come to learn – so why such a name?' Explaining that students would observe learning in classes and report findings to teachers and the broader school community seemed to further confuse – 'Students telling teachers their job?' All seemed not quite as it should be – certainly to the Head Janitor and perhaps to how many more of the school community?

'Life and learning as normal' was the promise. Thinking back it was perhaps not normal life and learning in AHS. A Japanese research student observing a German conversation group, a South African observing a Higher class learn about his country, his city and a policy that subjected his fellow countrymen, a Swede interviewing students and staff about Higher Maths lessons. Indeed far from normal times – but fascinating times and never more so on each occasion when Learning School groups shared their findings with staff, students and interested parents. Parental participation in the process of looking at learning in the school has in each of the three years been revealing. Parents have in general shown no wish to participate in meeting the team of researchers, in being interviewed or attending meetings proposed to discuss how they may contribute to the research. Clearly the Learning School has revealed the need to build a more effective learning partnership with parents.

The rapport and contact established between Learning School teams and students have been really effective, strong and exciting. Fifth year students talking about learning – how they experience or do not experience it – in classes and how they think they learn and what they feel they want to learn is a tremendously positive impact on and for the school. Researchers engaging

students in informal discussion about learning on weekend nights while socialising quite wildly is another success measure of the Learning School.

As the term Learning School gains familiarity with all – janitors included –
as schools become part of learning communities – let us hope that the emphasis
in schools shifts from testing what young people know and measuring what
schools do or do not do to helping young people and schools learn more and
more effectively.

Stewart Hay

All over the world schools confront the challenge of 'How does learning occur?'
And what can schools do to help students learn? In confronting this challenge
schools need to construct new approaches without wholly dismantling existing
approaches. In the school year 1999–2000 along with partner schools located in
three European countries, South Africa and Japan, Anderson High School in
co-operation with Professors MacBeath and Sugimine asked a student from
each of the then six partner schools to collaborate on a ten-month quest of
how learning occurs in each of the schools. This marked an important step in
helping Anderson High become a learning organisation and was the beginning
of the Learning School, an international student research project.

The project is based on the belief that a 'good school' is one which, itself,
learns, it is a *learning school* that changes in order to be an organisation that
encourages learning. Enabling and empowering a team of post-High School
students to spend two months in search of aspects of learning in Anderson High
School marked an important step in the process of making the change to a
learning school. Introducing the project to all staff in autumn 1999 Professor
John MacBeath advised that 'change is learning – and is loaded with uncertainty. It is also a journey not a blueprint.' The 'journey' in AHS has been and
remains fascinating.

'How can students who have no knowledge of this school or Scottish education comment on learning?', 'Most not speaking English will make this difficult,
if at all possible.', 'What next?', 'How will this help us teach and students learn?'
These were some of the questions and comments asked by teachers in Anderson
High at the outset of the Learning School project. They reflected real and clear
concerns about the feasibility and viability of the project. Beneath them also lay
some uncertainty and hesitancy about opening the classes of the school to
global eyes and ears and some uncertainty in terms of thinking of Anderson
High as a learning organisation as well as an organisation teaching knowledge
and hoping for understanding. The Learning School from the outset has aimed
to achieve this goal.

Anderson High School was the first school in which the team of six – later
seven students with the joining of Carla Soudien from Cape Town – began the
first Learning School. It was for school, researchers and co-ordinators a first. In
advance, the two universities had established a research pattern over three years
beginning with research of links between ethos and effective learning and

developing this in the second Learning School to search for motivation and in the third for Student self-evaluation.

With focus on the fifth year – the year of study for entrance to tertiary education in Scottish secondary schools – all Learning Schools have set about similar research procedures. This involves establishing student perspectives of each of the research themes by the distribution of questionnaires to each member of the year group. This provides the qualitative part of the research. For Anderson High this part of the research has given rich and invaluable insight into student perspectives of school ethos, motivation and factors affecting it and student perspectives of self-evaluation.

The impact of the quantitative data can be to challenge perceptions held or wished for. After presentation and publication of their findings by each Learning School, discussion, debate, questioning – valuable dynamics in all schools – follow. More than half of the fifth year do less than one hour of homework, a majority of the fifth year feel that the teacher's role is to motivate and student self-evaluation is to be found – but in a small number of fifth year students. These small parts of the extensive quantitative data gathered by the Learning School have fired debate, discussion and gone on to prompt review and change. It adds to the dynamism that schools need to develop, adapt and change.

The gathering of qualitative data – observing classes, shadowing students, carrying out spot checks of aspects of learning and behaviour – brings the research and the critical review of what is done and how it is done under the close and direct scrutiny of the international team of students. This also adds and contributes to the dynamics of school development but the process can prove challenging to manage and indeed to live through. A recurrent theme of the findings of all three Learning School projects' research in Anderson High has been of a teacher-led school. While it is encouraging that teachers promote and stimulate learning, it has also highlighted the need to promote a greater degree of student responsibility for their own learning. A determined drive is under way to share initiatives and ideas in and between departments on ways of helping students take greater responsibility for their own learning.

The research undertaken by the second Learning School group in session 2000–2001 on motivation stimulated interesting and lively debate among Heads of Department about the roles teachers and teaching learners and learning play in raising motivation. The research flagged up a tendency of students to be teacher dependent and learning to be teacher-centred. The evidence has been used by departments as part of their commitment to reviewing and raising achievement. A recent gathering together of ways departments are working towards raising achievement shows the stimulating effect of the work of the second Learning School 2 in prompting staff to 'think different'.

Anderson High, in common with schools globally, is an amalgam of people quirky and varied in their interests, enthusiasms and commitment to change – students, teachers and all alike. The varied agendas and aspirations of a large and diverse teaching and student body can make a complex 'organisational underworld'. The successive international student groups from three continents and now eight communities of the world bring a fresh set of eyes and ears to this 'underworld' and in turn provide rich and vital evidence and findings that hopefully have and will continue to help Anderson High be a listening and learning school striving to offer the best to all in it.

Harold Cressy High School (South Africa)
Lionel Adriaan, Former Head Teacher

I would like to share a few ideas and comment on the impact of the Learning School project on the South African schools, viz. Harold Cressy, Wittebome and Langa High. I am embarking on this assignment in the capacity as Staff Co-coordinator of the Global Classroom Partnership, South Africa, and am not actively involved as an educator inside a school but as someone 'on the outside, looking in'. The establishment of the Learning School was inevitable. It flows directly and naturally out of the educational, social and cultural bases/foundations of the Global Classroom Partnership.

Learning is a very complex and multi-faceted phenomenon. The fact that young students are engaged in doing research into various aspects of the learning process speaks volumes about the intellectual capacity and ability of the young people. It is also very impressive and highly commendable that these researchers are able to present their findings in a very articulate manner to several international audiences.

The pioneering groundwork and ongoing input by reputable academics enhance the professional and academic status and credibility of this project. I am convinced that the benefits that the researchers will accrue from their involvement and participation in this project will be tremendous – especially in the long term. It will ensure personal, social, intellectual maturity and growth that will adequately equip them to cope with all the challenges at university where incisive, critical and analytical assessment abilities are required. Carla Soudien, from Learning School 1 is an excellent example of a case in point.

The fact that researchers are from different partner schools working jointly and collaboratively across international boundaries meant that this was also a unique exercise in human relationships and interactions between people from different social and cultural backgrounds. It is essentially a case of researchers getting insight into 'how the other half lives' – an absolutely invaluable experience.

Very interesting comparisons can be drawn from the research done at various partner schools because the schools are obviously different in many respects. This can be a useful learning experience because there will be many common threads running through the results obtained from the research in various schools, bearing in mind that young people the world over are basically the same.

There were, however, many stark and startling differences between research results in South African schools compared to other partner schools. These differences were primarily the direct result of the oppressive 'apartheid' educational system that dominated the country for more than five decades. The

processes of rationalisation and retrenchment also caused insurmountable problems of overcrowded classes, demotivated and over-stressed educators, lack of
resources, discipline, etc. These differences are highlighted more pronouncedly
this year because a disadvantaged 'black township' school – Langa High – came
on board as a partner school.

Ministries of Education in other countries are providing meaningful support
for the outcomes of the Learning School research. This support, whether financial,
a sympathetic ear or eagerness to implement some of the recommendations of
the research, is totally non-existent and lacking in South Africa. There is no
way I can see the state improving or changing its education policy to inculcate
'a zest for learning' in order to raise student achievement.

I also got a strong impression that the hierarchy in South African schools felt
intimidated and threatened by young foreign students researching and assessing
learning in their schools. We might have to give this factor some consideration
– maybe look at a way of reassuring schools and make them feel at ease and
comfortable about the project. The fact that we have two diverse schools as
South African partners obviously means that some attention must be given to
the language question. Many Langa High school learners did not understand
the English idiom used in the questionnaire and left many blank spaces. Langa
High school learners are predominantly Xhosa speakers who lack the skills and
proficiency in English.

More time will also have to be devoted to doing research in South Africa
because there are two schools involved with special characteristics. Finally, I
also feel that this research should be followed up with checks and balances as to
how the research results had been used inside the schools. It will be disappoint-
ing and sad if schools are not going to use the research results meaningfully
and if the report on the research is imply going to gather dust on some shelf in
an office.

Graf Friedrich Schule (Germany)
Hans Gevers

Influence during the research

The LS influence on the school may be seen as both positive and negative. The
presence of the researchers during classes probably increases the motivation and
the engagement of teachers and of students. The interviews and questionnaires
force those involved to face different or even new views of school life. However,
some – teachers and students – may be disturbed or even annoyed because of
the presence of 'strangers' in their classes.

This has led some teachers to talk about the improvement of their teaching
style and the Learning School may be credited with stimulating these ideas. It
has led some teachers to think about the daily routine in their lessons and to
become more motivated to try out new methods. Moreover, new approaches
towards a general conception of their work may come as a result of this. On the

other hand, several colleagues have been critical of the small amount of data collected and have argued that the LS group have not provided the 'necessary' certainty while some colleagues again think that the student researchers were not properly prepared and were just 'exploited'.

Among the students, several now talk more often about teaching and learning. They have become more aware of learning as a personal process that they could and should control to an increasing degree. Conversation with their teachers about learning goals can lead to some additional knowledge about the immanent structure of a teaching subject and about the context of teaching/ learning, that is the directives, set by the educational administration.

Some parents have been led to consider their role in the educational process more intensively. They may begin to have conversations about learning not just in relation to marks, not simply because of 'confirmed' success based on a test or exams, but because of the personal development their children will achieve.

Working on a school policy

In 2001 the effects of Learning School were rather limited. The preparation of the Global Classroom Conference in Diepholz took up a great deal of energy. As the headmaster was due to retire at the end of the school year, he did not wish to embark on innovation as a legacy for his successor. Intense discussions on the results of the LS research will probably take place at the end of February and on the 22nd and 23rd February the GFS staff, parents and students will meet and will discuss the aims and the policy of our school.

Summary

The Learning School research has initiated discussions. We cannot precisely estimate the effects of the project. But we do welcome the attempt to have student researchers investigate the learning process. It must be able to take into account different points of view, and a lot rests on the quality of preparation and preparatory meetings. This is especially relevant to Learning School 3 where two groups are working on the same topic.

Gymnázium Zlín (the Czech Republic)
Mirek Rafael

I used to be a student of this school. I started studying there only in 1989, which is not long ago, but the society in those days was very different. For example, my country as it is now, did not exist then. We used to be a federal country of two nations, Czechoslovakia. At the time, it was also most unusual for schools from Communist countries to have any partnerships with their counterparts from Western Europe. However, Gymnázium Zlín had already been involved in preparations for such a programme for more than one year. And in autumn 1989 the first group of students from the Shetland Islands arrived at our school.

And I had absolutely no idea about it. Only two years later I became involved in the programme of the annual exchanges between the two schools. I still do not actually know why I chose to visit the small islands far in the north. I met many pleasant and interesting people and some of them will have their part in the following text.

In 1993 I left for university and lost touch with both the school and the Shetlands for some time – apart from my memories. And it was again at the time I was NOT at the school when the next important step in the development of co-operation was taken. In June 1997 the first Global Classroom conference was held in Lerwick – once again, I had not the slightest idea of what was going on. I was just about to sit my final university exams. Having done so, I returned to the school, this time as a teacher of English. I became involved in the academic life and I heard about Global Classroom and I also heard about another journey to Lerwick as a part of the original annual exchange programme. I was astonished by the idea of students meeting every year and comparing their projects and opinions. However, different teachers had been already involved with the programme and I personally preferred visiting the Shetlands again so my active participation in Global Classroom was postponed for another year. Before the conference in Cape Town I volunteered to work with the students and go to South Africa and I got the chance.

In Cape Town I met all the staff co-ordinators. However, not all of them were new faces for me. Some seven years after my first journey to the Shetland Isles I met Stewart Hay again, who is the teacher working on the annual exchange programme as well. This was the first opportunity for me to hear about all the details of the Global Classroom, about the Extended Student's Exchange and also, for the very first time, about the Learning School. We had many discussions concerning this topic. Honestly, I must admit I had many doubts about it. Recently I finished my university education and I still remembered how long it had taken my professors to explain to me something about school and educating pupils. And now we would have a group of young people, some of them still students of secondary school, the others having just left it, after a short course observing lessons and, my dear!, evaluating me!

But as I learned more and more about it, I came to the point when I realised it would be a pity to miss this chance to have a look at our school, and particularly our students, through different eyes. And even if the project does not work exactly as everybody would like, we do not risk much. A group of young people would stay for a month or so at our school. We could only benefit from having them, informally talking to them and sharing our views. From the very beginning the project also had the full support of the headmaster of the Gymnázium Zlín, Mr Zatloukal. As for the English department, where most of the discussions about the Global Classroom and later on the Learning School would take place, most of the teachers were of similar opinion as me – it is definitely worth trying.

And thus, we joined the Learning School. We had enough time to do all the preparations for the group before they arrived. Probably the most important point was to find the host families for our guests. We managed to find enough and I would like to thank them again for their help. After that, I got in touch with the two co-ordinators travelling with the group – Debbie Moncrieff and Kotaro Nariai – with the assistance of the Czech representative, Robert Janícek. We tried to prepare as many things as possible before their arrival. Following their request we found a classroom which could be used by the group as their base. We also informed the teachers whose lessons and classes would be involved in the observations and explained to them what the research would focus on.

Nevertheless, most of the work was to be done after the arrival of the group itself. By the time they had arrived in Zlin they had developed a clear idea of the procedures they wanted to follow and aims they wanted to achieve. One of the most astonishing things for me was to see the group working – at least in front of me they always managed to agree on the programme in a very friendly, though professional atmosphere. Everybody was also very efficient and able to work on their own, afterwards bringing all the data together and summarising them. I dare say the members of the group just perfectly fitted together. All of them obviously have their strengths and they were always willing to employ them for the benefit of the whole project.

I personally also greatly appreciated the role of Debbie and Kotaro. First of all, they had a lot of responsibility for the academic success of the programme, but they also had to perform management tasks. But I see as one of the most important and difficult things that they succeeded in keeping the atmosphere I mentioned above – friendly, but working – in the group. It must have been extremely difficult to establish the right relationship between the group and themselves as people to a certain level responsible for the young people.

I assume that the role of the Learning School at school has come to be seen as a positive one. I did not hear about any occasion when they had any problems dealing with our teachers. All our colleagues tried to meet the demands of the project even though it influenced their lessons and they did so in a friendly way. Also, from the teachers, I did not hear any negative comments about the usefulness or sensibility of the research. I guess that they felt rather as I did. They were not sure what might be the result of it, but they decided to help the group.

Apart from observing the lessons and our pupils the group also tried to get involved in the life of our school a bit. We asked them to join some of the geography lessons in which they briefly introduced their countries. As I heard, this was not only appreciated by the students, but by the teachers as well. In this aspect I would say that they helped us to introduce the idea of the whole Global Classroom much faster and in a more natural way than we would be ever capable of. However, as a whole, I feel this is one of the things that was the weakness of the first year of the Learning School. We should not forget this is a group of young people among other youngsters, and I see it as a very natural thing that they would like to get more acquainted with each other. Because of the time pressure they probably do not have enough time for that.

When the group was about to leave our school we received a huge pile of sheets of paper with a great deal of information on our school. And this is probably the biggest problem we had to face. We received the report in English, but because of the past of the system of teaching foreign languages, not many of our colleagues speak English well enough to be able to read it. We could not afford to pay for professional help to translate the report and so we had to translate it into Czech ourselves. And, of course, that meant an immense delay in accessibility of the material for all the teachers at our school. It is a pity particularly when I take into account it helped me deal with one particular class the group observed. When they had read the report on themselves, they tried to change the behaviour which had been criticised.

The English department also arranged to meet the group before their departure. It was a very interesting session. And this is a point where I made a mistake in something which might have helped us to overcome the problems with the final report and the fact that it was in English. It would have been rather easy to arrange for somebody to translate for all the teachers. But I did not do so and was 'told off' for that by both the headmaster and some of my colleagues.

And then the group went away. I had a chance to meet them again in Nara where they gave their final presentations to the participants of the Global Classroom conference and the professors of Nara Women's University. And I was so amazed by the work that they had done that I decided to perform the presentation at our school. This is dealt with later in this chapter.

The Learning School 1 by far exceeded my expectations of the project. To work with the group was a very pleasant and professionally teasing experience and to read the report and see the presentations a most exciting one. I can only believe, and now I do believe, that the future groups will cope with their task at least as successfully as the first group did.

This chapter was written from a very personal point of view. There are many people that I am indebted to for working with the Global Classroom. I did not write their names down since I might forget to mention someone and it would also make the piece much longer. If they ever have a chance to read this, they will understand who I was talking about. But I would like to thank them all.

Turning the tables

Students as teachers, teachers as students
John MacBeath

One of the opportunities I valued most from my relationship with the Learning School was to participate in a teachers' in-service day at Gymnásium Zlín (GZ). It was the most unusual and imaginative session I have taken part in and possibly the only one of its kind. It was 1 September, day one of the new school year. The staff had agreed to be taught by their students for the day and to evaluate the different teaching styles which they experienced. My task, as a participant observer, was to comment at the end of the day with the whole staff present.

The six-period day was shortened to last for just the morning, the afternoon being set aside for feedback and discussion. Each group of about eight to ten staff had a timetable with a different order of classes to visit. Each of the six classes was taught by a student who had to repeat the class six times over (or alternate with a partner). Each class was structured not so much round a subject as a particular style of presentation so that one class would be a lecture by the 'teacher' with 'students' taking notes. In another class 'students' were given five minutes to prepare a speech and then asked to come out to the front and present their talk. In another there was a sofa and cushions on the floor, with Mozart playing in the background accompanied by a free floating (and heated) discussion on abortion. In a fourth the chairs were arranged in a circle and the lesson took the form of a class discussion but structured and directed by the 'teacher'. In the sixth the room was set up as a resource base with computers, reference books, articles and newspaper cuttings with 'students' being asked to research a topic.

In the first class which I attended the student leading it gave a rather dry lecture on Japanese history. The teachers-as-students kept their heads down taking notes but from my position at the back of the class I could see how often they looked at their watches. As the lesson progressed, there was a lot of shuffling and growing restlessness. One member of staff asked if she could go to the toilet. The 'teacher' said 'no' but the member of staff went anyway. At the end of the lesson the 'students' were given a couple of minutes to complete an evaluation sheet which rated the lesson as too long and boring although it was half the length of a normal lesson in GZ. Leaving the class, some of the teachers self-consciously staggered rather than walked, and one said he didn't know if he could take much more of this. Another said that he couldn't believe how slowly time had dragged and that it took him back all too vividly to his own school days.

Later we were to experience a dramatic contrast. In the room with the couch and baroque accompaniment the discussion was so engaging that when the bell went there was a sigh and a general air of surprise. At the end of the period people looked at their watch for the first time. One member of staff protested that this period had been shorter than the others.

Later, again, in the circle discussion time went by very quickly. The student leading the session on international politics was very directive, picking on people (including myself) at random to keep them on their toes. She managed the discussion brilliantly and maintained interest and engagement throughout. We were given time at the end of the lesson to discuss our response to her style of teaching and to review our own learning. Two of the staff said they didn't like to be picked on and would prefer to volunteer or to remain silent if they chose to do so. One of them admitted that she was embarrassed having to talk in front of the class.

There was a buzz about the afternoon session and a great deal of debate. There was an argument that some topics were naturally more interesting than others and that some didn't lend themselves to interactive methods. There were defensive comments about caricatures of teaching and that their own lessons were not so boring, but these were countered by others who claimed that this had been the most sobering and salutary experience of their teaching career. A teacher said that it had held a mirror up to herself and that she, and perhaps some of her colleagues, would need to have a long hard look at their own reflections.

Three key issues emerged from the discussion:

1 The inter-relationship of teaching and learning

What emerged most clearly from the teaching sessions was the questionable nature of the learning that took place. Staff could recall little of what they had been 'taught' in some or all of the sessions. While there was some powerful learning going on, it was at the emotional level, the experience of boredom or time passing slowly, or what might happen next, or thoughts drifting off to matters of importance – things undone, things to attend to at home, feelings of frustration, impatience, wanting to getting on with other things, not seeing the relevance of what they were being required to pay attention to, the irrelevance of Japanese history to their professional or personal lives, an absence of goals. At times they were engaged and enjoying learning but even there it seemed like a suspended moment in time without connection to the rest of the day, or the rest of life. One enjoyable period, swiftly over and soon forgotten.

All teachers were able to identify their preferences for the climate of the room, the nature of the teaching relationship and their own preferred learning style. There were significant differences among them. Some didn't like being picked on by the 'teacher'. Some resented being brought out to the board to be 'shown up' in front of the rest of the class. Some didn't respond well to the free-floating nature of the resource-based classroom, wanting more structure and direction. Some didn't feel comfortable in the relaxed atmosphere of a room with couches and background music. None liked to be lectured at for a long unbroken period. These were powerful recreations of the student experience and could not have shaped the learning/teaching relationship more accurately.

2 The nature of engagement and disengagement

Teachers-as-students were acutely aware of when they were most and least engaged, acknowledging how they drifted off, what held or regained their attention and to what extent information washed over them as they became absorbed in their own thoughts and personal priorities. This reflection on the conditions of their own learning was helpful in accepting and making sense of the findings of the Learning School students. 'Walking in their shoes' as one teacher put it, had brought it most powerfully home to him. He would, in future, be much more alive to the student experience and to their views.

3   The relativity of time

Time has an objective quality which is hard to deny but its most salient aspect is its subjective quality because the passage of time is one of our most important experiences: when and how often people look at their watch is a very significant indicator of their engagement. The high watch count was very obvious in the classes where 'teachers' delivered a lecture and lowest in classes where there was interaction and opportunity to think critically and out loud.

6 Expert witnesses

Many different people have been at presentations by the students of the Learning School. Here a few of them describe the impact it had on them.

Thoughts from the seminar presented by young researchers
Professor Jean Rudduck, University of Cambridge

Never underestimate young people! I am constantly writing variations on the same theme: that schools have changed less in the past twenty years or so than students have changed. School improvement is not just about enhancing grades; it is also about updating structures and ways of relating so that there is a better fit between schools and students. New structures create opportunities for new ways of seeing and valuing the capabilities of young people today and they can open up spaces in which those capabilities can be exercised in support of learning.

Young people in school have been described as 'uneasy stranded beings' and as 'inadequately socialised' beings. The historian, Ariès, said that being in school was like being in quarantine, in a limbo world that still reflects early cultural assumptions of childhood and control and where it can be difficult for young people to demonstrate their maturity and make constructive use of the breadth of their out-of-school experience.

Increasingly, schools *are* seeing the logic of the link between students' commitment to the school's purposes and practices and their being respected as young adults, listened to and being taken seriously.

The presentation that I heard in Cambridge a few months ago is a good example of just what young people can achieve when trusted with a task that is 'for real'. What struck me – and I doubt whether my reaction is different from anyone else's – was how much they had learned. First, about research: research design, selection of informants, ethical issues, observation techniques, interviewing, analysis and interpretation of data. Then, equally important, was another kind of learning: the ability to work in pairs and as a team, and to work patiently and courteously with a range of participants.

These things I gathered from the retrospective accounts given at the seminar, but during the presentation itself I witnessed the confidence and poise of the young people, each doing their bit of a connected whole – and, remember, most were not presenting in their native language. There was a strong feeling of mutual respect and fairness so that no one person dominated the event. Perhaps the most demanding and most revealing section of a presentation is the questioning where responses have to be spontaneous (although we do tend to ask, even in different settings, the same questions!) and here again the team was impressive.

When students go out on work experience, teachers who visit the workplaces often comment on how different some pupils are: they talk about them as more reliable, more responsible, more capable. I remember being at a hairdresser's where there were young people on work experience placement and saw how readily they took on 'the style' of the professional culture – which is what the young men and women in the team did in relation to being researchers. It has made me think about what professional styles are open to young people as students in school other than the traditional passive–conformist style and the very different styles of student subgroups which are active but anti-work.

My one concern is that although schools were the focus of the enquiry, these young people were working *outside* the boundaries of formal schooling. I hope that their evidence of what is possible will encourage schools to find ways of releasing young people's potential by offering them, within their everyday structure, the right balance of challenge and support in the context of 'real' tasks.

Just pupils?
Archie McGlynn, formerly Her Majesty's Chief Inspector, Scotland

I had the privilege of discovering, through the eyes and minds of an enterprising 'illumination of students' from diverse cultures and different continents, of just how free-thinking and inspiring students can be if given the opportunity. Here I was, twenty years an inspector and a long-term advocate of the need to listen to students in evaluating schools, enthralled by the innovative and practical approaches to the evaluation of learning and teaching developed in a short space of time by . . . yes, a novice group of 'evaluators' called students. Of course this confident and articulate group had enjoyed advice and encouragement from the leaders of the Learning School initiative, but their insights and revelations of what makes a good school and what is good learning and teaching could only have come from years of being 'just pupils'.

I was taken by the way the students had approached the task within schools. It was clear to me that they had invested a considerable amount of time in gaining the confidence of staff and, in particular, their fellow students. In my experience, students are wary about being evaluated by other students and it was illuminating to hear how the group went about the job of involving the school student population and in this way adding to their evaluation judgements. They openly shared their evaluation instruments like the questionnaires, sought views on what would be most appropriate for individual schools and, indeed, individual classes in some instances.

The young are often criticised for having closed minds but the grey-haired among us could have learned from the openness of the 'Learning School' students. I was struck by the number of times I said to myself during the presentations 'there is no one best way' as student after student demonstrated how they had adapted to different circumstances and cultures of the classroom. This group, 'just pupils', made me think again about how we inspect schools. Do we have what we think is one best way? Do we adapt to the needs of different schools? Do we take account of changing circumstances? How can I improve our established questionnaires to reflect what I am learning here and now with this 'illumination of students'?

Inspired by the students, my thoughts turned to – what price the Scottish Inspectorate trading in a few inspectors for a student evaluator or two? The very next day I wrote a memorandum to my senior colleagues suggesting that we should pilot the idea of 'Student Assessors' with a view to students becoming an integral part of our inspection teams. While the Scottish Inspectorate has to take the credit for leading the way in getting schools and inspectorates to gather the views of students, the response to my initiative suggested that we were not quite ready to embrace 'Student Assessors'. I still have that memorandum and, like the Learning School, the day of the 'Student Assessor' will come.

Unthought-of questions
See-Ming Tsui, formerly Deputy Director Education and now a Director of the International Network for Educational Improvement, Hong Kong

I was deeply impressed by the findings disclosed by the group of international students who came to give a presentation of the Learning School in Hong Kong in May 2001. The methodology used in the Learning School project to support school's self-evaluation is very original, well designed and I would say very powerful – judging from the findings made by the group.

Peer observation of classroom teaching has already been found to be very useful. In the case of the Learning School, classroom activities are observed by students coming from other schools in different parts of the world with different cultural backgrounds and they are bound to bring with them interesting perspectives and sometimes unthought-of questions which help to stimulate the thinking of teachers and administrators. I am sure that Hong Kong schools find such a concept both challenging and useful for their own development.

As a side effect, I certainly got the impression that the group of international students were personally well rewarded by their one-year stay with the Learning School. Each of them is so confident and had so many interesting stories to tell. After the presentation, some of the audience were heard to remark: 'I wish I could send my child to the Learning School.'

Evaluating by changing places
Professor Michael Schratz, University of Innsbruck

What makes young people travel around the world looking at schools with an evaluative agenda? What brings them together from different countries of the world to do just the one thing: trying to understand the quality of processes and products thereby struggling for agreement about what are the goodness criteria? What is a good school, what is good teaching and, last but not least, what is a good teacher anyway? What's missing is the question which troubled the students most in their quest for quality in and around schools: *What is a good learner?*

I found answers to these questions in the presentation of the Learning School Project, which makes it a unique source of wisdom in school research *from below*. As a researcher I have rarely had so much insight into what is really going on in schools as I did while listening to the students' presentations of what they experienced on their way around the world looking closely at the schools in all the countries they visited. Who can judge better what's going on in a student's mind when teachers deliver boring lessons? Who knows most about what supports and hinders learning?

Evaluation has to do with values, and value judgements are tricky: either they are subjective and therefore biased, or they are (quasi-) objective and therefore of little relevance for the individual situation. Whose values are they anyway? Changing places gives the travellers the chance to experience the jungle of feelings by going from one school culture into another one. Therefore value judgements are more based on comparative and contrasting experiences, which turns decisions about quality into an intersubjective experience and thus makes them more human.

In this sense the Learning School Project has a pioneering function for school improvement at large, from which school can learn a great deal. What I have learnt listening to the students' presentation I want to summarise in the following way:

- Evaluation gains in quality if actors in the field of teaching and learning make the effort and change places by looking at what is well known from a different cultural point of view. This need not be a trip around the world, but changing places between two neighbouring schools might do a good job in getting an idea of what it means to experience a different school culture. Or even less ambitious: changing classes in one school from an evaluative perspective.
- An ethnographic perspective in school research asks for new ways of looking at what really counts in schools with a particular view of teaching and learning.
- If evaluation is understood as an endeavour to understand the quality of processes and products, negotiating meaning (values) and exchanging supporting evidence become key factors for the learning school.
- Evaluation therefore seems to work better in an arrangement of a community of learners rather than in isolation.
- School development depends on the dynamic forces in the fields of tension between continuity and change, between internal and external and between bottom-up and top-down processes.

I wonder, what's the fabric of a global network of schools being prepared to accept students travelling around the world as experts in learning and even more so of teaching?

Learning about the Learning School
Professor Louise Stoll, University of Bath, England, President of ICSEI

The evidence is increasingly clear that students have an important role to play in their own schools' improvement; not as passive recipients of what their teachers, school leaders and the school system decide is right for them to learn, but as active agents in their own learning process.

I was fortunate enough to attend a session about the Learning School at the International Congress for School Effectiveness and Improvement's (ICSEI) annual conference in Copenhagen. The conference theme was Democratic Learning. This session appealed to me because it was to be presented by students – very appropriate to the conference theme, I thought. I found a group of young people from all over the world who were participating in an exciting project and taking a huge personal risk (but then learning involves risk taking). They were leaving their homes for a year and travelling around the world experiencing and learning about schools in other countries and, most important, learning about their own learning.

The focus in Year 3 is student self-evaluation. The young people told us that when they asked their peers about their learning, many commented: 'I've never thought about that before.' As one of the project leaders noted: 'We're chasing something we can hardly find.' Why is it, when learning is so difficult and so important, that time is not devoted to helping learners understand what facilitates their learning and what gets in the way of learning?

The students told us they fed back results to participating departments in the schools they visited. Responses varied and in some cases not many teachers showed up for the students' presentation because they found it difficult to take criticism of their school. What a missed opportunity – and a lack of risk taking. These young people are keen learners. I hope some of them become teachers. I can't help thinking that younger and, perhaps less engaged learners, do not have the opportunity to move on to another school in another country when someone does not want to listen to what they have to say about learning. They often have to conform to someone else's view of them as learners. The trouble is, many respond by disengaging from the learning process.

Can this kind of initiative be rolled out to a large number of schools (or scaled up, as it is described in some countries)? This is a funded international project, but has been carried out on a small budget, with huge commitment from participants and host schools. In a sense it's not really a learning school; it's a learning network, although one hopes that the participating schools are learning from it. It would be interesting to see whether it could be carried out within one country – indeed, students might even become involved as members of inspection teams. Alternatively, an LEA (school district) might try it with its schools. Finally, and most powerfully, a school might decide to try the experience. Many schools are already involved in self-evaluation. This would just take it one step further. Then they really would be learning schools.

Crain Soudien, Consultant, Cape Town, South Africa

Coming as it does out of the Global Classroom initiative, the Learning School might be seen as yet another opportunity for schools and the students and teachers inside the Global Classroom community to strengthen their bonds with one another. To be sure, the Learning School is that but it is also a great deal more. It is a far-reaching attempt to initiate new forms of learning, using new research approaches and putting this new knowledge to use in interesting ways. Innovation, however, is always risky. While it breaks new ground and so seeks to redefine convention, it also has to convince sceptics that the new ground it is laying down is fertile and rich.

In terms of the fertility of the project, two features of the Learning School interest me. The first is the peer researcher idea. The project places young researchers into schools and classrooms where they are expected to operate as serious data and information gatherers and interpreters. The idea has enormous appeal because one has young people interviewing and observing other young people with the hope that they will reach much more deeply into the complexities of their peers' minds and perceptions. The approach is considerably more advanced than those research approaches where young people are used as 'authentic ethnographers', such as the technique of giving people cameras to photograph the world as they see it. What makes it more advanced in this instance is that young people are expected also to make sense of what they find out and to put this into an interpretive frame. This is where the risk comes in. There is much to be gained by having young people working as researchers of their own contexts. They have access to insights and experiences which older people will struggle to achieve, simply because they are the same age as their 'subjects'. At the same time, however, and this is where a discussion arises, they don't have immediate access to the sociological and pedagogical frameworks with which they can make deep sense of the information they are gathering. They can synthesise a lot of the data to generate what one might call first-level understandings, but they are always going to struggle to go beyond the surface information to draw deeper conclusions about why things are the way they are. This is a real challenge to the project and raises questions about the induction of the student researchers into the exercise. How much 'academic' preparation (social, contextual, theories about learning) does one want the student researchers to have? How much of the interpretation of the data can one expect them to do? What does giving student researchers the responsibility for the whole project mean? What is lost and what is gained in the process? Alternatively, coming from another point of view, are concerns about students' roles as data-gatherers and data-interpreters out of place and somewhat precious? The debate on these questions is immensely important and should not be avoided.

The second issue which interests me relates to the larger question of school improvement. Schools can benefit immensely from the Learning School in so far as it gives them an opportunity to understand themselves, what happens inside their schools and to evaluate one or other aspect of the way in which they function as learning organisations. This is an aspect of the project which has enormous potential. Schools can use the Learning School to evaluate and diagnose how teachers and pupils are dealing with one or other dimension of the learning process happening within their four walls. Very few schools anywhere have access to opportunities such as these. They have the potential to put relevant, fresh and – depending on how the Learning School packages its findings – provocative information at the school's disposal. And, critically, the people who are gathering the data are not strict outsiders with punitive agendas. They are people within the community. It is possible for this part of the project to be taken to another level with more participation of the schools in the design of the Learning School. Creating more opportunities for buy-in from the schools will arise from this.

Having raised these issues, it must be repeated that the Learning School is a unique learning initiative and ought to be of great interest to parents, students, teachers and academics who have an interest in cross-cultural learning and in finding innovative ways of improving their schools. All of us can only grow from what it has to teach us.

The untapped potential
David Mansfield, Deputy Headteacher, St Edward VI School, Chelmsford

I was very privileged to be invited to attend the report back session of the Learning School Project in Cambridge on 19 June 2001. As a Deputy Head overseeing a large sixth form in the Home Counties, I was already aware of the untapped potential lurking within many of our students, but nothing had prepared me for the sheer quality of what this team of 17 and 18 year-olds had achieved.

The team travelled internationally to seven schools to research, 'What makes a student want to learn?' The research instruments used were particularly impressive, attaining a level of sophistication that would have graced a Master's dissertation. The group wrestled with creative ways to assess student motivation qualitatively and quantitatively. They ended up using a combination of questionnaires (from school leaders as well as pupils and parents), observation of classes, and individual shadowing. This process also comprised almost hourly spot check interviews on student motivation levels, in which the researchers, as students themselves, returned very honest and instructive findings.

Perhaps most impressive, however, was the comparative work done using the extensive range of data produced. Each school was profiled in terms of what appeared to be the dominant motivational factors against a number of generic headings. The team stuck closely to the empirical data and produced wonderfully accurate portraits of national characteristics. Indeed, further identification and integration of the external, national socio-economic/political context into their conclusions would have been interesting. The findings informed us, for example, that the Swedish school, Bobergsskolan, placed great store on individual human relationships as an extrinsic motivation factor, whereas the German school, Graf Friedrich-Schule, saw 'the Good Person is a Working Person', emphasising the ethic of work as an intrinsic driver.

In conclusion, a number of observations stand out from this year's project.

- It shows that researchers like Jean Rudduck are correct to emphasise the importance to school leaders of listening to the student voice in school improvement. These sixth formers had their fingers on the pulse of the schools they researched and quickly raised issues that, as in the case of Anderson High, on Shetland, rattled a number of cages that more traditional evaluation methods might carefully have avoided or not even have picked up. Should school leaders be releasing their school councils to make more strategic recommendations on school development based on thorough research? Should students be seconded to Leadership Teams for periods to assist in driving up standards? This project raises some very radical possibilities for consideration.
- The confidence with which these students presented their findings, and the dignity and maturity with which they conducted themselves demonstrated the impact of their year off timetable in an international environment. The breadth of their understanding and multi-cultural perspective will shape them for the rest of their lives. Surely we must look at more international exchange as a route to sixth form extension work.
- It seems irrefutable that to draw the best out of our young people we need as educators to be more flexible in the opportunities given to students in their formative years. These students have been fully empowered, trusted with an authority that enabled them to grow in stature. Surely young people need to be given responsibility that goes beyond the mopping up of jobs unwanted by members of staff that prefect duties can quickly deteriorate into.

In short, the Learning School Project is a path-finding approach to not only understanding the global classroom better, but also extending students to the limits of their potential. These are aims we can all applaud.

Part II

Insights into the school experience from the Learning School students

So what did the Learning School students find? What did they discover that may enhance our understanding? What of their findings might penetrate the policy agenda? What should feed into professional development opportunities for headteachers, for teachers, for school governors or school boards and for parents?

The chapters which follow start with the place called school and how it is seen from a student perspective. The commonality of student experience is perhaps even more surprising than the differences. Students in all countries tend to like school, largely because it is a social place, a place to make friends, a compensation, in part at least, for the common feeling that school life is 'stressful' and 'difficult'. Schools have a remarkable similarity across the globe, especially secondary schools with their subjects, timetables, examinations, age-related cohorts, lessons, usually in the context of one teacher one class. We are led inexorably to question the value and effectiveness of that age-old way of packaging and transmitting knowledge, curiously inappropriate for a twenty-first-century world.

What students appreciate about their teachers seems also to be universal in character. The world over, teachers are people who are themselves interested in learning, student-centred, people who make their classrooms relaxed as well stimulating places, enjoy a joke, vary their teaching and listen to their students' points of view. Judgements of teachers are made predominantly in the context of 'lessons', the well-worn, traditional structure of teaching and learning, but the exploration of lessons reveals how ineffective that can be for some students who find themselves left behind, disengaged, and in a situation out of sympathy with their learning needs and learning styles, studying subjects in which they have no interest and in which time hangs heavily. Teachers themselves profess to be caught, along with their students, in this trap, time rushing too fast past them to really engage with deep and meaningful learning.

As we move through these chapters we get progressively closer to how young people strive to make meaning of their classroom experience, each student living out his or her individual life in their classroom. We get a picture of what the school day means for them, peaks and troughs of motivation and of learning. And as we follow them from school to home we get a fascinating glimpse of their parents' expectations and what these mean to students, again with themes and insights that resonate across national boundaries.

One of the valuable contributions of these chapters, relevant to teachers and schools throughout the world is the toolbox of instruments which help to get closer to the real experience of students and teachers. It is through the spot checks, shadowing, on-the-spot interviewing that LS students were able to dig deeper than inspection or testing can afford. These tools may be used by any school in any county for their own internal evaluation purposes. This is self-evaluation at its best its most penetrating, its most honest.

7 A place called school

Saeko Yoshida and Joe Williamson

This chapter begins with comparisons of ethos ratings from four of the schools. 'Ethos' is a word that has passed into the educational vocabulary in the last few years. It is a term hard to define and one even harder to pin down in any hard measurable sense because it is such a subjective phenomenon, a feeling, an impression, something visceral. But it is none the less real for all that because how we feel about our surroundings is powerful and deeply affects how we learn and whether or we are motivated to make the effort.

These judgements of ethos are made by both the Learning School students and the school students, in all cases showing some strong points of difference between the outside and inside perspective. Consistently LS students are more positive than school students in all schools and on all items, raising questions as to where the 'truth' lies, if indeed there is 'truth'. Are students by nature more critical of their own situation? Do they bring to their judgement an historical perspective? As senior students are they reflecting a view that they have grown out of school and desire a more adult environment?

We find, as in many self-evaluation projects, that toilets are a recurring theme. It can be a most significant indicator of school ethos, saying much about the priority given to this inescapable, and sometimes uncomfortable, facet of human life. There are some marked, and perhaps surprising, contrasts among the four schools.

These quantitative data are followed by a more qualitative picture from one of the schools. All of these different snapshots tell us as much about the students perhaps as they do about the school, but they do provoke questions about the place called school.

The four schools

LS1 investigated school ethos in four of the five schools – Sweden, South Africa, Scotland and Japan. The process of our inquiry is illustrated in Figure 7.1.

Anderson High School

The questionnaire was handed out to students in their fifth year of high school in October. The school profile shown in Figure 7.2 contrasts student opinions about their school with those of the LS1 team. There tends to be a fairly close

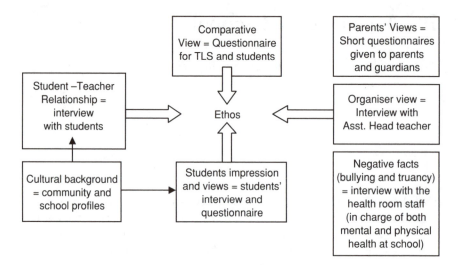

Figure 7.1 Investigating ethos

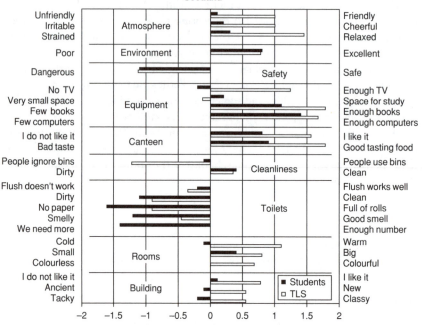

Figure 7.2 School profile, Anderson High School

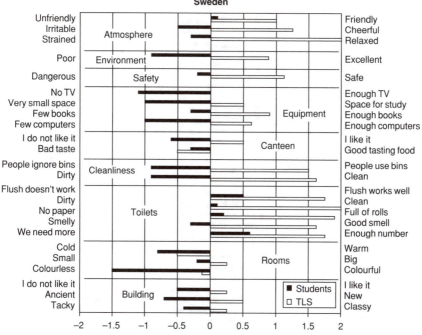

Figure 7.3 School profile, Bobergsskolan

agreement between the two sets of perceptions. The LS1 team are consistently more positive except on the question of use of bins.

Bobergsskolan

In Bobergsskolan 80 per cent of the fifth year students filled in the questionnaire. The items on their profile in Figure 7.3 were mainly similar to the profile used in other countries but there were a few local variations. The contrast between the LS1 team's evaluations and those of the students is very marked. LS1 students are generally very positive while the school students are highly critical. LS1 saw the school as very relaxed, cheerful and friendly and only on the subject of food and temperate warmth gave slightly negative ratings. The most striking data is with regard to toilets. It is surprising to see toilets being rated so positively given the general tendency for toilets to be so poor. There are even grudging positives from the school students.

Nara

A third example comes from Nara where 110 questionnaires were returned. Again, a similar discrepancy is found between schools students' judgements and

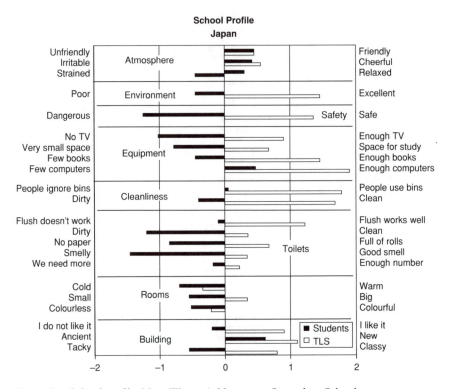

Figure 7.4 School profile, Nara Women's University Secondary School

those of the Learning School team. Only on 'friendly' and 'cheerful' is there agreement and on the newness of the school building (see Figure 7.4). The LS students are clearly impressed by the level of resourcing but students seen dissatisfied. While LS students see the school as relaxed, that is not the students' view. Analysis of these data may help to shed some light on the discrepancies in judgement. We have chosen the South African School to explore further.

The South African context

The questionnaire was distributed to 120 students, as well as Learning School researchers. Here we get a slightly different picture again – agreement between LS1 and schools students on some aspects and disagreement on others (see Figure 7.5). The Learning School students tend to be more positive overall in their evaluations but the differences tend to be fairly small except in relation to cleanliness and use of bins and judgements of classroom size. The striking feature is a positive view of the social, or collegial, ethos of the school as opposed to the resources and school building, toilets and overall resources available to students. These reflect a school struggling to maintain a fitting environment for

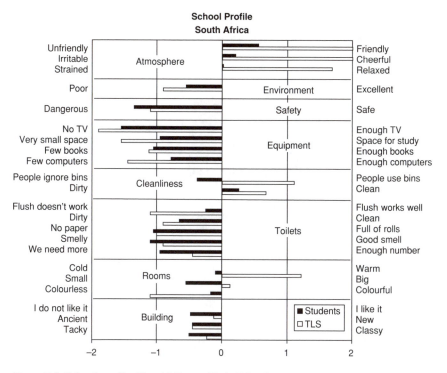

School Profile
South Africa

Figure 7.5 School profile, Harold Cressy High School

students and teachers in a socio-economic context which miltates against that. So much of what is presented reflects things beyond the school's control.

When asked to choose a word to describe the atmosphere of their schools students used words such as sociable, stressed, strict, uneasy, busy. The most common choice, as shown in Figure 7.6, was 'sociable', showing again that the collegial dimension of the school is its single strongest feature although a cluster of terms such as 'stressed', 'busy' and 'tired' suggest that it is also hard work.

Behind the data – Harold Cressy High School

A fuller view of the school in South Africa emerges from interviews with students and teachers.

School buildings

As shown in Figure 7.5, the marks for the school buildings are negative. The building was rebuilt in the last decade but as the profile suggests, the building does not *feel* very new. There is a big hall in the centre of building but the ceiling has got many holes so that rain can drip into the hall. There also are many things that need fixing.

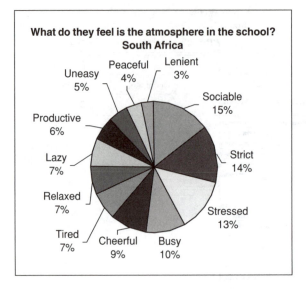

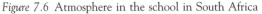

Figure 7.6 Atmosphere in the school in South Africa

Some of the students' comments about the school building were:

> It could be in a better shape.
> It looks like Alcatraz.
> It's too dark inside.
> It makes me feel welcome.
> Close the roof completely in the forum.
> Re-do the whole building and add a swimming pool.

From the LS1 point of view the building was also seen as uncongenial. One of the LS1 team said that the building made the noise echo because it seemed to have been built without consideration for noise insulation. So it makes for a disturbing environment, especially at the breaks.

Classrooms

Most of the rooms in the school have no decoration unless the students them-selves put up posters. The walls are painted in a neutral cream colour. The students also feel that the rooms are too small and crowded as there can be up to fifty students in one classroom.

The question we asked about how hot or cold the rooms are was not such a suitable question because the climate is usually warm in South Africa. However, it can be quite cold in winter and the classrooms do not make allowances for temperature changes. The students wrote:

Needs air conditioning.

The rooms are very small considering the fact that we have more than 40 in our class.

I think we should get curtains for the windows.

Need to transform upstairs classes.

Toilets

The toilets were an issue and students made many comments such as the following:

The toilets smell of smoke.

The toilets are very disgusting.

Need more paper.

We went to look at the toilets and found many of them locked because they were out of order. While there are plenty of toilets, there are only six available for all the girls. There were cigarette ends so it is obvious the students use the toilets as a smoking area as smoking is not allowed inside the school.

Cleanliness

The answers from us about the cleanliness were mainly positive and even after the break time there was little mess and the school seems to be kept clean. The school hires five cleaners who are janitors at the same time, and they clean the school continually. You don't see rubbish lying about in the school and it seems that students are using bins properly. One student did suggest, though, that the school needed more bins because they produce so much rubbish at the two daily breaks.

Equipment

The equipment available is insufficient say the students. We went to have a look in the library and while they do have books, it is often used as a classroom. So, the students do not get the chance to get in the library much and they also cannot get access to the computers. The school does have one computer room but the models of computers are old and slow. The students told us that there is only one TV in the school and although watching TV is one of their preferred learning styles there is limited access.

The students' comments about the equipment were:

There is only one TV.

Very little school equipment for everyone.

We cannot actually use any of the computers.

We need to have more computers because there are some grades that are willing to learn but they don't get the chance.

Safety

This was seen very negatively and taken seriously because it is common to have belongings stolen. These are again a reflection of social conditions outside the school. The students said:

> You cannot feel safe because there are students who have the nerve to take other people's belongings and don't care at all.
> There are too many long fingers in the school.
> Things got missing very quickly in the class.
> MYTH – schools are safe.
> I left my ball in a class for one period and when I came back it was punctured.
> Some people at the school get kicks out of stealing.
> People steal your belongings, even things as simple as your notepads.
> We need lockers in the school.

During one observation period the class had a test and went to a different room to do it and when they finished and came back to their homeroom some of the students' wallets were stolen. Lockers are not the solution, the students told us, because there is a group of thieves in the school and unless these lockers have very secure padlocks, they would be able to break in them anyway.

Environment

How do these things affect the environment of the school as a whole? In view of the negative marks and comments about the facilities, it is not surprising if the environment for learning is also seen as negative. It appears that facilities and resources have a great influence on environment for learning. However, we could see the students are trying to live well with what they have, sticking newspaper on the windows to block the strong sunshine, maintaining a relaxed and cheerful attitude.

The students were, on the whole, friendly to one another and to the visiting team. Very often students just came and spoke to us. It was second nature to them and they didn't think of it as anything special.

What they want

In other schools we could hardly get comments from students as to what they would like to change. In Harold Cressy High School, the students had a lot to say about likes and dislikes and what would make it a better school:

> Change nothing. It is good as it is.
> Most of the teachers are friendly and motivate very well.
> I dislike our past.

I dislike the principle if it rains, it rains in.
I hate the bars on the windows it makes me feel like I'm in a jail.
I dislike the fact that there is no smoking.
The desks should be much bigger.
It's a bit strict.
I like that the school has strict rules.
The school has a bit stupid rules but it's okay anyway.
I hate going to detention when it was the train's fault.

I think that the teachers should think more about the students.
Some of the teachers are cool and they motivate me well.
There is rivalry between students and students, teachers and students and
    teachers and teachers.
The school starts too early.
There aren't enough functions in the school, i.e. social gatherings.

Of all the improvements it was the relationship between some teachers and students that students saw as the most important area for growth. This was seen by them as coming from both sides and not just the responsibility of the staff. Students needed to work on their attitudes and their respect and understanding. The very good relationships that existed with some teachers could be built on and spread through the school.

The school has to struggle against lack of funding and resources and, despite the problems of the building, strenuous efforts are made to keep it clean. Toilets are, as in many other schools, an issue but students cope with adverse circumstances and seem on the whole to be cheerful, friendly and welcoming to visitors. The warmth of the school in its relationships shows how much can be done to counteract the bleakness of the physical structures, a legacy of apartheid, and a huge gap between rich and poor, the privileged and the disadvantaged.

8 The school day

Gregor Sutherland, Duane Henry and Mary Lee

In this chapter we get a feel for the different structures of the school day in different countries. The five schools presented here are in highly contrasting cultural settings – Scotland, Sweden, Japan, South Africa and Hong Kong – and some of the differences are immediately striking. They range from the very open-ended and flexible school day in Sweden to the highly structured day in the Hong Kong school, reflections more of the general culture than of the school itself. But beneath these obvious differences we are also struck by many of the apparent similarities – subjects, periods, classes, tests, pressure – things we have come to accept as defining the place called school. This does raise some fundamental questions about ways in which schools have traditionally structured learning and teaching and continue to do so. It prompts us to ask what the alternatives to this traditional school day might be.

Anderson High School, Lerwick, Shetland

A day at the Anderson High School begins with the arrival of staff and students. The latter come either on foot, by bus or get dropped off by car. Which mode of transport you use depends on where you live. Those who come by bus might live a few miles away or out in the more rural parts of Shetland – for them, the day began long before their arrival at the school gates at 8.45 a.m. For those who live close by, they walk, and for the students who live in the halls of residence on campus, that literally means a minute between bedroom and blackboard.

By 8.30 a.m., some half an hour before registration, there are many students at school, gathering in their designated year group areas or in the canteen to catch some breakfast before lessons. Students continue to arrive during that half hour period, and some are still getting out of cars in front of the school as the first bell of the day rings.

As in most schools, when the bell goes there is a slow moving process as the corridors fill and the occupants flow from their year area to their designated registration classes. Registration is at 8.55 and usually just takes the form of a brief attendance check, the passing on of any information to the class for the day or coming week, and covering various administrative matters. Afterwards, the move begins again as students make their way to their first class of the day.

The Anderson timetable is quite simple. The day is divided into six periods, with a morning break after the first two, and a lunch break before the last two. The end of one period and the start of the next is marked by one bell, and all classes are the same length, apart from the fifth period on Wednesdays; which is devoted to social education and is a bit shorter than all other lessons, meaning that the school day is over fifteen minutes earlier on that day.

No morning is complete without the regular announcements read by one of the senior management team over the school public address system. It is a regular feature of the school day and occurs before the end of the second period, just as students are turning their attention to their mid-morning break and beating the queues at the tuck shop or canteen.

Students are allowed off the school grounds for their lunch break between 12.50 p.m. and 1.45 p.m. As the school is within reasonable walking distance of the town centre, many students go there to buy lunch and meet friends. Those who choose not to dine in town can do so in the school canteen. Quite a few students seem to use the canteen, and its popularity is probably increased during the winter months and when the weather renders the short walk down into town unpleasant.

The senior students in the school (those in fifth and sixth year) have a few free periods in their timetable – typically four a week. During these non-timetabled periods, the students can spend their time in different places doing one of two things. Some choose to relax and spend the time socially with friends chatting or playing a game, or alone listening to music or reading. For these students, their common hang-out zones are their year group areas or the school canteen. Other, perhaps more motivated students, can go to designated study rooms to work or make a start on homework. On occasion, students go to see their teachers, and have been known to get some extra tuition and help if the teacher happens to be available at the time. This use of a free period probably only applies to a small minority in Anderson High though. Some might spend the time using computers to access the Internet and do some e-mailing. It is quite common that free periods are timetabled at the end of the day. For some this means the chance to go home a little bit earlier.

Years one to four don't have free periods so the end of the day is generally marked with the same mass movement of people as the students flow from the various exits. Within a few minutes of the bell going at 3.40 p.m., the school is virtually empty and the cleaners outnumber the students. Actually, many of the cleaners are students as some of the senior students have after school part-time cleaning jobs. For those with dual roles as both student and staff, they finally leave the building at 5.30 p.m.

Nara Women's University Secondary School, Nara, Japan

The school starts at 8.30 a.m. and usually finishes at 3 p.m. and twice a week at 3.45 p.m. Students have either six or seven periods a day. Between each period they have a ten-minute break plus one hour for lunch. From the observation it became clear that the students get tired as the day progresses and some fall asleep in class. This may be attributed to exhaustion from the club activities, studying at home long into the night, or simply their way of dealing with daily stress.

Morning classes are much more lively. Students seemed to be more interested and worked more willingly. Afternoon classes were quite different. Right from the very beginning we were struck by its calmness. Students tended to be very passive, sitting, some watching the teacher and some laying their heads down on the desk. Some tried to take notes but the majority were avoiding that as well. The teachers, we assumed, recognised this and made allowances because we never witnessed students being told off and the teaching was at a much slower pace than usual. In the morning classes that we observed the teacher changed topics and questions very rapidly, creating a very productive and fast-paced atmosphere. In the afternoon class the teacher did not seem to be as concerned to meet the lesson's requirements. The spot check figure for tiredness in the afternoon was very much higher than in the morning and students were much more likely to say that time was passing very slowly. On other items there was, surprisingly, not such a great difference.

It did seem to us that the teacher relied on the morning classes to cover the ground while the afternoon classes took more the form of additional help, checking up what the students remembered but not teaching any new material.

Bobergsskolan, Ange, Sweden

Students attending Bobergsskolan come from all across the Komune and use various means to get to school, from buses and trains for those who live further away, and cars and by foot for others. The school day begins at 7.55 a.m. with the first class of the day. Those who have spent a long time travelling to get to school can have breakfast in the canteen prior to the start of classes. Around the school there are mounted television screens that display various types of information for students. When students arrive at school they have a look at one of the screens to see if there is any information relevant to them and their school day.

Student timetables vary depending on what year and programme they are in. The length of timetabled classes varies also, from 60 minutes to 120 minutes and can be any length in between. The number of lessons timetabled also varies from day to day. The overall result is that the length of lessons vary throughout the day, the frequency of lessons varies from day to day, and those differences are determined by what year and programme the student is in.

Because the start and end times of lessons are staggered, the corridors and public areas of the school rarely seem to be very busy. Lunch, which typically is taken at about 10.30 a.m., is one of the few times of the day when the majority of the students seem to have some time out of classes together. But the exact start time and length of the lunch break vary according to year programme and day of the week. In the early afternoon, the canteen re-opens to serve light options. During this time, depending on the timetable, the canteen can become a little busier again as students gather for another bite to eat.

The timetable also includes a significant amount of free time for each student, though this varies from day to day. This free time, or study time, may be spent in a number of ways. There is a quiet room in one of the main corridors which is referred to as the 'monkey cage'. Here, students can come to study in assured quietness. Others may spend their time in the library where the atmosphere is slightly less orientated to study than in the 'monkey cage'. There are also a number of areas around the school where there are sofas, and students can be found reading or chatting with friends. Outside the canteen there is an area furnished with tables and chairs which is used as an extension of the canteen during its opening hours. When the canteen is closed, however, this area is also used by students who are not in timetabled lessons.

The Swedish school day could be described as very flexible. During shadowing several interesting things were revealed. Occasionally some students arrived late for classes, by up to half an hour in some cases. This was, from time to time, also true of teachers. As responsibility for learning is always thrown back on the student, the purpose of this is to foster a greater sense of independence. It is also quite common for classes to end before the designated time, with the class perhaps being told that they can study elsewhere at their convenience. For one student, his day began at 8.20 a.m. and was over by 10.40 a.m. He began his first class of the day a little later than timetabled and his second of the day ended sooner that it was supposed to. He had no more scheduled lessons so went home early. Whether or not he used his time at home to study is uncertain as we could not shadow him then.

Sometimes a class just does not take place for some reason. Some students use this extra free time very productively while others spend it wastefully, just listening to music or chatting with friends. Others, however, fit things into the free time, like another student who had a large gap in her timetable in the middle of the day due to a cancelled class, so went to the music department and had an unscheduled and impromptu lesson.

The school day ends for different students at different times on different days. Sometimes, as the case above illustrates, the day can be over after just a few hours at school – though this is an extreme example. The official end of the school day is 2.55 p.m., though by that time many students have finished for the day and have already left the building.

As observers, coming in from different school systems, we felt the Swedish school day was chaotic and lacked structure. Over time, however, we came to appreciate its flexible approach and room it gave individuals to learn and take responsibility for their own timetabling and use of free time.

Harold Cressy High School, South Africa

The timetable

The timetable at Cressy is limited by the teachers available to teach the subjects. If a teacher leaves, his or her subject may have to be withdrawn from the timetable if there is no one left to teach the subject. A good example of this is woodwork. The school is equipped with full facilities for this subject but currently there is no teacher who is qualified to teach it.

Eleventh grade students study six subjects. There are three compulsory subjects, these being English, Afrikaans and Biology. Three of the four classes study Maths as well. The other subjects on offer are Geography, History, Accounts, Economics, Physical Science (which includes elements of both Physics and Chemistry, Typing and Needlework, although students do not have a completely free choice of these subjects).

The timetable is structured in a six-day cycle with subjects rotating according to which day in the cycle it is, rather than which day of the week it is. In each day of the cycle students study each subject six or seven times, usually once per day but for some subjects twice. The most frequently studied subject is Maths and this occurs eight times in each six-day cycle.

Structure and Subjects

The students we interviewed generally thought their timetable was fine and most had little to say about the way in which it was structured. Those who commented said they thought there were too many periods of Maths in each cycle, and they didn't like double periods in some subjects, especially Maths. However, double periods happen quite infrequently, at most twice a week. Quite often students study the same subject twice in one day even though these periods are not placed together. Again, some students think that this is too much and say they don't enjoy these periods.

Two groups made the point that there is only one period of PE for eleventh grade students in each six-day cycle and they felt that this was not enough. One group was disappointed that the Life Orientation and Guidance periods were no longer being taught. Until last year there were periods planned by the Guidance Department to give students advice and knowledge about current issues. This year they were not included in the curriculum.

Most of students we talked to would prefer to study fewer subjects but would also like to add further subjects to the curriculum. Some thought that six subjects was a satisfactory number. When asked what extra subjects they would like to include, there were many suggestions. The most popular were: more languages, for example, French and Italian, Accounting, Business Economics, Home Economics and some practical arts subjects such as dance, drama, music and art. The majority of students made comments about Computing too. At present there is a computer room in Cressy but eleventh grade students do not have access to it. Virtually all of the students thought it would be extremely beneficial if they had the opportunity to study some kind of computing.

The six-day cycle

The majority of the students are happy with the six-day cycle. Previously the timetable followed a seven-day cycle until last year when it was changed to six days. One group said that for a while it was confusing, not knowing what day of the cycle it was. Another group felt that it was less monotonous than the typical five-day schedule and made time go faster while yet another group preferred the Monday to Friday timetable as it made them feel more organised.

Free periods

All groups except one said they would appreciate some more free periods. Presently students do not have any free periods. Each of the seven lessons every day is taken up with academic subjects. One group said that one free period per day would be ideal, but even if there were three or four in each six-day cycle, they felt that students would make productive use of this time. Other groups did not suggest how many free periods they would ideally like but said that they would like some at least. Some students said that if they had some free time they could spend those periods doing their homework, leaving them more time in the evenings to pursue other activities. The majority of the students said they would use their free periods either studying or socialising, with about 4 in 10 opting for more sports. One group specifically said they would not study in this time because the break times were not long enough. One student warned that most people would just leave the school and not use the time productively although this might change as exams approached.

Length of lessons

Generally, students thought that 45 minutes was an ideal length for each lesson. Some thought that each lesson should be only 30 minutes, and one group agreed that 40 minutes would be better. They said that it was difficult to remain focused for a full lesson and that they tended to get bored towards the end, so less than 45 minutes would be ideal. It was agreed, though, that the appropriate length of lesson very much depended on the teacher. There were those who could make the class interesting while for those who couldn't maintain interest, shorter lessons would be appreciated more.

Public Secondary School, New Territories, Hong Kong

The school

The school operates a timetable on a six-day cycle. Students attend classes from 8.30 a.m. to 3.30 p.m., Monday to Friday, with a 15-minute morning recess and a one hour and ten minutes lunch break. Each class is 40 minutes in length, with no time allotted for changing classes. Most classes consist of approximately 30 students, with the occasional advanced class of six students. Classes are conducted primarily in Cantonese using English textbooks. Most teachers use a microphone, amplifier and loudspeaker system when addressing classes.

Preliminary impressions

The Hong Kong education system is a high-pressure system in which students are graded from an early age. At the high school level all students must pass through a series of what students colloquially call 'hell' (also known as exams) in order to achieve 'heaven', also known as graduation. In high school, students are streamlined after the third year according to exam results. Students are either placed in the arts or the science stream. Within this system, it became apparent during our research that students have little or no opportunity to be flexible in their learning. Whereas the findings from Europe suggest that students do not take enough responsibility for their learning, our research in Hong Kong suggests that the extent to which students have the opportunity to take and use responsibility for their learning is quite limited.

Many students of the secondary school say that the Hong Kong education system is too restrictive for their learning. They find the curriculum is too densely packed with unrelated information, and the tests too numerous and dominant. As students must continuously work towards achieving assessment-based criteria in frequent exams, they have little room to explore or develop their learning. This system actually works against learning development. In such a system, the development of a student's self-based learning criteria is severely restricted, therefore the development of student self-evaluation is also necessarily limited.

Most of the handful of students selected from the sixth grade for in-depth interview felt that they lacked freedom to make use of interests in their learning and said that the system relied too heavily on memorisation techniques to pass through it. In English and History, for example, students are required to memorise lengthy model answers in order to pass the exam, which consumes most of their time in these subjects.

Students feel they have become too dependent on teachers to give them information to pass the rigorous, rigidly test-oriented system. One example came from a contracted English teacher from New Zealand who experimented with different teaching methods with the aim of encouraging students to think more about their learning. Students responded with interest to this teacher's class, but after a couple of classes the students insisted that he simply give them the material they needed to 'underline', 'highlight' and 'memorise' in order to pass the examination. Students express a desire for change within the school and the Hong Kong school system, but find it difficult to deviate from the norm or take risks.

On the positive side, teachers often have fairly close teacher–student relationships. No researched student mentioned this directly, but our international student research group have observed and discussed this frequently. It may be related to the fact that most teachers are relatively young. Some teachers have made attempts to be flexible within the system and promote discussion about learning development and personal development, but they also admit that time for this is too limited.

It should be noted that the Hong Kong Ministry of Education has implemented several initiatives to introduce meaningful and wide-ranging change. Being a government-owned school, it should be at the forefront of any change. During Learning School research, students and staff took part in the initial stages of the IQEA School Improvement Study which is designed to promote a greater sense of ownership among teachers and students. Time will tell.

9   Layouts for learning

Debbie Moncrieff, Kotaro Nariai and Gregor Sutherland

The point has been made in previous chapters that context matters. We respond to the environment in which we find ourselves in very different ways, but never neutrally. What makes a classroom a place for learning is never a simple matter, as seen in the length to which some teachers will go to make it a more congenial place to be, a comfortable and enjoyable place in which to learn and a stimulating place. Classrooms may be seen as 'behaviour settings', and even when they are empty of people they send quite clear messages about how people will behave when they enter. Children will go straight to desks and only the cheekiest or uninformed will presume to occupy the largest chair at the front of the room. While there is a predictable similarity of classroom space from country to country, the Learning School students also documented differences in classroom layout and furniture, raising questions about why such differences exist and what underlying pedagogy they assume. These are some examples.

A Swedish school

Figure 9.1 shows what one classroom looks like in the Swedish school. The layout signals choice. You can choose where to sit, or possibly even lie, round a table, face to face with friends, in a relaxed posture on a sofa, or at a more conventional desk. How does this seem to affect what students do and how they learn? Based on an observation of one 45-minute class on a Friday we noted the following.

The class began ten minutes late. As the students came in they were very sociable to each other and looked as though they were enjoying being together in the classroom. The layout of the room is such that with the free seating the students can decide as they enter the room how well they want to work. It seemed to us that those who were feeling sociable went and sat on the sofa, while those who wanted to work sat at a desk.

When class began, the students settled down and everyone listened; some taking notes and others not. Several students were making productive comments to the teacher. As the lesson continued many students began to become less interested in the lesson and more interested in socialising with those nearby. Interaction between the teacher and the students occurred quite frequently but

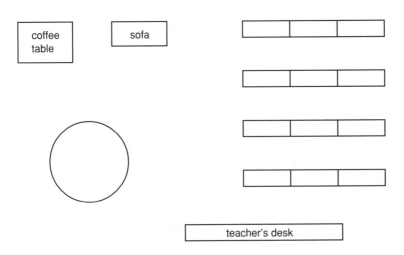

Figure 9.1 Classroom layout in a Swedish school

most of the class was spent listening to the teacher. By the end of class many students seemed to have lost concentration and were quite eager to leave the room.

We observed five types of students in the class:

1   Those listening carefully to the teacher, taking notes, paying attention and staying quiet throughout.
2   Students who were listening well but interacting with the teacher, asking questions and making comments.
3   Those who were chatting with students who sat near them but also listening and taking notes.
4   Students not interested in the lesson, chatting for most of the time.
5   Students doing other things, either sleeping or listening to music.

With some exceptions, we observed that the students who were seated on the right of the room and the pair on the sofa were mostly of the first type, concentrating throughout. Those around the circular table were of the second and third type, with also one student who was not interested at all. Those who were on the sofas at the back of the room were mostly distracted and chatting, the fourth type, although they were taking notes for some of the time.

A Japanese classroom

In all the classes we observed the seating arrangement was similar, rows of indiividual desks facing the front, girls mixed randomly with boys. As hardly any interaction was taking place, the fact that the genders were mixed did not seem of any relevance. On the whole, students were well behaved, mainly

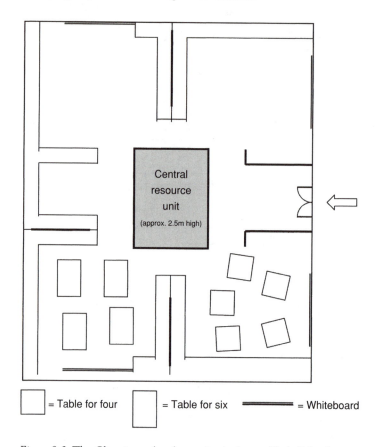

Figure 9.2 The Chemistry class layout in Anderson High School

listening to the teacher, and if not paying attention they tended not to disturb the others.

In one class, however, we saw a very clear division between the socialising students and students productively working. In this class all the relaxed and talkative students were sitting at the back of the class and were disturbing the lesson. Even the more destructive group at the back was further split into two groups. One group, of mixed gender, were enjoying the lesson in a very relaxed way while at the other side of the class there was a group of boys who were quite loud and disruptive. While the teacher reminded them several times to pay attention the boys were not told off.

A Scottish classroom

In the Chemistry department at the Anderson High School the classrooms are all in an open plan area. It is a new department and is the only one with open plan classrooms in the school. In D-block, the chemistry and biology block, there are two open plan wings. Figure 9.2 shows one of them. They are separated by a central concourse from which each wing is accessed (see arrow on right).

There are no ceilings in D-block so the roof beams can be seen which creates a feeling of height and openness. In the centre of the wing there is a large resource block of shelves and cupboards. Dividing and surrounding each class space are built-in worktops and more cupboards. Above worktop height there are dividing partitions (shown in thicker lines) that add some more privacy to classes. Tables tend to be arranged in groups and there is an absence of an obvious teacher's desk in each space.

The teacher thinks that this style of classroom is great and she would not change it for the old style of classrooms. There is lots of equipment nearby and the school does not need so much of it because two classrooms can share the same equipment. The teachers from the other classrooms sometimes wander into the class to help out some of the students that need help when they have free time. If it was not open plan, then the other teachers would not be able to see the other class and it is very beneficial for the students to have two teachers available sometimes. The teacher also does not have a desk in the class so there is no obvious front to the room. She said that she did this on purpose so as not to have a front area of the class where many teachers feel comfortable just staying in and dictating to their students. This allows her to move around the class and not have to worry about what and where her students are looking. As there is no front to the class, group tabling is encouraged and this is a big part of the way that the teacher teaches. The teacher can address each group individually according to what particular topic or problem they are working on.

However, the open plan area does have some bad points as well. The noise level can get very high as four lessons can be going on at any one time and obviously voices carry between one working area and the next. Sometimes there may be younger students in the next area and not only do they get noisy but sometimes they wander around the department and enter other working areas. This means that it is quite easy for someone to get distracted by other classes. The other classes are not actually visible from the desks of the students but if they want, they can easily move to see what's going on elsewhere. The noise level does take some time to get used to but when you have been in the class for around two or three weeks you don't really notice it. Another observer came to the class one day but said that she could not observe the class well as she was finding herself getting distracted by the things going on around her. The open plan does have many advantages and some disadvantages but overall it seems to be working well in this class and no one is really bothered by it at all.

The History class offers a different kind of layout for learning (see Figure 9.3). The grouped table arrangement is not uncommon in Scottish schools particularly in arts subjects, signalling a certain kind of discursive content in which

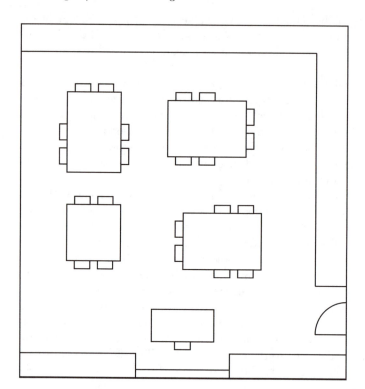

Figure 9.3 The History class layout in Anderson High School

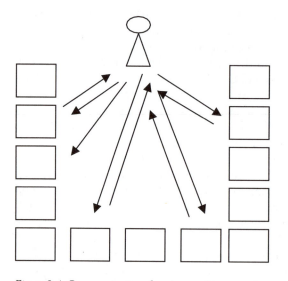

Figure 9.4 Communication flow in one German classroom

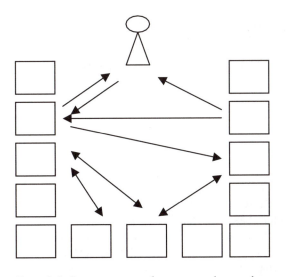

Figure 9.5 Communication flow: a second example

students are encouraged to share ideas with one another and work collectively on tasks. It allows the teacher to work with groups as well as address the whole class.

Quite typically in German classrooms students sit in a horseshoe formation rather than in rows (see Figure 9.4). This means that you are never looking at the back of anyone's head and also that it is much less easy to hide behind such a neighbouring obstacle which can shield you from the teacher's line of sight. More positively, however, the set-up suggests that there will be interaction across the class from student to student as well as student to teacher.

The focus of the horseshoe is, nonetheless, still on the teacher who occupies the central space at the front and dictates the interaction and flow. Figure 9.5 illustrates a different teaching and learning style which the horseshoe arrangement permits.

10 Subjects, subjects, subjects

Miki Nishimura, Duane Henry and Colin Bragg

All secondary schools in all countries structure their time around the study of 'subjects'. In fact the curriculum has a familiar look from one country to the next – languages, Mathematics, Science, Social Subjects, Art, Music – timetabled in periods with classes of students – a school structure that would be comfortably recognisable to an octogenarian returning to her old school. The variation from school to school is primarily in the range of subjects studied, length of school periods and balance of subjects within the school day but the underlying similarity does allow for a common set of data as to the preferences and dislikes of school students, male and female. In this chapter data are presented on what students said about their school subjects. One of the most interesting findings is on reasons why some subjects appeal more than others – intrinsic interest, and why subjects are least liked – pressure for extrinsic grades. There are echoes here of Csikzentimihalyi's (1998) study of motivation which showed that the top three reasons for engagement in school subjects were, in order, enjoyment, satisfaction in getting better at learning, and interest.

What students said

In each country students were asked to name their most and least favourite subjects, followed by reasons for their likes and dislikes. The patterns between the sexes are interesting in both similarities and differences from one country to the next. Across the six schools there were some close agreements as to favourite and least favourite subjects. Figure 10.1 shows an aggregate of favourite subjects.

As can be seen, creative subjects together with social science and physical science are most often chosen. Foreign languages follow in fourth place. Native language and Mathematics, generally seen as the two key or 'core' subjects, figure low in the favourites list. However, these overall data conceal some significant differences between one country and the next. Table 10.1 illustrates these differences.

The most striking difference shown in Table 10.1 is Foreign Languages, seen as important and valuable by the European countries and Japan but rated very low by the two English-speaking countries. Bobergsskolan is out of step on

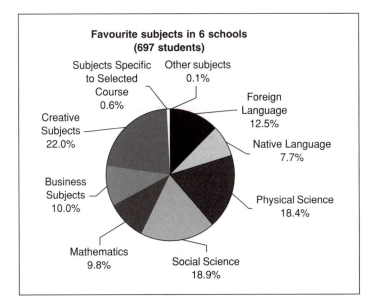

Figure 10.1 Favourite subjects in six schools

Table 10.1 What is your favourite subject? (% within each school)

	Scotland	Sweden	Czech Republic	Germany	S. Africa	Japan
Foreign Language	2.4	27	23.1	17.2	3.4	15.7
Native Language	4.3	11.1	1.7	5.4	14.5	10.4
Physical Science	21.3	1.6	22.2	23.7	17.2	16.5
Social Science	22.6	4.8	16.2	8.6	29	20
Mathematics	4.3	12.7	7.7	14	9.7	14.8
Business Subjects	7.9	6.3	13.7	1.1	24.8	0
Creative Subjects	37.2	30.2	15.4	30.1	1.4	21.7
Subjects Specific to Selected Course	0	6.3	0	0	0	0
Other subjects	0	0	0	0	0	0.9
Sample size	164	63	117	93	145	115

Physical and Social Science while Harold Cressy is very low on creative subjects but comparatively high on Business Studies.

But what is that makes students choose their favourite subjects? Again, over-all results from six schools give a general picture, as shown in Figure 10.2. As can be seen from Figure 10.2, nearly three-quarters state that it is intrinsic interest that drives motivation. The only other substantial group is the 12 per cent who say they are motivated by grades. But a more varied picture emerges when we look at differences from school to school, as shown in Table 10.2.

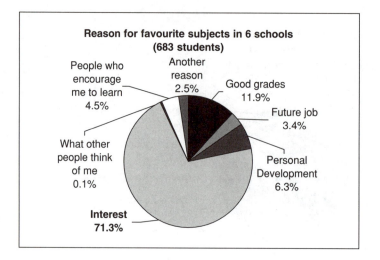

Figure 10.2 Reason for favourite subjects in six schools

Table 10.2 Why do you like it? (% within each school)

	Scotland	Sweden	Czech Republic	Germany	S. Africa	Japan
Foreign Language	2.4	27	23.1	17.2	3.4	15.7
Good grades	8.6	9.7	4.3	23.1	13.3	15
Future job	0.6	0	7.7	4.4	4.2	2.8
Personal Development	4.9	6.5	2.6	0	9.8	13.1
Interest	80.4	72.6	77.8	67	62.2	65.4
What other people think of me	0	1.6	0	0	0	0
People who encourage me to learn	4.3	4.8	3.4	3.3	8.4	1.9
Another reason	1.2	4.8	4.3	2.2	2.1	1.9
Sample size	163	62	117	91	143	107

While there are differences, the most striking aspect of Table 10.2 is the high figures for interest, by far the most important factor in all of the schools. Good grades are seen as relatively important in the German school while personal development and the influence of other people are given a much higher rating in South Africa than elsewhere.

Least favourite subjects

Least favourite subjects are in some respects a reverse mirror of the positive but that is not the whole story. These are shown for the six schools in Figure 10.3. Again, despite the common factors, there are differences among the six schools.

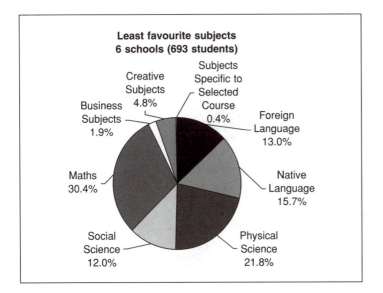

**Least favourite subjects
6 schools (693 students)**

Figure 10.3 Least favourite subjects in six schools

Table 10.3 What is your least favourite subject? (% within each school)

	Scotland	Sweden	Czech Republic	Germany	S. Africa	Japan
Foreign Language	2.5	13.7	7	20.2	22.9	14.5
Native Language	41.1	2.7	8.8	5.3	2.8	20.9
Physical Science	12	15.1	46.5	17	25	14.5
Social Science	5.7	13.7	19.3	26.6	1.4	13.6
Mathematics	17.2	42.5	14.9	24.5	43.1	31.8
Business Subjects	3.8	0	0	1.1	4.2	0
Creative Subjects	7.5	8.2	3.5	5.3	0.7	4.5
Subjects Specific to Selected Course	0	4.1	0	0	0	0
Sample size	158	73	114	94	144	110

Native languages is markedly most unpopular in Scotland while in Sweden and South Africa it is Maths that is significantly more unpopular than elsewhere. In Germany it is physical sciences that are least liked (see Table 10.3). These are not necessarily national or even local differences but may simply reflect the individual school, its curriculum, its teaching, peer group influences, or the pressures to achieve in these areas.

The reasons students give for their least favourite subjects does throw some further light on these questions, as shown in Figure 10.4. It appears from Figure 10.4 that it is pressure of grades that most detracts from a subject's

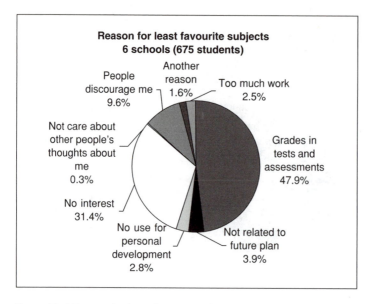

Figure 10.4 Reason for least favourite subjects in six schools

interest. Nearly half of all students are in this category while another 30 per cent simply say they have no interest in the subject. This is perhaps related to compulsion and pressure to achieve.

When we look at it school by school (see Figures 10.5 to 10.10), while there are common reasons, the Swedish students are noticeably less demotivated by grades than the others but are most likely to cite lack of interest. This is not a surprising result in a school which puts subject motivation, interest choice and responsibility at the centre of its educational philosophy and practice.

Gender differences

There are significant gender differences in choice of favourite and least favourite subjects (see Figure 10.11). Girls are more likely to favour Foreign and Native Languages while boys are more inclined to choose physical science and Maths. These results are not perhaps surprising given research and international comparative data which continue to show consistent gender biases in mathematics and languages, often seen as having genetic origins.

Tables 10.4 and 10.5 show how these gender preferences break down school by school. They show what the aggregated data hide, for example, the very big difference between Anderson High and Graf Friedrich Schule on Foreign Language and between the Swedish and German schools and Physical Science, again reflecting national cultures as well as individual school cultures. Similar differences hold true when it comes to comparing girls' preferences school by school. These show that gender is less of a determining factor than the

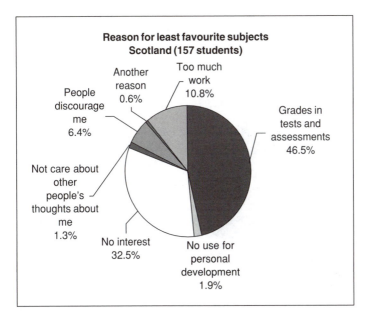

Figure 10.5 Reason for least favourite subjects (Scotland)

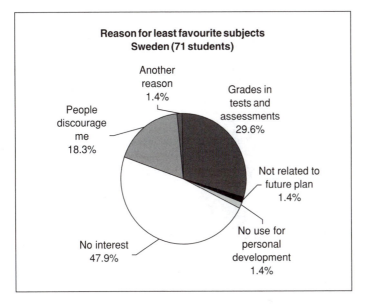

Figure 10.6 Reason for least favourite subjects (Sweden)

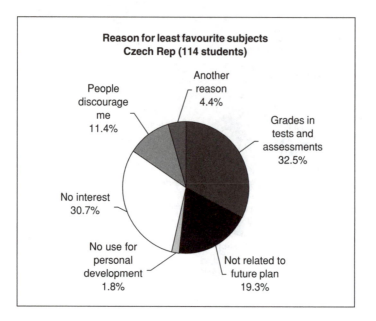

Figure 10.7 Reason for least favourite subjects (Czech Republic)

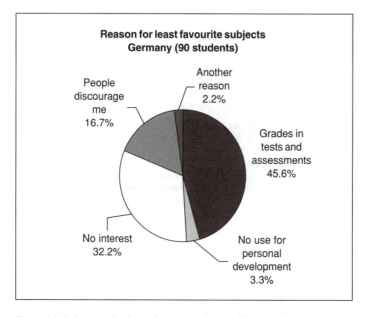

Figure 10.8 Reason for least favourite subjects (Germany)

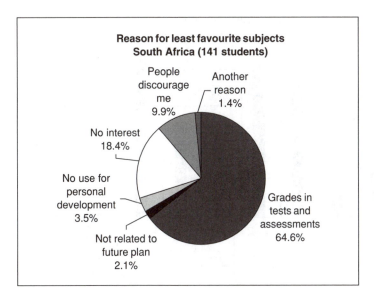

Figure 10.9 Reason for least favourite subjects (South Africa)

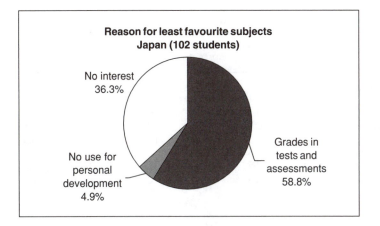

Figure 10.10 Reason for least favourite subjects (Japan)

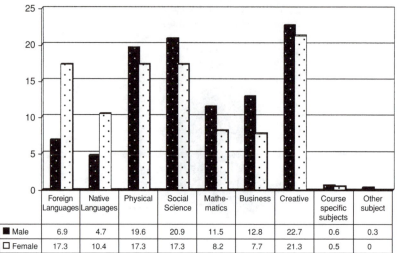

Figure 10.11 Favourite subject by gender in six schools
Note: males = 321; females = 376

Table 10.4 What is your favourite subject? (boys)

	Scotland	Sweden	Czech Republic	Germany	S. Africa	Japan
Foreign Language	0	18.8	13.2	2.6	4.5	8.8
Native Language	0	3.1	1.9	2.6	9	10.5
Physical Science	23	3.1	15.1	36.8	19.4	17.5
Social Science	17.6	6.3	18.9	18.4	32.8	22.8
Mathematics	5.4	12.5	5.7	15.8	13.4	19.3
Business Subjects	12.2	12.5	26.4	2.6	19.4	0
Creative Subjects	41.9	37.5	18.9	21.1	1.5	19.3
Subjects Specific to Selected Course	0	6.3	0	0	0	0
Other subjects	0	0	0	0	0	1.8
Sample size	74	32	53	38	67	57

Table 10.5 What is your favourite subject? (girls)

	Scotland	Sweden	Czech Republic	Germany	S. Africa	Japan
Foreign Language	4.4	35.5	31.3	27.3	2.6	22.4
Native Language	7.8	19.4	1.6	7.3	19.2	10.3
Physical Science	20	0	28.1	14.5	15.4	15.5
Social Science	26.7	3.2	14.1	1.8	25.6	17.2
Mathematics	3.3	12.9	9.4	12.7	6.4	10.3
Business Subjects	4.4	0	3.1	0	29.5	0
Creative Subjects	33.3	22.6	12.5	36.4	1.3	24.1
Subjects Specific to Selected Course	0	6.5	0	0	0	0
Other subjects	0	0	0	0	0	0
Sample size	90	31	64	55	73	58

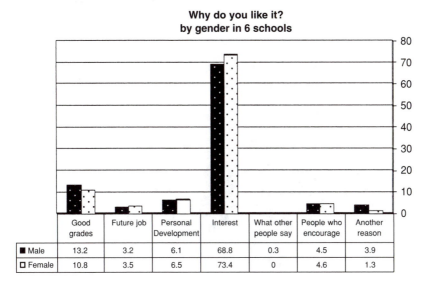

Why do you like it?
by gender in 6 schools

	Good grades	Future job	Personal Development	Interest	What other people say	People who encourage	Another reason
■ Male	13.2	3.2	6.1	68.8	0.3	4.5	3.9
□ Female	10.8	3.5	6.5	73.4	0	4.6	1.3

Figure 10.12 Why do you like it, by gender in six schools?
Note: males = 311; females = 372

individual school, as shown, for example, by the fact that in Bobergsskolan no girl chose physical science (and only 3.1. for boys) while in Gymnázium Zlín it was 28 per cent for girls and 15.1 for boys!

When we look at reasons for likes and dislikes by gender (see Figures 10.12 and 10.13), there are fairly close similarities suggesting that girls and boys tend to be motivated and demotivated by very similar things and that, when it comes to issues of gender, while significant, gender differences are less of a consideration than other factors. What lies behind these figures we can only discover by

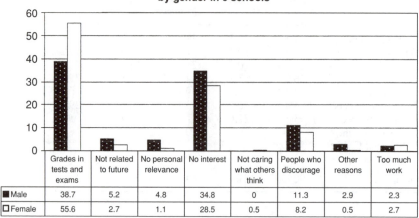

	Grades in tests and exams	Not related to future	No personal relevance	No interest	Not caring what others think	People who discourage	Other reasons	Too much work
■ Male	38.7	5.2	4.8	34.8	0	11.3	2.9	2.3
□ Female	55.6	2.7	1.1	28.5	0.5	8.2	0.5	2.7

Figure 10.13 Why don't you like it, by gender in six schools?
Note: males = 310; females = 365

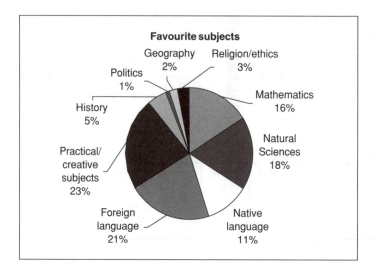

Figure 10.14 Favourite subjects in Germany (LS3)

using more fine-grained instruments, the findings of which are illustrated in Chapters 12 to 18.

Postscript

There is an interesting postscript to this LS2 study. It comes from the LS3 students and their data from one German school. As it was with a different

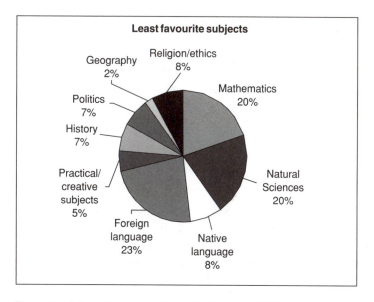

Figure 10.15 Least favourite subjects in Germany (LS3)

cohort of school students and conducted by a different Learning School team, it is a useful test of data reliability. Although the questions put are not quite the same, very similar findings emerge. The German school's choice of favourite subjects is shown in Figure 10.14.

Creative and practical subjects were chosen by nearly a quarter of all students with Foreign Languages a close second. Mathematics is chosen by only 1 per cent. But when to comes to least favourite subject, Mathematics is out in front with 23 per cent along with Native Language and Natural Sciences (see Figure 10.15).

There is an irony in the fact that it is the three subjects of the curriculum internationally regarded as the 'core' that are least chosen, not only by German students but typically by others too. Perhaps it is because these subjects are seen as the core and most emphasis is put on them. By contrast, it is the creative subjects, least emphasised, least measured in international league tables, that are most favoured by students. We are bound to ask: are these things by any chance related?

11 Lessons, lessons, lessons

Jimmy Karttunen, Carla Soudien, Robert Janícek and Joe Williamson

Lessons are what happens in school. In secondary schools all around the world students move from one lesson to the next, typically four or five in a day. Each of these tries to condense into a small time frame, and often a congested classroom, the maximum amount of information and knowledge acquisition that can be managed with the spillover being what students have to do on their own time as homework or home study. Many catch up in after school classes, tutorials or private lessons. However dedicated the teacher, he or she is constrained within the dictates of the classroom, the timetable and the urgent need to cover the syllabus. Demands of university entrance push teachers towards methods of which they do not always approve, as we learn from teachers talking about their teaching and their students' learning. In this chapter three different kinds of lessons are observed, one a language class where the demands of written language and grammatical accuracy prevail, the second a Czech class in which a common way of ensuring student participation is to bring them out to the blackboard, and the third example from Sweden, the adult class in which teaching and learning take on a different dimension.

Two Japanese classes: learning English
Jimmy Kartunen and Carla Soudien

This observation of English classes in a Japanese school raises a fundamental question about the purpose of language learning. It contrasts a facility in written language for the purposes of university entrance with the more pragmatic issue of communicative competence in the language.

The majority of students in Nara Women's University Secondary School are planning to study at university and therefore will be taking the difficult entrance exams required before entry to university. These exams demand a high level of English competence and so students have to push themselves hard in order to pass them. The curriculum in the English classes observed is aimed at students being able to do well in these exams and thus has to be of the highest level.

Emphasis not on communication

It was immediately noticed that while the level of English used in the classroom was of a very high level, the emphasis of classroom work was not on improving the students' communication abilities. The teacher commented to us that, for the students, 'English is not a communication tool but is just for the exams.' We observed that the usual path of communication was for the teacher to address the students in English and for the students to respond or discuss in Japanese.

Some of the students were quite confident with their English speaking ability and would give answers to the class in English. However, the majority did not choose this option and instead spoke in Japanese. The way in which the teacher dealt with this situation meant, however, that students who wanted to improve their communication skills could still do so while others in the class could listen to the Japanese. If a student answered in Japanese, the teacher would immediately translate this into English and relate it to the class as he wrote it on the blackboard. To make this more natural and comfortable for the student who was replying, the teacher would often change the first person answer into the second person so an atmosphere of a conversation taking place was created. For example, if the student said in Japanese, 'I think Science is the most useful subject,' the teacher would say something like, 'Oh, so you think Science is most useful' in English. In this way students who wanted to listen to English could do so and those who were finding it difficult could understand the Japanese. It was also a subtle way of teaching both first and second person in the second language.

The teacher told us during a short interview that he would prefer it if more communication skills were being taught to the students. Unfortunately, for this to happen the whole university entrance procedure would have to be modified. As it is, English ability is only tested through two of the four language skills – reading and writing. This is unfortunate for the students as their aim is to pass the entrance exams and as a consequence many do not see the importance in learning to communicate well in English. English is only seen as a subject in school, it is not viewed as a useful skill for daily use.

To compound this view it is interesting to note that in the school there are two native English speakers who teach lessons in only first, second and third grade. After entering fourth grade the emphasis clearly lies on the improvement of reading and writing ability. Operating within the confines of the course we think it is clear that the students really are learning well in the classes we observed, but because of the limitations imposed by the system, this means that the emphasis cannot be on communication.

The Global Classroom can help the facility with spoken English by exposing the students to authentic everyday English. By involvement in Global Classroom topics the students can practise real English in all its applications and even if they find it difficult, at least they are able to develop a better appreciation of language as it is spoken.

Relevant topics

Closely related to the above point is the nature of lesson content. The topics contained within the topic all help students recognise the importance of learning English. Two distinct examples of this were seen in the classroom. Students were asked, in groups, to list the six most important subjects that they study in school. High on the list of many groups was English. By considering this point, which probably the majority of students had never thought of before, students could begin to appreciate their English study and realise that actually it is going to be beneficial to them in the future. Hopefully this will have a positive effect on their motivation level, since sometimes it is difficult for students to become motivated if they do not see the relevance of the subject being studied. Another example was seen with the students studying the government report discussing whether or not English should be introduced as a second language in Japan. Of course the students, when they fully understand the contents, can see that it is in fact a realistic option that the government will officially introduce English to Japan. Again, this can help them appreciate their English study and will lead to better learning.

Student confidence

The issue of student confidence has been touched upon several times already. The confidence level of the students is a major factor in their hesitation in speaking English. In the classroom there is a very relaxed atmosphere in which students do not feel nervous to express their opinions. Indeed, if students are selected by the teacher to answer a direct question, they tend to answer well and openly. However, we noticed on numerous occasions that if students were asked to give their opinion on a topic, they would be much more hesitant in replying. This may be to do with factors that lie outside the English class specifically, that is factors that are present in every lesson, in every class and habits that have been formed over many years. Their hesitance in giving their own view is by no means specific to English.

This leads to another point. In every lesson students were selected to answer questions by the teacher. On no occasion did a student volunteer an answer or raise their hand to catch the teacher's attention or to volunteer a comment. Again, this is not specific to English but highlights something common to many Japanese classrooms. Students learn by listening, by doing as they are asked and by not interrupting. It is quite probable that some students had questions they would have liked to ask about the topics being studied, but for their own reasons did not ask questions. The teacher commented that he knows all the students do not understand everything happening in the classroom, but they understand enough to do well. Students are constantly being encouraged to talk, in English or Japanese, but unless they are selected, they tend not to do so.

Relaxed atmosphere

The fact that the classroom atmosphere is relaxed and open contributes greatly to teachers' attitude to students answering or talking in class. In virtually every lesson it is reiterated that it is OK to answer in English or in Japanese. The teacher constantly repeats that it if students don't know the word, expression or answer in English, they should answer in Japanese. A constant effort is made to make the students feel comfortable, relaxed and confident.

Also contributing to the relaxed atmosphere is the students always knowing what is going on in the lesson. If they are going to do any kind of work which is not teacher led, whether it be individual, pair or group work, the teacher will always tell the class the time frame that they have to do it in. Throughout the activity also, we always heard him say, 'You have ten minutes/five minutes/two minutes left.' The students knew exactly what speed they should be working at, and also knew at what depth they should be working, according to how long they had for the task. It seemed that from the students' perspective, this worked very well, since they always knew exactly what was expected of them.

Also, at the end of a lesson the students were usually told what was going to happen in the following lesson. This allowed them to begin to think about the topic if they wanted to and helped create a good atmosphere at the start of the next lesson since students knew what was going to happen.

Homework and tests

Students also do a lot of their learning of English outside the classroom. They are given tasks to do on a regular basis, sometimes finishing off a task that hasn't been completed in class and sometimes doing work in preparation for a new topic. Usually the students have several days in which to complete their homework and the teacher commented that he usually gave the students homework before the weekend. In general, they are expected to do about thirty minutes of English homework per night. Going by the answers that the students gave in class, it was clear that they had done work out of school, especially in trying to understand parts of a difficult written text.

On a few occasions we observed in the classrooms the students doing 'minitests', usually of vocabulary words which would be corrected either by themselves or by the person sitting next to them. These helped students see how well they knew the new words of vocabulary, if they did well, they could feel pleased with themselves and, if they did badly, they knew they had to look over the words again. These only took a few minutes to complete and check and were good for the students to do.

Over the course of one school year the students will have five English exams which, when combined, will form their final result. It is therefore clear that students have to study well throughout the year and cannot, as in some countries, make a final burst towards the end of the year to catch up.

At the blackboard – the Czech Republic

The device of bringing students out to the blackboard is common in many countries. In Czech schools numerous observations were made, some with positive effect and others evaluated quite negatively. The following extract describes the response of three students in one lesson.

When the first student went up to the board a lot of interaction occurred between the student at the board and the teacher. The student had to explain what they were doing to the rest of the class and we found out later that this was used as a test and students were given marks according to how well they knew the work and how well they were able to explain it to others. The class seemed to be comparing the student at the board's answers with their own. A few students in the class seemed not to be fully concentrating and this was probably because of the use of classwork only and not much variation in the styles of learning and teaching. Some of the students also said later that they did not like the subject very much and therefore did not feel compelled to be very attentive.

The second student at the board had obviously not done his homework and did not know how to tackle the problem. The teacher, however, insisted that he come to the front of the class. The student used humour to cover up the fact that he was embarrassed and the teacher continued questioning him even though she knew that he was unable to answer the problem. The student was only allowed to sit down after a few minutes of questioning by the teacher.

The third student at the board was a girl who seemed to know her work really well. She was able to explain her problem with ease. At this point quite a lot of quiet, private conversations began occurring. The atmosphere in the class had become progressively more uncomfortable and the students seem less inclined to be in the class.

Whether coming out to the board works or not seems to depend on a lot of different factors and it is not easy to keep the whole class engaged if one student is struggling with something everyone else knows, or when a student is very good, as in the last case, it may also be difficult to follow. For example, if the rest of the class also knows the answer, they may not feel they need to pay attention, or alternatively if they do not know the answer, they may find it difficult to follow a student who gets there with ease or they may resent learning from a student who is seen as simply 'showing off' how good she is. This does not imply that the blackboard strategy cannot work but that it is not an easy technique to employ successfully.

An adult class – Sweden

To find out about learning which comes from pure motivation and not from compulsory attendance, we visited an adult class. This class takes place in the school and the students in it try to reach a certain academic level to finish high school. This class was attended only by women on the day we visited but several people were absent, so possibly there are males as well. The class has two different rooms for studying. One of the rooms is quiet and the other room is for the more sociable students who like to talk while they study.

The students' views on the class were interesting. They said that Swedish was their favourite subject and the least popular classes were Maths and Computing. However, they said that they didn't find the curriculum too demanding. The atmosphere of the class was quite relaxed with the students being able to drink coffee and move around the class. On this particular day group work was the most usual learning style but it must be kept in mind that we were only there for one day and we cannot really comment on any learning style patterns.

We encountered a very interesting feature of the class which took the form of learning diaries. These are given to all of the students and they have to write about feelings, emotions and just generally comment on anything they want. These diaries are given to the teacher and she reads them over and then adds her comments. This makes the students more aware of what they are doing and helps them to feel more comfortable with the work and their school life. It also helps the teacher build up a closer relationship with the students because they share personal thoughts and comments.

We observed three classes that day which were Swedish, Geography and English. The first class was Swedish. Students were working in groups preparing a report about six famous writers and poets. The whole class was concentrating well and all were doing their work.

The next class was Geography and it was mainly based on group work. They had to join together in groups, choose a country and then give a presentation on it. This meant that they had to go away and research the country themselves. This was good for showing the students how to use the process of learning while also finding the factual data. They used many different sources to find this information which allowed them to work with a variety of learning styles. For example, some used the Internet and others just worked from books in the library. When presenting their information, the attention of the students was held for a longer period of time because they all had to prepare the presentations on their own.

The last class that we attended that day was an English lesson. The teacher used a relaxed style for teaching because he wanted them to use the language and he didn't care about the accuracy of grammar. He was quite happy for the students just to be talking among themselves as long as they used English. We saw this as a good way of teaching a language because it encouraged conversational English, something which will be of most use to them.

From the spot check we found out that the class was extremely positive. The most interesting points on the spot check were that the students all wanted to be there and were happy. The least positive points from the class were the alertness and the energy level. This can be explained by the time of the day, but these points were still on or above the average. The students told us in the interviews that they found it very interesting and enjoyable to be in the class. This was partly because it was an enjoyable social experience but they also

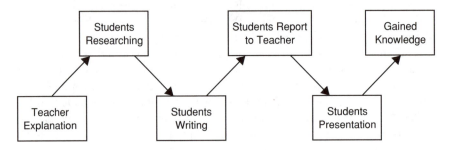

Figure 11.1 Structure of the class in Sweden

benefited from being able to upgrade their knowledge. The structure of the class is shown in Figure 11.1. It demonstrates the flow of the class in structuring learning for the students.

The relationship between the students and the teacher was a very important factor in this class. The teacher told us in an interview that an important hurdle which the adults have to overcome is in admitting the need to upgrade their level of education. Because of this, their self-confidence was low but their level of motivation high, and getting stronger as the course went on. To keep their spirits up the teacher said that she was always giving them compliments and when criticism was needed it was given in a very constructive way.

Overall, the class was very positive and 'pure' motivated learning was indeed taking place. This we saw as a prime example of lifelong learning in this community but it also taught us something about the relationship between learning, motivation and confidence.

12 Who do you learn most from?

Kataro Nariai, Carla Soudien, Colin Bragg and Miki Nishimura

This question – Who do you learn most from? – was put to students in different countries with some surprising results. Most students did not immediately think of teachers. This was unexpected because we might assume that learning is so closely associated with school that this would be the obvious response. It is all the more surprising in countries like Japan and the Czech Republic where students tend to evaluate their learning in relation to how much the teacher tells them. But, in fact, students defined their learning and sources of their learning in broader terms, thinking of family and friends and as driven by their own interests and motivation. What emerges as a singular strand throughout these inquiries is the intrinsic drivers of learning – you learn, in school or out, because you are interested.

The second half of this chapter which focuses on teachers specifically has strong resonances with much other research into what makes a good teacher (Rudduck, *et al.* 1996; MacBeath, 1999; Wragg, *et al.* 2000) although the question 'What teachers do you learn most from?' evokes a more pointed response than the more general question 'What kind of teachers do you like?'

Who encourages me to learn?

Students in the six LS2 schools who were asked this question gave quite different responses. In all countries, except Japan, parents got by far the highest rating, nearly as high as teachers, comparing very sharply with all the other schools but most noticeably in comparison to Japan where no one chose teachers.

This does not mean that teachers are not seen as an important source – indeed, all the evidence from all classrooms shows how much good teachers are valued by their students. It does mean, though, that students' desire to learn is driven first and foremost by sources outside the school (see Figure 12.1).

In the four countries where parents were cited as the strongest influence we asked how strong that influence was. Judgements varied as Figures 12.2 to 12.5 show.

In the four countries in which friends were seen as a significant influence, the strength of that influence also differed from school to school (see Figures 12.6 to 12.8).

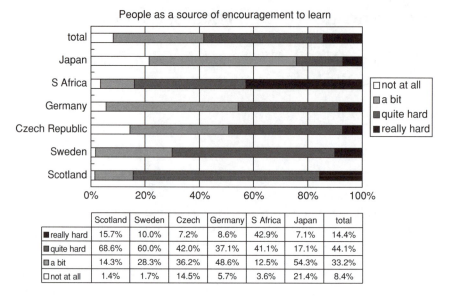

	Scotland	Sweden	Czech	Germany	S Africa	Japan	total
■ really hard	15.7%	10.0%	7.2%	8.6%	42.9%	7.1%	14.4%
■ quite hard	68.6%	60.0%	42.0%	37.1%	41.1%	17.1%	44.1%
■ a bit	14.3%	28.3%	36.2%	48.6%	12.5%	54.3%	33.2%
□ not at all	1.4%	1.7%	14.5%	5.7%	3.6%	21.4%	8.4%

Figure 12.1 Encouragement to learn

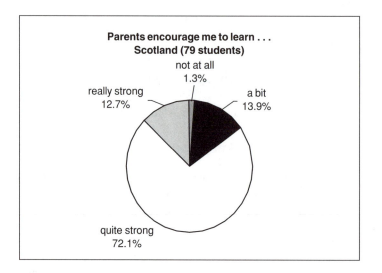

Figure 12.2 Parents' encouragement to learn (Scotland)

Teachers were mentioned less than parents and friends in five of the schools but in one, Anderson High School, teachers were seen as virtually on a par with parents. For those who answered 'teachers', we asked how strong that influence was. Do teachers encourage you to work 'really hard', 'hard', a 'bit' or 'not at all'? The results for Anderson High are shown in Figure 12.9.

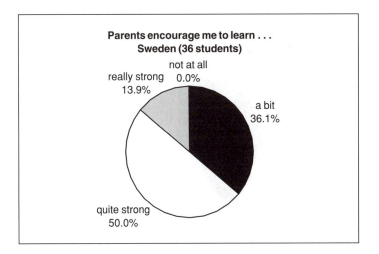

Figure 12.3 Parents' encouragement to learn (Sweden)

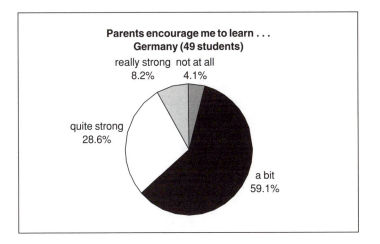

Figure 12.4 Parents' encouragement to learn (Germany)

What kind of teachers do you learn most from?
Kotoro Naraia and Carla Soudein

We asked students in different countries about the teachers they liked and learned from. LS1 went into this issue most in the Czech Republic. Interviewing Czech students about what kind of teachers they liked and what kind of teachers they learned most from gave us some interesting answers. We found that the most important qualities of teachers who are liked are being understanding and

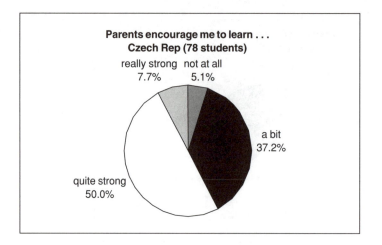

Figure 12.5 Parents' encouragement to learn (Czech Republic)

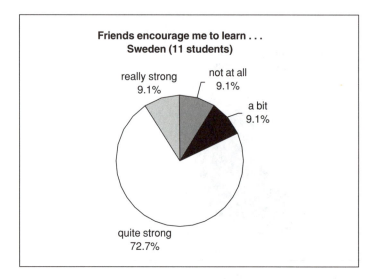

Figure 12.6 Friends' encouragement to learn (Sweden)

friendly, although this group felt that this was not true of all teachers they had dealings with. They emphasised the following:

*   A teacher who varies the lesson and can keep it interesting is most liked.
*   A teacher who is interested in his or her subject and interested in the needs of the students is appreciated, also someone who realises the students don't like classes where only writing is done.

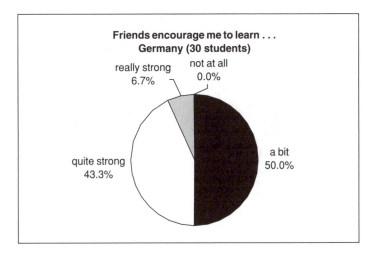

Figure 12.7 Friends' encouragement to learn (Germany)

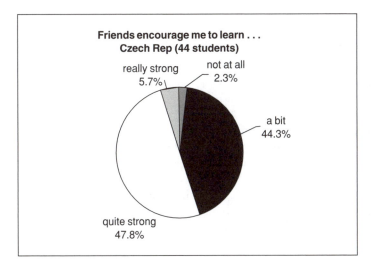

Figure 12.8 Friends' encouragement to learn (Czech Republic)

- Teachers who are knowledgeable and have teaching skill. However, it is not important for the teacher to make the class feel too relaxed and at ease as this leads to the classroom being an ineffective study place.
- Young, funny and sympathetic teachers who encourage discussion and let the students get to know him or her on a personal level are most liked.
- Teachers who introduce interesting topics, who use a variety of teaching techniques and who sometimes teach topics other than those in the textbook.

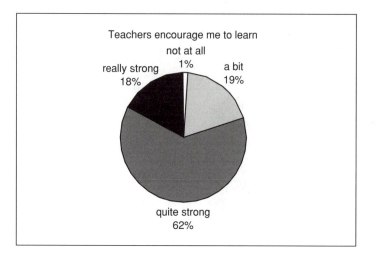

Figure 12.9 Teacher's influence on working (Scotland)
Note: N = 74

What kind of teacher do you learn most from?

Many students differentiated easily between what kind of teacher they liked and those they learned most from. Some of the opinions on the kind of teacher students learn most from were as follows:

- Teachers who are friendly and understanding.
- Teachers who prepare well for the class and work hard for the class – you feel more motivated to work for the teacher.
- A teacher who goes beyond merely teaching and actually gives an insight into the subject so that students can really become interested in the subject itself.
- Teachers who are direct, honest and funny.
- A strict teacher who demands rather more from the students helps them learn a lot.

It was said that most is learned from teachers who give a lot of information in class so that students are not required to do too much study in the evenings at home. A second group made a similar comment. A different group, however, felt that they learned quite a lot with lessons structured in this way and therefore didn't mind taking notes in class and studying them at home.

Other comments

From the points that followed on from these questions, many more opinions emerged. Some students felt that sometimes teachers put too much pressure on them, demanding a lot from them in their particular subject and seemingly forgetting that the students have many other subjects to study and prepare for.

With regard to teachers' personalities, some students, a group of girls, said they would like to have a more friendly relationship with their teachers. At the moment they felt that the teachers were generally not interested in their problems. However, in contrast to this, a group of boys said that it is not necessary to get too close to their teachers. They just wanted to know exactly what to do and how to do it and keep their relationship with the teacher strictly on these terms. A group of girls said it was necessary for the teacher to be an important or main figure in the class. This, they said, acts an incentive for the students who feel that if the teacher is not authoritative, the students don't know what is important in class and what is not.

Concerning the actual work done in class, two groups offered opinions on this. One group felt that doing classwork for the majority of the time was fine but sometimes they wanted to take a break from only writing. These students enjoyed working in groups, especially in languages and in the laboratory. The other group, a boys group, thought that when a lot had to be learned it wasn't appropriate for the students to have control of the class, but they would like to have opportunities to speak in longer length classes.

One group commented that they thought it was very good that they usually have the same teacher for the full four years of their time in Gymnázium Zlín. They spend the first year getting to know each other, then from that time on the relationship is usually quite comfortable

Comments from other schools

What students said in the Czech school was very similar to what students said in other schools, most of the issues seeming to cut across national boundaries. Most of the students we talked to, no matter what the country, wanted a teacher who was objective, that is, non-discriminating, without favourites, friendly and in no way egoistic or giving a feeling of being superior to the students. A common theme was also teachers who were strict – but not too strict – and respectful as well as funny and 'looking happy', 'looking as if they enjoyed their job'. While some students wanted their teachers to be serious and a bit strict, they did, at the same time, want them to be sociable, easy to talk to and good listeners.

Students saw it as very important that the teacher was good at explaining things, used new and different ways of getting ideas across, used a variety of teaching strategies and encouraged different styles of learning. Other words that were most frequently used to describe qualities of good teachers were:

- caring
- respectable
- organised
- helpful

13 Who likes school?

*Jimmy Karttunen, Robert Janícek and
Saeko Yoshida*

Following on from the discussion of school ethos, this chapter by Learning
School 1 students probes more deeply into students' views of their schools, their
liking for schools, their sources of satisfaction and dissatisfaction, and their
general motivational level. This is a valuable contribution to our understanding
of student motivation through comparisons of high and low motivated students
and the range of attitudes to class work and homework, to teaching approaches
and learning styles which are associated with that. The similarities between two
schools of very different types and in very different countries are striking. The
differences also raise important questions. Gender differences in and out of
school are also explored in both countries and again some of the constants pose
questions about issues that lie deeper than the individual school or classroom
and its power to shape human beings.

The Czech Republic

There were 100 questionnaires circulated around the school and 69 of them
came back to us to be processed. From these a variety of viewpoints have arisen.
For us, who have seen different educational systems and schools, the atmosphere in this school seemed a bit more tense than elsewhere but the view of this
school from the students came across as very positive. It seems that the school
creates a good working environment; 65 per cent of students said that they liked
school and not one of the 69 answered that he or she hated the school. We also
asked about motivation and found three groups – the highly motivated, the
quite motivated and the unmotivated. These responses, shown in Figure 13.1,
refer to a general feeling about school work but obviously fluctuate with different lessons, different teachers, different contexts.

There was no difference in attitudes to school between females and males,
and when it came to motivation, there were also no gender differences. We
have seen from other data that the motivation of boys is often lower than that
of girls. In Sweden, for example, we found that boys were not as motivated as
girls but this was not the case here.

These general data on students' feelings and motivation may be taken as
very positive but it must be stressed that these are overall opinions. In further

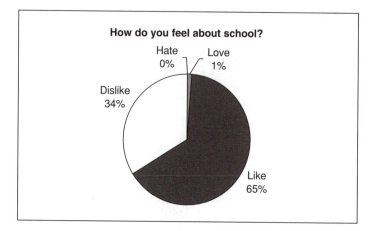

Figure 13.1 How do you feel about school? (Czech Republic)

questioning and discussion we found many specific things that students were unhappy about or would like to see changed. Gender differences are also present when it comes to specific issues.

High school life

We asked right at the beginning of our inquiry what the students actually thought about school life. The fact that 55 per cent of the students used the word 'stressful' suggests something negative but, on the other hand, quite a high percentage of students also describe their school life as 'interesting', 'sociable' and 'enjoyable'. It may be said that high school life in total is quite positively assessed. Examining data further, comparing the most positive and the least positive groups, we see quite distinct differences. Many more of the 'negative' (dislike school) group find school stressful, difficult and boring than do their 'positive' counterparts. Exactly the same scenario occurs when we compare the high and low motivation groups.

Free time

How students spend their free time out of class during the day also says something about motivation. Nearly all the boys who filled out the questionnaire said that they spoke to their friends in their free time. Half of the girls, on the other hand, said they spent their free time studying. This suggests that the boys were less motivated than girls to spend their own time studying.

Looking at studying more generally, the highly motivated students have the highest figures for studying whereas the unmotivated students study the least.

Regarding the amount of free time which students had, none of the highly motivated students said that they had no free time whereas in the quite motivated and the unmotivated groups it was common for students to say they had no free time. Could this be because more motivated students are able to be more productive than less motivated students? It would appear that the less motivated spend more time catching up on school work while more motivated students have covered the work at a more appropriate time. It is worth mentioning that 100 per cent of the students who selected the term 'productive' to describe school spent their free time studying while only two students from the 'stressed' group did the same. They tended to talk to friends.

Although terms such as 'stressed' and 'busy' occurred quite often, the word with the highest choice was 'friendly'. It must be encouraging for this school that the students are not daunted by its very fast pace and intense curriculum and that they feel surrounded by friends. There was hardly any difference between male and female opinions. They contrasted only in one response which showed that the girls felt more 'busy'. Students who most often found the atmosphere stressful and uneasy expressed negative feelings more often than the motivated ones and 'stressed' students were more likely to be found among the unmotivated group.

There was less of a divide, however, when it came to out-of-school time, homework aside. We wanted to know what preference students have during the week and at weekends. As it happens, no matter what gender or motivation level, or even whether they were 'positive', 'stressed' or 'social', there were no differences in what they said about division of school and out-of-school time. They all said that during the week their focus was mainly on school work with hardly any social activities. A rapid change takes place at weekends when nearly the only activity for everyone is socialising.

In the whole week span most of the students study five to ten hours no matter what their level of motivation is. Furthermore, at all three levels of motivation 10 per cent of students study more than ten hours a week. But when we compare the amount of daily study we find that some students study more sporadically, with some doing more at weekends. The usual time is spent on doing actual homework, but they do not seem to divide the work proportionally across the week. Of the small group (5 per cent) who study more than two hours a day, all were girls. The highly motivated students (80 per cent) do attend a lot of extra classes in the afternoon.

Most of the students who spend a lot of time on homework come from the highly motivated students (70 per cent of the highly motivated group) and they spend quite a lot of time alone in their room. Looking at the student group who describe themselves as 'social', they are much more likely to spend time with friends and do less homework and their figures for daily study as well as weekly study are consistently lower.

The highly motivated students appear to divide into two groups. One group is composed of smart students who do not need to study as much and are successful in school anyway. The other group includes students highly motivated for their school work and getting good results, but to reach this level they have to try harder and they spend a lot of time on homework and revising. The quite motivated and unmotivated students spend about the same amount on home-work daily but compared to the highly motivated, a little less.

We were also interested in who students did homework with. A vast majority (94 per cent) study individually rather than with friends or classmates. We thought that maybe students who were considered 'sociable' would elect to study with someone around but even these students, otherwise spending lots of time with their peers, do tend to study on their own. It may be the demands of the system which makes these students behave as they do because they are asked to memorise a considerable amount of factual information which they believe is probably best done individually. Do they believe that this is the most effective way to get good grades? Is it most beneficial for the students them-selves? Is it simply what they are used to and encouraged to do? Could they learn to study socially and learn, even memorise, more efficiently?

Their preference is to study at home; 92 per cent of students study at home rather than than elsewhere which seems to be quite normal as there is no special study room established in the school or in the community.

Study to be done outside school is considered by 63 per cent as too much, by 37 per cent as just right, but none said too little. We found it very worthy of note that the highly motivated students and students who study more than three hours a day actually think that they are asked to do too much, although they cope well with it. It might be just their feeling because in comparison to the average, they study excessively which makes them feel overwhelmed by it. Some 76 per cent of the 'stressed' students considered the amount as too much.

What was the nature of their study? The students mostly spend their time outside school study revising for tests. Unmotivated students spend more time revising for tests than highly motivated students do. We found this surprising but after closer examination found that unmotivated students revise more be-cause they know that they have to in order to to get by. However, they tend not to engage in other types of studying. They focus only on what is necessary and they do not see beyond this. School work is boring but has to be done and they do not try to find new, interesting or just different ways of studying. So they satisfy themselves and the school's requirements. On the other hand, the highly motivated students want to get the most out of their learning and want to learn to the best of their ability. They of course still revise for the tests because that is at the core of their success in this school but they also leave some time for doing supplementary studies. This, they say, can help to improve their develop-ment of different strands of knowledge. They also feel negatively about the exam-driven style of learning at this school but since they are so motivated, they try to find untried forms of studying as well. These students do not pay as much attention to the tasks given by the teachers and decide themselves what and how to study. That seems a remarkable sign of students' confidence and responsibility for their own learning.

When?

Most studying for tests is done at the last minute. While 20 per cent do their studying in advance, as soon as they can, 80 per cent of students do so at the last minute because the skill they are being asked for is memorising loads of facts in a short time. Many factors such as too many subjects, timetable and intense syllabus do influence this. Students say they do not have any time to learn properly, nor to reflect on what they are studying. So memorising has to be left to the last minute. The only students who seem to slightly divide their workload bit by bit are highly motivated ones. As we have seen before, these students add to their revision a noticeable part of supplementary study so they seem to learn extraordinary aspects as well as those needed simply for revision.

It was mentioned before that a lot of the students attend extra classes. The class most frequently attended is English. It was interesting to see that students attend them because they do not do enough in class time. They find it important as preparation for exams and for university entrance as it will give them an edge over their rivals. Some of the students study English because they just like it or because of their personal development.

Learning inside school

We found out that 55 per cent of all the students cope with the workload well. For the motivated group the figure is 80 per cent. Both boys and girls seem to cope equally well or badly while the more unmotivated students struggle.

When it came to seating arrangements and work habits in the classroom, we found that the highly motivated students were more likely to want to study individually or in a pair, disliking whole class work, perhaps because it distracts them and holds them back. The unmotivated group, on the other hand, prefer a bigger group, possibly to ease the tension of a strictly individually focused class where responsibility rests with the individual. In whole class or group work the responsibility is divided among several people, therefore it mentally relieves them of being solely responsible for completing a task. They realise that the group can help them. The last, maybe not significant but certainly interesting, point is that boys answered more than girls that they preferred group work.

Most of the highly motivated students felt confident whereas the unmotivated students were much more likely to see themselves as shy. The unmotivated students do not get good marks and tend to feel self-conscious within their class environment and with their peers who are achieving better results. These unmotivated students try to attract as little attention to themselves as possible and avoid being selected in class. It is probably because they feel insecure about the school work and do not want to make mistakes when called upon in class. These unmotivated students also told us that they felt uncomfortable in class and would like to mix more and work more with others. They feel they would work better with more variety or a change in environment.

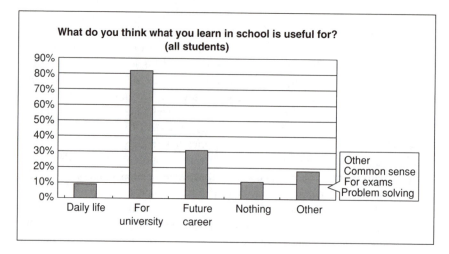

Figure 13.2 What do you think what you learn in school is useful for?

School activity

By far the most common school activity was to listen and take notes. More than half who were questioned said they would like to have the opportunity to express their individual opinions and 60 per cent said they would like to be able to discuss, do practical work or present themselves. They said they were treated as a group of students and not as individuals. This is especially true of the highly motivated students who would like to learn and study in different ways. They think about their learning and want to find more effective ways but are content to stick to one stereotypical style.

This was also shown in their attitude towards the supplementary study which was mostly done by these highly motivated students. Their least favourite way of studying was written tasks given by teacher or learning by simply looking at information and writing it down.

When it comes to the purpose and use of studying, over 80 per cent of the students think they will use what they have studied for further and higher education (see Figure 13.2). All the students who completed this questionnaire want to go on to further education and 45 of them know the type of university they would like to study at. None of this is surprising as the entire curriculum is geared to passing entrance university exams and the students enter school with this goal. The most popular courses were technical, natural science, medicine, languages, economics and computing.

Scotland

The questionnaire asking about feelings about school was handed out to students in their fifth year of high school in October. The 121 returned are the

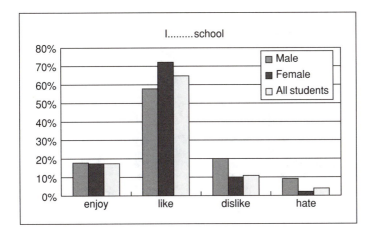

Figure 13.3 I . . . school

basis of this report (see Figure 13.3). The gender return was 40 : 60 males to females, an accurate reflection of the balance of boys and girls in the school.

Motivation

Most of the students in the fifth year have a positive feeling about school. Less than 20 per cent either dislike or hate school while the majority of the students, nearly 80 per cent like it. The males give a broader spectrum of answers. More of them answered hate, dislike and enjoy school than the females who mostly answered 'like school'. In general, the females have a more positive impression of school than the males. When asked about motivation, there was only a small highly motivated and a small unmotivated group. Over 70 per cent fell into the quite motivated group.

When looking at motivation level and the students' feeling for school, it is clearly seen that the highly motivated group is much more likely to have a positive feeling for school than the unmotivated group; 95 per cent of the motivated group were positive while just 45 per cent of the unmotivated were positive.

We are left to consider the reason for this. Is it the students' good feeling for school that makes them motivated or do motivated students like school because it is a place where they can fulfil their study needs? And is it because of a lack of motivation that unmotivated students see school as something boring, something to dislike?

Only 5 per cent of the students who like or enjoy school are unmotivated, and 14 per cent of them are highly motivated. Of the students who answered negatively, 30 per cent are unmotivated and only 5 per cent are highly motivated. Males are surprisingly more numerous among highly motivated students, although they also have the highest number of unmotivated students.

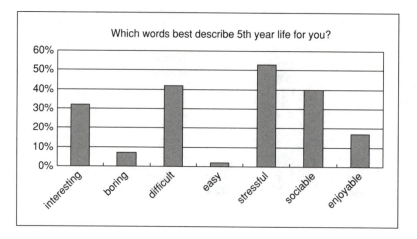

Figure 13.4 Which words best describe fifth year life for you?

Description of school

The word that was used most frequently when the students were asked to describe their school life was 'stressful' (see Figure 13.4). More than the half of the students used that word. Something that should be taken into consideration is the fact that neither prelims nor exams were close when the questionnaires were handed out. This circumstance probably gave a lower number than the answers that would have been given at the time before the exam periods.

The second most often used word was 'difficult', used by 42 per cent of the students. There are more females that find school stressful and difficult, 60 for females and 50 for males. Over 80 per cent of the unmotivated students used both the words 'stressful' and 'difficult'. It is understandable that these two words usually go hand in hand, because if you find your schooling hard, you more easily feel pressure and because of that, stress.

The most regularly used positive words were 'sociable' and 'interesting', both of which were used as description by more than 30 per cent of the students'. It was the highly motivated students in particular who used positive words such as 'interesting' and 'enjoyable'.

Some 30 per cent of students could be called 'positive' because they used only positive words to describe their school life. Surprisingly perhaps, it was more likely for females than males to be negative.

Homework and school work

All the students questioned in the fifth year spend their intervals and lunch times with friends. They are much more likely to be just socialising or doing other things than studying. They said they very seldom used these times for school work. Motivated students were more sociable than unmotivated students during lunches and intervals. This can be interpreted in two ways. It may be because the motivated students are usually seen as cheery and happy students and because of their light mood, they are more sociable. An unmotivated student is more likely to be talkative and sociable during classes and so the breaks are not all that much of a difference.

During lunch a lot of the students leave school to go to the town, which is as likely a venue as staying in school. Students also go home for a while or go to the hostel. The majority of the motivated students, however, stay in school.

Three-quarters of the students prioritise schoolwork before social life during the weekdays. Only 8 per cent let their social life go before homework and there are more males than females who do that. Otherwise there are no big differences between the two genders' priorities.

The unmotivated students are much more likely than the rest to find social life more important than school work, while almost three times more of highly motivated students place a higher priority on school work than the rest. More surprising is that 73 per cent of unmotivated students, despite their low motivation, still see school work as something important and therefore have prioritised it during the weekdays.

The number of Higher exams that the students are planning to take also influences their priorities. Of the students who take four or more Highers, 80 per cent put school work as their priority while 60 per cent of the students with less than four Highers have the same priority.

When the weekend comes the students' priorities are drastically changed. Then we see the other side of the coin and three-quarters of the students consider social life more important than school work. Only 1 per cent prioritise school work during the weekend.

A lot of the students in fifth year, 65 per cent of them, have a part-time job outside school. Females and males are equally likely to have a job and this also goes for unmotivated and well-motivated students. One-third of them with a job say they can not see their employment as affecting school or their social life while 35 per cent of them said that it badly affects their school work. The social life of 32 per cent of them suffers, although 23 per cent said that it had a positive effect on it.

Students spend their spare time doing a lot of different activities. The most popular one is a sport of some kind and that is engaged in by the majority of the students. Other things many of the students do is socialising, especially at the weekend. They also enjoy music, either listening to it or playing instruments. Computing is more likely to be done by males while females prefer to read a good book. Some 7 per cent of the students feel that their spare time activities interfere a lot with their school work. Of these students, all of them except one are performing some form of sport.

More than half of the students spend less than an hour on homework and the rest one to two hours. The amount of time these fifth year students spend on homework is very individual. Some spend less than one hour per week while others spend over ten. Most spend one to two hours a day. Females are more likely to spread out their work than males. A small group, 12 per cent, spend more than ten hours per week doing homework. These are likely to be doing either four or five Highers and most of them have a high level of motivation, although there are some from the low motivation group too. How is it that students with no motivation can study? Maybe they find satisfaction in the subjects they do but don't have any aims and goals and do not have any real motivation. More likely is that they they find the subjects difficult but feel the pressure to pass more and a need to study more. It is boys who are more likely to do less than one hour of homework per day and also in a weekly perspective are less occupied with homework.

Stressed students are more likely to spend longer on their homework than the average and think the amount of homework is too much. Only 12 per cent of the students with more than four Highers spend less than one hour on homework. For those with less than four, the figure is the 36 per cent.

Whether the students have a job or not does not really affect the amount of homework they do. There are just slightly less students that do a lot of homework among the employed students and those without a job.

The majority of the students, 54 per cent, think the quantity of homework is just right. The rest of them, except one, feel there is too much homework. This single student wants more. The difference between the two genders' answers shows that more females are likely to feel the quantity is too much than males. When we look at the level of motivation, the students who feel there is too much homework increases in step with their lack of motivation. From 33 per cent for the highly motivated, it increases to 55 per cent for the unmotivated students. The percentage is even higher for stressed students than unmotivated students.

When the students are given homework, they are most likely to spread it over the week. Half the students do it that way. A few students do not do the homework at all while the rest do it either at the last minute or as soon as they are assigned it. Motivated students have a much higher figure for doing it as soon as possible than the rest and the unmotivated have a higher percentage for doing it at the last minute.

Almost 60 per cent of the students turn to the teacher when they need help with their homework. The others turn to friends and classmates. Other family members are sometimes seen as giving support and of them it is most likely to be parents. Females turn much more often to friends and classmates than males do. For males the teacher is the main person who gives them help.

Influences

Teachers are incontestably the biggest source of the students' academic knowledge with 96 per cent saying so. All other options are much less than 10 per cent, and of those, the family got the highest percentage.

When looking at the source for the students' personal development and from whom they learn most personally, the teachers drop down to last place with only 5 per cent. Here friends are the most important people with 62 per cent and parents not far behind. The students who learn personal matters from the teacher turned out to be only females. Well-motivated students have parents as their greatest source. Other things and people that influence their personal behaviour are their siblings, the general public, the Internet, TV and magazines.

About three-quarters of the students feel most comfortable studying at home by themselves. To study at school is preferred by 20 per cent of the students, and they are most likely to be males. Many unmotivated students would rather study with friends than alone. This is probably because the other students can help and keep up the pace. Although to be with a friend during studying can lead to more chatting than studying.

There is a big difference between the answers given by males and females on the question whether they learn from the media or not. The majority of the male students say they learn a lot from TV, radio, newspaper, etc. and only 2 per cent said very little. Among females, on the other hand, only 15 per cent learn a lot and the majority of the females learn some. They also have a much bigger percentage on very little, 16 per cent.

What is it then the students learn from the media? Do males and females value the information given by media in the same way? Is that the reason why males learn more? Do they only see academic knowledge as something to learn? To know how a character in a soap opera got through personal problems, is that something valuable to know? The questions are many and the only way to answer them is to do follow-up questions.

Learning Inside school

More than half of the students in the fifth year, 52 per cent of them, are doing four Highers. Eleven per cent are doing two or less, 22 per cent are doing three, while 16 per cent are doing five Highers.

There are slightly more males than females that are taking four or five Highers and strangely the unmotivated students are taking the most, all of them have three, four or five Highers. None of them feel that they are doing well in school, three-quarters say OK and one quarter, not very well. This last fact can, together with the large number of Highers, be part of the reason they feel unmotivated. There must have been some kind of motivation behind these students otherwise they would not have taken so many Highers. As said before, over 80 per cent of them described their school life as stressful and difficult. All this together must make the students feel overworked and not really good about themselves and in the end their motivation is dragged down by it.

The two student groups who feel they do either well or OK in school are the well-motivated students and students with positive descriptions of their school life.

Almost everyone in the fifth year thinks that their present year is important. Students who do not feel that way explained their answer by saying that schooling up to S4 is enough, and that Highers are not needed in their future career. Most of the students who said it was important meant it because of university entry and future career plans.

The way of working in class the students prefer is individual and differs from student to student. Therefore it is hard to give a general picture of their preferred way of learning. Quite a lot want to work individually or in pairs. More than two-thirds of the students see these working forms as their best way of learning, especially pair work. The opinions differed only slightly for different motivation levels and genders.

Two-thirds of the students learn most by learning constantly throughout the year. The rest learn the most during their study before the exams. This is more likely to happen for students with less motivation. Gender does not have anything to do with the part of the school year the students learn the most in.

When looking at the students who learn most throughout the year, it is seen that more of them than those who learn most before the exams spend a longer time working on homework during the week. This could be a reason why they learn more throughout the year.

Almost every student in the fifth year wants a calm classroom atmosphere. They do not want to feel the stress or panic that can occur during some periods. Most of them also want it to be a relaxed environment, while the rest prefer a more serious atmosphere. There are no noticeable differences between the answers given by different genders or motivation groups.

Future hopes and plans

The majority of the fifth year students, 96 per cent of them, plan to go on to further education and higher education after high school. It is only males that said they would not continue their education and only one female said she was not sure. All the highly motivated students, 100 per cent, will continue in their future while unmotivated students are still at 91 per cent.

Of the students who are going on to further education, 80 per cent know whether they want to study at a university, college or somewhere else. Many of them also have a preferred city where they want to study. The larger Scottish university cities are the ones most of the students have in mind, although universities and colleges like Oxford and Scalloway Fisheries College were also mentioned.

Some 78 per cent of the students know what they want to do in the future. This is something that helps them decide what and where to study. Quite a few do not know the future job they want but at least the area of career. Most popular are careers in engineering, science, teaching and especially primary teaching, business, nursing and the media.

14 Two classes compared

Jeremy Barnett, Joe Williamson and
Robert Janícek

In this chapter two classes in the Swedish school are compared. One is a vocational class, the other an academic class. The careful observation of teachers and students and the use of the spot check reveal some important differences and raises a whole series of questions about motivation, independent learning and the role of the teacher. It prompts our thinking about the balance of teacher intervention and student choice, structure and freedom, challenge and support. Embedded beneath these issues is the question of culture so that what may appear questionable to a British or Japanese or Czech perspective has to be set within the Swedish frame of reference.

This is followed by a short extract comparing two Japanese classes where the quite different responses of students to the same lesson raises questions about undercurrents and dynamics which are not easily observable or explainable but are nonetheless very significant for the quality of student learning.

The two Swedish classes

We observed seven Swedish classes over two weeks and compiled results from five of them. Three classes were from a vocational course with first year students. Two classes were from an academic course with second year students. The general response by the students to our presence in the classroom was in both cases positive. They were helpful, interested and apart from a few minor exceptions took our research seriously.

The vocational class

In this class there were around thirty students. This class is rather exceptional in that it is made up of students who are experiencing some difficulties either in their academic or personal lives. The course is designed to focus on different learning styles and to help students find a method or strategy of learning that will best suit each of them. At the beginning of the course two main learning environments were established, these being a silent room and a room with music playing in the background. If the students wanted to suggest other environments they could.

The syllabus of this course is not particularly demanding. In this class the emphasis is not placed on high academic achievement but on trying to arouse and promote a level of interest within the students. Students spend quite a lot of time on a single task, developing it on their own or with a group if they choose to. They put their own thoughts and ideas into the work they're doing so that by the end students know the work is their own, and are inspired by this and with a heightened level of interest. Two teachers teach this class, sometimes both of them present the lessons and sometimes neither are in the room. Both have equal responsibility for the class and share the work in the classroom between them.

We observed three vocational classes and all followed a very similar procedure. At the beginning of the lesson the teachers gave an explanation of what was to be done in that particular class. This explanation usually took around five minutes and everyone was absolutely clear on what to do and how to proceed. After this the class split into two groups depending on the mood they were in. Those who wanted to study with music would move to another room and those who preferred silence would stay in the same room. This choice by the students was not a final decision and they could change rooms if they felt that their mood was changing. Sometimes during the lesson the teacher would change the task that the students were doing and at times the focus of the lesson moved away from the Swedish class and on to other topics.

The students had the chance to take an optional break. In all three lessons the majority of the students took advantage of this. The students were able to take a shorter break after 30 minutes or a longer one after 50 minutes. The class usually finished with a friendly talk between the teachers and the students. On one occasion a deal was made so that the students could leave the class five minutes early if they finished their work before the next lesson.

The academic class

In this class there were thirty students. All members are studying the SP2 course, an academic programme focusing on social sciences. We observed two lessons in this course.

Both classes began with a five to ten minute explanation of the task. Students generally listened carefully and some took notes. The teacher made sure that everybody knew what to do and then usually let the students work on their own. After the explanation the teacher's role was one of support and help if the students asked for it, although the majority of students tended to work independently. Again the students had a choice as to their preferred working environment. In this case they could leave the room and go to work in other parts of the school, usually the library but sometimes on the sofas, the quiet room or any other place. The majority of the students took advantage of this option and went elsewhere to work.

Students usually began the required task very conscientiously. They would remain focused for quite a long period of time. However, by the end of the lessons they usually required some help from the teacher in order to maintain their level of concentration. The teacher would assist by changing the teaching/ learning style or developing a discussion to talk about an issue partly related to the Swedish class and partly related to real life.

The structure of the lesson allowed for a variety of learning styles. The lessons did not finish in any particular way and the students just left the class.

Observing in the vocational class

When we first entered this classroom we felt that the students were unmotivated, noisy and disruptive. By the end of the lesson, though, our opinion had changed dramatically. On the surface this class might appear to be difficult to manage, but beneath this impression we found many positive aspects. The results from the spot check were very positive. In the three classes we observed the student spot-check data revealed them to be concentrating, active, productive, sociable, motivated and cheerful. However, the students also recorded that they were often bored and that time was passing slowly. These spot-check results raise some interesting questions.

In the beginning we considered these students to be rather 'problematic'. They didn't seem to be comfortable with being in the class. But the spot checks suggested that they never felt lonely and, on the contrary, were extremely sociable, relaxed and happy. This is indeed encouraging information for the teachers who were trying to help these students. Students who were shy, having problems relating to people and with school began to have a more positive outlook even in Swedish lessons.

However, these positive aspects have to be set against another of the spot-check findings that students quite frequently felt bored and that time passed slowly for them. We wondered if this was due to the instrument, its wording and meaning. Was there some stigma attached to the word 'bored' itself? Perhaps students in this class, and possibly high school students in general, assume that because they are in the classroom they should be feeling 'bored'. Might it be that being bored is so associated with school and study that is the 'right answer', and that even if they are feeling somewhat neutral they still circle that they are bored? On the other hand, given that on the spot-check sheet the opposite of bored is 'excited', perhaps students felt that because they weren't feeling excited they must be feeling bored.

If the above explanation is not the case, it can be assumed that the students are, in fact, feeling rather bored. Or that they think they are bored. These are students who have had difficulties adapting to school life and some have re-peated the same school year several times. We could see that the students were trying hard to enjoy the class and make progress but, given that many had disliked school for a long time, it must surely be difficult for them to remain interested all the time. Even if they realised that they must try hard in order to graduate from high school, if they are not genuinely interested in the subject, it is easy to feel bored. The main point to take from this is that the students are obviously trying very hard and are positive in many areas of the spot check, but that their underlying feelings, perhaps at a deeper level of motivation, are negative.

We also noticed a clear difference in motivation, enjoyment and positive feelings between these students and the students in the academic class. The vocational students, whatever their deeper commitment, remained positive and motivated throughout all three observed classes.

Perhaps in their high school life they will not reach the same level of academic achievement as their counterparts in the SP2 class, but within their level of ability we observed that they do work better. They seem to enjoy what they do, are inspired by it, interested in it and are very positive about the whole classroom situation. The academic class, on the other hand, does not appear to try as hard, perhaps because they are more aware of their academic ability and realise that they do not need to try so hard to reach the same standard. It seemed to us a pity that the same productive mood and atmosphere noticeable in the vocational class could not be transferred to the academic class. Perhaps the academic students feel less challenged by the work given to them. It is interesting to consider what might happen if the academic class were challenged more. Would they respond more positively?

A change of mood

In all the classes we observed students came in feeling negative either because of the previous class or because of their bad mood. There is usually about 20 per cent of students tired, 17 per cent hungry, 15 per cent bored. There are not many positive feelings in evidence. However, rapid change seemed to take place in the classroom because the spot-check results taken in the middle of the lesson were, on the whole, positive, showing that students were interested in what they were doing. The timing of the lessons varied but interest remained at the same level and the judgements of the two researchers, the teachers and the students' feelings were mainly similar and only differed in some cases.

Some comments on features of the vocational class

The explanation at the beginning of each class achieved three main things:

- The students were 100 per cent clear on what they had to do.
- The students all knew why they were doing the task and the time that they had to do it in.
- The students knew what would happen if they didn't do it.

This opening explanation time took place in every lesson. Obviously the teachers feel this is a good way of helping the students learn more efficiently. It also prompts the students to work on their own. The role of the teachers then becomes minor if the students do not specifically ask for help. Of course, if the students are absolutely clear on what they are doing, then it is much easier for them to complete the task fully and to the best of their ability. This explanation time in the beginning of class is also the only practical way of addressing all the students at once since there is a large number of students in this lesson.

With two teachers and their two classes mixed, it means that the number of students is quite high but it did not appear that class size affected the learning because of the clarity of what was to be done right from the beginning. This means that the teachers have less to do and can take time moving around the class and helping the students. The teachers told us that it is the less able students who attend this class so the normal way of teaching, standing in front of the whole class and talking to the whole group would not be beneficial for this class at all. We also thought that it was much more suitable and effective for this class when the teachers walked around the class and helped individual students when needed.

For these students it seems to be very important to have a role model to look up to and respect. More time spent with an individual student allows both teacher and student to deal with specific difficulties, to build up trust between both for further work and it also avoids anyone being left behind because everyone can work at their own pace.

In this class there is a problem with concentration with the students although the students themselves did not say that. We observed that students in this class could not remain focused for the full length of a lesson. They walked around, talked and daydreamed but from the spot check we could see that they still felt very positive. The students do not consider themselves to be distracted, remaining motivated and happy, trying their best. However, both teachers realise that there is a need to keep students concentrating as long as possible so they have some techniques which they use:

- to have one or two optional breaks depending on the lesson length;
- change tasks from time to time to maintain focus;
- totally change the subject when the concentration has almost gone, for example, mind stimulating games and riddles;
- open and accepting attitude by the teachers towards the students.

Students have the choice over how and when they take their optional breaks. They can take it in two five-minute breaks, one ten-minute break or they can use all of the time and leave ten minutes earlier. We think this is a good way of doing the breaks as it is totally on the students' terms and they can feel that they are taking responsibility for their own time. This idea is also just to give the students a break from their studies and make them feel refreshed.

When the teachers notice that the students are tending to chat they change the task so as to regain students' attention and boost their concentration. This also shows the students that there are many different styles of working inside a classroom and that they can experiment with a variety of learning styles. Therefore in this class there is no predominant learning style, no single trend or pattern but the crucial element is a change in task when required so as to keep motivation and focus at high levels.

Especially in the long lessons there comes a point towards the end when the students cannot get motivated to do anything so the teacher changes the whole idea of the lesson for five minutes. This is the way of keeping the students' interest alive. From the teachers' point of view, the purpose is not only learning here and now but also in motivating the students through a variety of activities which will have relevance for life after school. If the lesson gets to a point where no learning is taking place, the teacher is not so much bothered about teaching Swedish. The teacher tries by every possible means to make the students active in any way and avoid unproductive passiveness: 'There is no point in the students sitting in the class doing nothing at all. If I can make their minds active in anyway about anything, then it is better than them sitting around doing nothing' (Ola Sund).

These teachers have a very open and accepting attitude towards the students in their class. They take their feelings and attitudes into account and work with the students to get the best from them. They have taken this approach because they realise that they are dealing with students who have problems, whether these are school-related or not. This is the only way that they can get the students to respond without making them feel intimidated or different from 'typical' students. This approach appears to be the most suitable and to work well in this class, but it does make us wonder if this shouldn't be the usual way of dealing with students in all classes and in learning that takes place outside the school.

Misbehaving and disaffected students

In every class there are usually some disaffected students. If the students start to misbehave and move around, then they have a greater chance of disrupting someone if there is such a high number of them. Obviously they cause an effect and reactions from the rest of the class. There are many different types of disaffected students. The ones that we encountered were disruptive students and shy learners who didn't want to work in the class. The disruptive boys were not tolerated for long by the rest of the class. Usually at the beginning of the lesson these students were quiet and worked a bit but as the lesson progressed they became more physically active. However, the teacher always came and tried to settle them down. We thought that there was some very clever handling of these particular students in this class. The teacher did several things:

- played along with the students;
- dealt calmly with possible problems;
- motivated students by giving them an interesting task (searching on the Internet) and they stopped disturbing others.

'I have to play along with them and not lose my temper because if I do that then I would lose their respect and trust in me as a teacher' (Olo Sund).

We observed that the option of moving to another classroom is on the one hand effective, but we thought that it might be better if students stayed in the class for the whole lesson after their initial choice as this would avoid these disruptive students moving between the classes and disturbing other students. In the classes where students stayed, the disrupters would only disrupt the class for a short time and then the rest of the students began to ignore them. At that point they usually stopped being disruptive. We saw that they did not have such a big influence over the rest of the class and that the class as a whole was strong enough to deal with them. On occasions when the whole class became involved in the distraction, then the teacher would step in.

There is also one boy in the class who is very shy. Perhaps the typical way to deal with his shyness would be to make him work at the same level and pace as the rest of the class but in this case the student received some individual attention. He was allowed to work on the computer throughout the lesson and searched the Internet, researching his own ideas. After the lesson was over he could complete the work at home and hand it in the next day. This method seemed to be working well for this particular student. It allowed him to see that the teachers were helping him in a way that suited him very well.

It was very encouraging to see how positively the students in this class felt about learning but the length of lessons was an important factor in sustaining their interest. Towards the end of the class students became distracted and learning decreased. But each time this happened, the lesson finished with a change of task to something less related to Swedish, perhaps an informal discussion, mind-stimulating games and on one occasion even a deal. The teacher allowed the students to leave five minutes early if they spent that time doing their homework before the next Swedish class.

Observation in this Swedish class was very interesting. The approach taken by the teachers is quite different to other classroom situations given that the teachers take into consideration the students' personal and academic problems. In this class emphasis is not on learning itself but on learning how to learn and the teachers work hard to make students interested, inspired, motivated, productive and comfortable with themselves.

Comments on the academic class

We looked at information collected in two How Are You? sheets from this academic class and the found the results to be quite different from the vocational class. The first class we observed took place at 12.30 and lasted for one and a half hours. The results were not very positive from the students' point of view. They were often thinking about other things, drowsy and bored. They thought that time was passing slowly and that it was difficult to concentrate. This is interesting because the two researchers as well as the teacher thought the opposite on many points although we all agreed on the lack of concentration. The reasons for these findings might be:

- The teacher wasn't present for the whole lesson.
- The students weren't interested in the task (reading and writing).
- The length of the lesson.
- Students' mood from the previous class.

The fact that the teacher spent most of the lesson with a few students who were sitting a test didn't seem to be a drawback in this case. The teacher spent the first thirty minutes with the whole group and helped them with revision for a test. Afterwards they were told exactly what to do and they seemed to be interested in this task because they took notes during the explanation. When the teacher left the room the students began to work. They were alone and had been given responsibility for the class and so were in a position to use the time wisely or waste it. We thought they seemed comfortable with this.

On the other hand, their reported lack of concentration may be because they now felt freer to chat. They indeed chatted for some of the time although it seemed to us an understandable break from work rather than lazy time-wasting. This is clearly shown in the spot-check graph where the students give very negative responses as to their level of concentration but are extremely positive on items such as relaxed, sociable, happy and cheerful.

The second class we observed was shorter, only 55 minutes long, and the response of the students here was much more positive. They had a lot of freedom in this lesson and worked for a long time alone. At the beginning the teacher explained the task and the students chose where, how and with whom they did the work. Some of the students stayed in the class with the teacher and worked either in groups or individually. Sometimes they asked the teacher for help.

The whole class was working well and seemed to enjoy it. This is shown in the spot check where the student data show them to be concentrated, alert, relaxed, active, productive and willing to participate. The task was full of variety, student inputs, sharing with colleagues and seemed to be interesting. Sometimes chatting took place as well and this is shown on the spot-check graph where students said that they were sociable, happy and relaxed. Compared with the amount of the work done, the minor chatting was not a problem and in this case it positively contributed to a nice atmosphere in the class. In this lesson the work was combined with enjoyment. An informal discussion took place at the end of the class to which students reacted very positively and seemed to be enjoying it.

General comments on the academic class

The academic class is structured in a similar way to the vocational class. The explanation at the beginning is considered crucial. Students are given a large amount of responsibility for their time and study. Being absolutely clear about the task reduced problems in getting on with it. Taking notes during the explanation suggests that students found it important and useful.

After the explanation the role of the teacher is minor. Often the students are not even present in the classroom after this, having gone somewhere else to study. We observed that this has a positive impact on the students:

* They have the freedom to organise their time.
* They do not need to be told to do something but do it on their own.
* They can choose a place to complete the task.

For Swedish students it seems very important for them to have responsibility, which gradually increases as they get older. Students in this academic class were able to work well with just a little help. They were good at working independently and putting their own personal opinions into their work. By contrast, there was one particular occasion when students spent a considerable part of a lesson listening to the teacher. Students' focus and interest in this learning style were much less than the one in which they had a set task in the beginning and they could deal with it in their own way, either by individual, pair or group work inside the class or even outside it.

Students were in a position to use the time wisely or to waste it. We thought they seemed comfortable with this. On the other hand, the low concentration might have meant that the students felt free to chat. They indeed chatted for some of the time but it seemed an understandable break from work rather than lazy time-wasting. This was clearly shown in the spot check graph where the students are so negative about their concentration but extremely positive in answers such as relaxed, sociable, happy and cheerful.

In this lesson the students certainly might have not been interested in the task itself. This would explain why they were somewhat distracted in this lesson, whereas in the second lesson the same learning styles occurred and the class as a whole responded very positively. This leads to the conclusion that the length of the lesson or some factors outside the classroom may have caused the students to be distracted. The first class was very long and on several occasions some students were stuck as to what to do. They stopped working and began chatting.

The second class we observed was shorter, only fifty-five minutes long, and much more positive. The students had a lot of freedom in this lesson and worked for a long time alone. However, at the beginning the teacher explained the task and the students chose where, how and with whom they did the work. Some of the students stayed in the class with the teacher and worked either in groups or individually. Sometimes they asked he teacher for help.

The whole class was working well and seemed to enjoy it. This is shown in the spot check where the students are concentrated, alert, relaxed, active, productive and willing to participate. The task was full of variety, student inputs, sharing with colleagues and seemed to be interesting. However, sometimes in the group chatting took place as well. This is shown on the spot-check graph where students said that they were sociable, happy and relaxed. Compared with the amount of the work done the minor chatting was not a problem and in this case it positively contributed to a nice atmosphere in the class. In this lesson the work was combined with enjoyment. An informal discussion took place in the end of the class. We cannot ascertain its effect but students reacted very positively to it and seemed to be enjoying it.

Students could also choose somewhere to finish their work. For students who did not feel comfortable with sharing ideas with a peer group it was a good chance to go away and complete what was needed in a more effective and suitable way for them. Students could go to the library and use all of the school's equipment if they wanted. Not only is this interesting and motivating for them but it is also a good chance for lifelong learning to take place. They learn how to find information which can help them to finish a set task. The actual process of carrying out a task is much more efficient for memory than just factual memorising of a book.

The students in this class remained focused for quite a long period of time. However, the teacher still used some techniques when their concentration level went down:

- informal discussion;
- changing of task – seen in the learning cycle;
- individual help.

The informal discussions were very effective when time was limited. The teacher initiated a discussion using the plot from the *Decameron* that the class were studying. This developed into a discussion concerning current life styles – affairs and jealousy.

These academic students are generally motivated to study and usually work hard. We observed that when they were working at their best the class was following several different learning styles. We developed this idea and found that a learning cycle pattern had taken place as shown in Figure 14.1.

This learning 'cycle' includes several learning styles which followed each other. In this case it was listening in the beginning, reading of a text, writing up

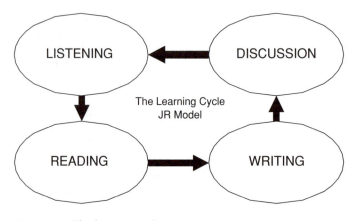

Figure 14.1 The learning cycle

about the text, then a final discussion about the whole task. Students knew that they would have to back up information from one learning style to do the other properly, therefore the whole work in total was more effective and productive. They read a text more carefully, because they knew they would have to write an essay about it. They had to raise good points in the essay because they knew they would have to use them as good arguments in the formal discussion.

The individual help was beneficial when students got stuck even after the explanation, or when the students thought of original ideas and asked the teacher if they would be applicable to the task. The teacher would give the student an initial boost and he or she would work well without distraction.

We did not observe any real instances of disaffection in these lessons. The atmosphere in this class is surprisingly relaxed and nice. There was one girl who did not take part in classwork or group work but she worked excellently on her own. There was no peer pressure on her, the class liked her and respected her. From that she gradually developed and we saw her actively participate in the class discussion on jealousy and affairs. The teacher established the right kind of atmosphere where no one felt intimidated or nervous about voicing their opinions, which certainly helped this girl to feel more comfortable with in presenting her ideas and taking part in classwork.

The students and the teacher have nice kind of relationship on what feels like even terms. The fact that the teacher does not patronise and can relate to the students without judging them is instrumental in establishing this relationship. The trust in this class is a very important factor but we found this also in the vocational class.

In the vocational class we did not notice any difference in concentration due to the timing of the lesson but this was not the case in the academic class. As described above, the students appeared much more negative in the longer class that in the shorter one. The teacher did well in keeping the students' attention for so long, but it seems as though long classes are much less productive than shorter ones, as much time is spent on trying to keep students focused by frequently changing tasks, giving them breaks, and so on.

In conclusion, we think that this academic class worked very well. We were able to observe many interesting points. These students need to reach a certain academic level to get into college or university. However, the teacher not only teaches factual information but also tries to give the students other skills and information by looking at the subject from many different angles. By the end of the course the students from this class should have a full appreciation of the subject – they should be able to communicate very well, express their opinions on paper and also be aware of the historical background of literature.

What's the matter with 5B? Two Japanese classes compared

In this excerpt a comparison is made between 5B and 5C, two classes in the same school with the same teacher and following the same lesson content. One, however, appears much more efficient than the other. In seeking explanations we are reminded of the significance of context, the vital effect of the composition of the peer group, and the importance of the relationship established between teacher and class. These are not three separate factors but, as can be seen in this passage, interact with one another in a dynamic way.

On the last day of observation we observed two lessons in the afternoon, both with exactly the same contents. The first was with 5C, the second with 5B. Both classes were studying the same section from the English textbook.

During the first part of the lesson in both classes the teacher explained the text to the class and selected students to answer questions. In 5C the selected students answered immediately and usually correctly. In 5B the students struggled with the questions and were often unable to answer. This was surprising and unusual because in other lessons 5B usually had no problems with answering the teacher's questions. On this day they were distinctly different. Trying to understand this, one possible explanation is that 5B perhaps had other work to do for that day and did not have time to prepare sufficiently for this lesson. Perhaps something had happened in a previous lesson to distract them.

Other explanations for the difference between 5C and 5B class are that 5C class is the home room class of the Japanese teacher and the students enjoy a very good rapport amongst themselves and with the teacher. Students and the teacher seem to have established a very productive way of learning and teaching. The teacher also seemed to be more relaxed with his own class than with 5B. The students appear to feel more comfortable with asking questions even to us in front of the whole class and the whole lesson with 5C proceeded in a consistently productive way. On the other hand, in the 5B class, the teacher had to spend more time settling the class down and less was being taught. Students were, throughout the lesson, more talkative and less concerned with Japanese than mucking about. This was confirmed by the spot-check results. While 5B students frequently answered that they were relaxed, happy, cheerful, excited, they also reported that it was difficult to be productive and they were generally unmotivated and passive.

Although 5B is markedly less involved than 5C, the level of interaction is still relatively high compared to the other countries in which we have observed classes. Even if students are talkative during the class, they would try to ensure they had covered the ground, for example, if a student were uncertain about anything, he or she would come after the class was finished and speak to the teacher personally. This happened both in 5B and in 5C and says something significant about the culture of the school and its society.

15 It all depends on your point of view

Robert Janícek, Kotaro Nariai and
Debbie Moncrieff

What students see and what their teacher see may often be quite different things. And the Learning School students who sit in classrooms and observe may also make judgements based on what they see and don't see. In this chapter we give examples of a number of different classrooms where the spot check shows both wide divergence of view and sometimes quite close consonance among the three sets of judgements. This does place a question mark over classroom observation which focuses on what the teacher is doing rather than what students are learning.

The spot check is filled out at one point in the middle of a lesson, perhaps half-way, to get a snapshot of what students are thinking and feeling at that moment. The teacher also fills it out with her judgement of student engagement while the LS student (or students) do the same. This gives a triangulation of judgements. Sometimes there is a close match. Sometimes, most typically, teachers over-estimate their students' involvement. Occasionally teachers under-estimate their students' level of interest and involvement. The first of the following four figures (Figure 15.1) shows a teacher significantly under-estimating her

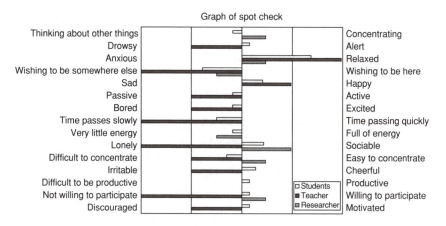

Figure 15.1 Spot-check graph by Ms S

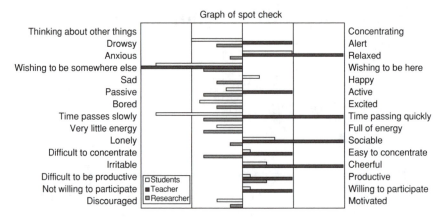

Figure 15.2 Spot-check graph by Mr M

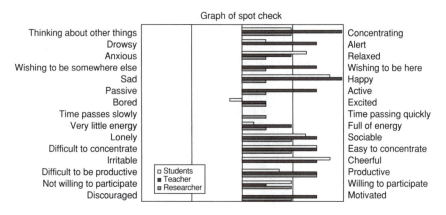

Figure 15.3 Spot-check graph by Mr H

students' mood and level of alertness and motivation. It is noticeable that the LS1 rating lies closer to the school students than to the teachers.

The second example (Figure 15.2) illustrates the opposite tendency. The teacher misreads his students' mood, level of alertness, mental activity and very significantly whether time seems to be passing quickly or slowly. From where the teacher stands, time goes by quickly. For the students it drags. The LS team's judgements here fluctuate considerably, rarely in agreement with the teacher and only occasionally close to the students' assessments.

The third example (Figure 15.3) shows three sets of judgements all on the positive side, except for one item where students cannot agree to being 'excited'. The teacher is consistently more positive than his students with the exception of their being relaxed and cheerful. The LS1 observers are often less

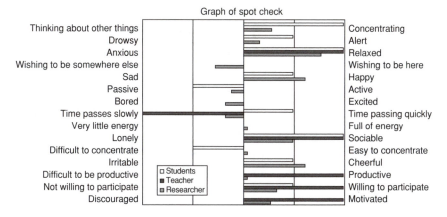

Figure 15.4 Spot-check graph 1 by Mr C

positive than either teacher or students, particularly on relaxed, happy, sociable, easy to concentrate.

Figure 15.4 provides a different pattern again, a striking contrast between the observers and the school students. The LS team judgements tend to lie quite close to those of the teacher but six items are dramatically at variance with the students. Their motivation and productivity are notably misjudged.

These examples illustrate the very subjective nature of evaluation when it comes to what is going on inside as opposed to what is visible from the outside. It does not mean that students' assessment represent the 'truth' and although they are certainly closer to knowing how they are feeling, they interpret their feelings in a context where they are rarely, if ever, asked to make such a judgement.

The data are very ambiguous and need to be followed up by conversations which unpack the perceptions and meanings lying behind the figures. The following are examples of such further exploration.

A week of English in Anderson High

There used to be twenty-one students in the class but five of them left for reasons of their own so that there are sixteen students at the moment. It is getting near to exam times so both teachers and students feel the pressure to cover the ground. Two spot checks were taken in this English class at two different points during the week (Figures 15.4 and 15.5). They show a different response from the class on these two occasions as well as a different judgement on the part of the teacher.

The most positive spot check of the week was on the Monday and what happened on Monday was playing out the drama of the book they had been reading. The teacher took one of the most important female roles in the play

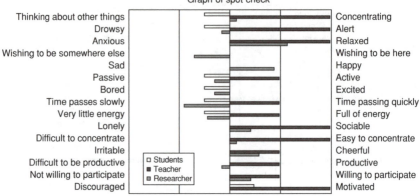

Figure 15.5 Spot-check graph 2 by Mr C

because the rest of the girls were shy and refused to join the play. The students who were playing the main roles looked more confident while the teacher showed in a very natural way how well aware of this topic he was by using lots of reference from the news about the IRA. He also picked one of the characters from the film that was very familiar to the class in order to shed light on the characters in the drama. The students looked more active and engaged when the teacher talked about these non-fictional examples and a few of the class asked him some questions about his story to find out more. The teacher did not talk about these things too long and went back to the drama work to continue the lesson.

The teacher used many examples from the daily life such as current events and up-to-date news. The difference from what was to happen later in the week was that the teacher dramatised the play and he did not spend a long time on explanations. The students were interested in the story through the drama, and the good sound effects that were added by the teacher who also had a good sense of humour and made it lively and interesting.

On the Friday the spot-check result was the most negative of the week. The class had finished the drama and the lesson was moving on to the next work so that the teacher gave a very long introduction before they started. From these students' responses, I think the students' mood depended on how easy it was to follow the lesson and how meaningful the lesson was for them. Simply listening to the teacher seems to present a very high barrier for some students. The students later remarked that their learning was limited to a lot of listening which did not always suit their own preferred style, and that as the lesson became more academic, the fun went out of it. They said that they were not supposed to look for fun like the younger students. When the teacher told them a non-fictional story related to the text that they were studying, he got their attention back. This also happened when he used lots of references from daily life with some jokes to re-engage their interest. The students looked more alert and were keen to listen to the teacher when he spoke about something apart from the book. It made the lesson more relaxed and the students remained enthusiastic at these points where he was speaking about something they could easily relate to.

On the other hand, the teacher sometimes went into very long explanations because he felt he needed to tell them the important points from the story even though the students were getting distracted. It is difficult to know how much they were actually taking in, especially as they weren't making notes. He later said that it was his practice to get them used to listening because he thought that previous students he had taught were more used to watching than listening – and it was important to develop their listening skills.

At the end of the week they finally finished the story and seemed to be satisfied with the fact that they had 'done' the book. They had been working on the book *Bold Girls* for about one week and it was not very long before they had become fed up with it. After the week the students who had taken roles in the play appeared more confident in talking to the teacher and this seemed to have involved them more than the others.

The seating had not been changed at all and the group of active students had not been separated. The first exam is getting close and the students have to study more at home to finish their RPR report. In the lesson revision is being done all the time and they are doing the same story *Bold Girls* as when I was in the class last time. The teacher thinks it is boring for me to observe lessons during this revision period, which means the teacher and the students have to do it for the exams even though they might not want to do so.

Spot-check analysis

The spot check at the beginning of the week was generally quite positive and the teacher's and students' version agreed on a number of the items. Students were on the whole willing to participate. They were motivated, alert, relaxed and concentrating (although students also say it is difficult to concentrate) – although on these last two points the teacher is less sure and gives a midpoint score on his spot check. On only one point is there is a marked disparity between the teacher and the class – that is on time passing. For the students time is passing very slowly.

As the week progresses and work becomes more academic and serious the spot check becomes more negative both in the view of the students and in the view of the teacher, although his is consistently more on the positive side. By the end of the week the spot check gives a much more consistently negative picture from the students although there are still some positive features about their mood. They are generally wishing to be somewhere else, are passive, and have very little energy. The English teacher is, however, noticeably more positive in his judgements of the students' engagement with his lesson. It is in this context that the teacher makes the point about student listening. He is aware that they find it difficult but his judgement that it is easy for them to concentrate stems from the fact that he thinks they are working hard at listening and they look as if they are. He also agrees that students can be very adept at looking interested even when they are mentally far way. The students, he said, found listening boring and they were not used to sitting paying attention for long periods of time. They live in a world where their attention span is acknowledged to be short and predominantly visual.

On the positive side, the students always answer 'sociable' and 'motivated'. They are also generally positive about feelings like happy, relaxed and cheerful and these feelings contribute to, and maintain, a relaxed atmosphere in the classroom. In the relaxed atmosphere, the sociable mood can easily turn to chat rather than productive conversation but in this class the students said that they don't chat in the class and the class is actually very quiet unless there is a disruption from outside. I think that the teacher's firm authority prevents them from chatting because the teacher is always in control and the lesson flows without interruption. From time to time the teacher reminds them of how close the exam is and how much, or little, they have done so far. He exerts pressure on to them to try to complete their own work and students seemed to realise that they have to concentrate.

Four lessons from the Czech Republic

These examples are very revealing in pinpointing the differences as well as similarities in the way the teacher reads the situation and how students see it. The various spot checks taken from the Czech school start with two very positive examples from an English and a Chemistry lesson followed by two (one Chemistry, one Czech language) where there are much more marked differences. All tell an intriguing story of differences in student engagement and illustrate how teachers' and students' evaluations can both converge and diverge.

English

In this lesson the English teacher gave students the opportunity to choose their own learning styles. The students responded well to this. Some chose to work individually, some in pairs. The time was not used to socialise but to speak to one another about the work in hand and kept focused on the lesson. Students were willing to speak out in front of the class and didn't need to be picked on by the teacher. At times there was a slight reluctance but once the ice was broken, opinions flowed freely. Students in this class had been together for a number of years and had greater confidence in one another. Their level of English is also of a very high standard.

The spot check in Figure 15.6 gives a generally very positive picture with only one small negative on the 'wishing to be here' question. While the teacher is, on five categories, markedly more positive than the students, on six he/she

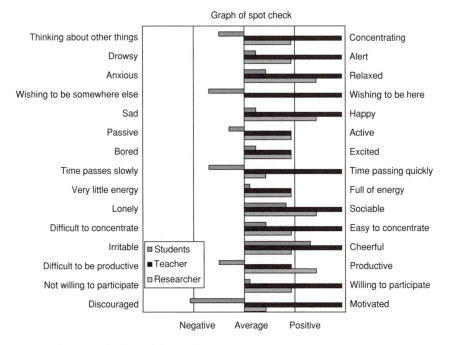

Figure 15.6 Spot-check graph by Ms H

is slightly less positive and in fairly close agreement on the others. This suggests a teacher pretty much in tune with the class and reading their emotional and motivational state pretty well. It is the kind of picture from a spot check that signals that this is a highly effective lesson for students and teachers alike.

Chemistry: example one

The lesson lasted for two periods with a small group of seven students. For the first five minutes the teacher explained what they were going to do and showed them the equipment. They responded well to her cheerful attitude and concentrated well. They participated well answering her questions and this was a short focused introduction so they stayed interested. For the next twenty minutes they worked on experiments, working co-operatively and productively. The teacher went round helping them individually. After twenty-five minutes one pair demonstrated the experiment for others while another student wrote on the blackboard and the rest of the class took notes. Over the forty-minute period students changed activity and position every ten minutes. All of the students understood what they were doing and when they didn't, they asked one another for help. They also had paired discussions with feedback to the rest of the class and for about ten minutes the teacher left the room, trusting them to get on with the work on their own – which they did.

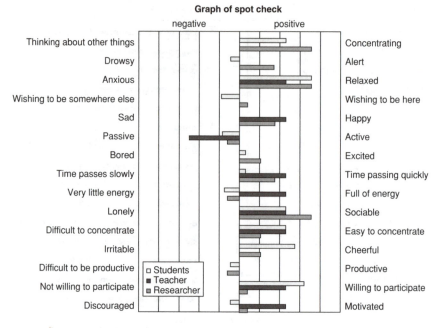

Figure 15.7 Spot-check graph by Mr N

The spot check in Figure 15.7 was done half an hour into the lesson when the students were all doing different things, doing an experiment, writing on the blackboard and taking notes. Overall the results were very positive both from the teacher and the students and after the lesson students said they had learned a lot, had been 'on task' for almost all the lesson and had enjoyed the relaxed but purposeful atmosphere.

Interesting points

1   The class atmosphere changes when students move from normal classes to more hands-on activity in the lab. There is a lot of change of activity and physical movement around the room. The atmosphere is helped by the small number of students, their opportunity to work together and their friendship with one another.

2   We noted that the atmosphere changed a bit when the teacher left the room. Students became more relaxed, laughed more and talked more sociably. However, they did not become rowdy, continued to work diligently and any pressure from the teacher disappeared during her absence.

3   There was a noticeable change in the teacher's role between the normal classroom and the chemistry lab. In the lab the teacher spent only a small percentage of time actually 'teaching' her role being mainly that of observer.

Students used each other much more as a resource than in the normal classroom while the teacher's contributions were more random and in response to students' questions or observations.

Chemistry: example two

The second Chemistry example shows a wide divergence of opinion between teacher and student (Figure 15.2 above). The teacher is not aware, of course, of the students' previous history and has to combat their lack of motivation and low expectation at the beginning of the lesson. But the teacher is more optimistic than the students that this lethargy has been overcome.

At the beginning of this sixth period lesson many students marked that they were not feeling very positive at all and many people were tired, hungry, anxious and cold. The fact that a couple of people marked 'anxious' suggests that they were not particularly looking forward to this lesson. One student marked 'bored' right at the beginning of the lesson. Only one student had marked 'happy' and nobody gave full marks for expectation. The mood for learning was below average suggesting that motivation levels were quite low right from the start of the lesson.

The spot check took place exactly in the middle of the lesson. It proved to be extremely negative overall whereas the teacher marked a large number of points very positively. This teacher, who received many positive spot checks from other classes at different times, gave the impression that he/she did not seem to tune in well to this particular class's feelings, confirmed by the fact that the students had marked that time was passing extremely slowly while the teacher marked 'time passes extremely quickly'. The teacher did, however, recognise that the students were not keen to be in this class and acknowledged that they were not particularly motivated or concentrating very well. He/she could also see that the students were not happy or excited to be there.

The spot check was done while a student was being tested at the board and this student as well as another student spent a total of twenty minutes at the board which began to drag on and this could help explain how negative the class felt. This period of teaching had been going on too long and students were finding it increasingly tedious and indicated that they did not want to be in the class any longer.

Interesting points

1   Time spent at the blackboard

While students were being tested, each one spent at least ten minutes at the blackboard either just writing or attempting to explain as well. Although the teacher contributed, he/she did not seem to be adding anything substantial or significant and during the students' time at the board most of the responsibility of class was transferred to that person being tested. If that person was successful at the board and was able to explain the material sufficiently, the time spent at the board was productive. However, when a student at the board was not very competent in the subject, the time spent was wasted and we wondered – was all that time spent by students at the board necessary?

2   The class atmosphere

The atmosphere in this class was not seen by the students as particularly friendly or comfortable and they did not seem to enjoy this class much at all. The teacher seemed to be having difficulty in establishing a positive learning relationship with these particular students. Those who came out to the board seemed extremely anxious and the teacher put a lot of pressure on them to be correct all the time. This atmosphere did not seem to be the most conducive for effective learning.

3   The mood for learning

The mood for learning figures before the lesson began at a low point and students seemed tired and a few were hungry, but surprisingly enough, the students' estimates of learning taking place were quite high despite their lack of motivation. Once we were able to understand just how much these students had been groomed to work, no matter what the conditions were, it made more sense to us. These students have a lot of work to cover and they are aware of this and work hard constantly to achieve results.

These findings raise some critical issues about the environment of learning, students' perceptions and the cultural context:

- Can students learn effectively in non-conducive conditions and with low motivation?
- Is such learning 'deep' and meaningful?
- What do students mean when they evaluate their own learning?
- Is their perception of 'learning' conditioned by their culture?

A lesson in Czech

The third example follows the same student into another lesson, this time in Czech. Many of the same themes emerge.

The teacher was slightly late but all the students stood up as he came in. The students were noisy and chatty as the lesson began but the teacher made it clear from the start that he did not want any chat at all during the class. He then started to give an explanation from a book which he held in his hand. All of the students took notes and had the same book as the teacher so they could follow what was being talked about. The teacher sometimes stopped his explanation and asked questions of the class. The female members of the class generally replied to these questions. To try and get more involvement from other members of the class the teacher walked up and down the aisle so that he could get a clear view of all the students and prompt some of them into answering his questions.

He then moved on to do some board work, which had a display of some authors' names. This board work did not last very long at all and he swiftly moved back on to the previous routine. This pattern was repeated several times with the teacher moving from long explanations to short board work exercises. This was the framework for the entire lesson and, from observation, spot check and post-lesson interview, this resulted in some of the students getting bored.

Most of the students took notes continuously but there were some students who seemed to have had enough and simply stopped taking notes. Most of the students who got distracted did so secretly so as not to let the teacher see them. They seemed to look around for something to distract them, using the spot check or doodling on their notebooks.

The girls in this class seemed to have a good relationship with the teacher and did try to communicate with him. Even after the lesson some stayed behind to see what he had marked on his spot check.

Spot-check analysis

The spot cheek was done near the end of the class and the teacher did this on purpose. Some students asked continuously whether or not they could do it but the teacher always said no and left it to the end of the lesson. There were lots of mismatches between the teacher's feelings and the students' feelings. The teacher did not think that the students were relaxed and they made him believe that they were concentrating and he thought they were totally motivated in this Czech class. The students, however, were actually feeling slightly discouraged and wishing to be somewhere else. The students were also feeling totally passive but the teacher saw them as very active. He even went as far as to give full marks (a 3) on students feeling active while their evidence was that they were actually tending to feel more passive throughout the lesson.

From our point of view the teacher has his own way of teaching and seemed to think that this is the best way to teach the Czech course. He thought that the students were following it well but we felt there were long periods of time in which students got bored and lost interest. The spot check was done just after a long explanation from the teacher so it is not surprising if they were not feeling totally active or productive at that point. On our spot-check sheet we marked that for the students the time was passing very slowly (a 3) but the students had actually given this a less extreme mark (a 2). Comparing our views to those of the students we may conclude that the students are used to this style of teaching and have adjusted to it better than we have.

Students were feeling sociable, cheerful, and strongly wanting to participate so that if the teacher had harnessed these feelings by some form of interaction we think that the motivation level would have increased in the class. Many of the students said that they had energy and motivation at the beginning but due to the long dictations from the teacher they used this energy to distract themselves.

The students' answers to the questions about how much they learned seemed to be at odds with the spot-check results. They said that they learned a great deal. This was explained by the fact that most of the work that was done in the class was note taking so when they left the room they felt that they had lots of information. Even though they thought it was a boring way to learn, it still gave them what they needed from the lesson. This was a different view of being 'productive' from our own as observers, but is seemed to be the only teaching style that students were familiar with, in this class at least, and they accepted being bored as part of learning, or acquiring information.

There were two negative boys in this class. They both felt unhappy before the class and their spot-check answers were very negative. They also mentioned that they did not feel that they learned anything. They were fairly passive. They did not chat and they indicated that they were willing to participate but had lost interest and couldn't be bothered being in the Czech class any more.

Interesting points

1   Students looking for distractions

We noticed that there were some students who were looking for distractions. These were engaged in secretly. They tried to keep out of the teacher's line of sight and did so by sending messages to their friends or writing on their notebooks. Some were reading magazines under the table and so on. The teacher was not aware of these distractions but because they seemed to be scared of him they were very careful to hide what they were doing.

The teacher asserted his authority while the lesson was underway as all of the interaction was teacher to student, him asking questions and them responding or him talking or dictating notes.

2   Layout

The classroom was set up for receiving information and copying notes as they were all seated facing the blackboard. The room itself was also really too small for the number of students in this class. There was very little room for us even to fit in. This classroom set-up restricts learning and teaching styles are restricted as they cannot move any furniture in the class. The tables were long and had to be in the position so that it would be difficult for any group work to take place.

16 A life in the day of three students

*Karolina Landowska, Stepan Hlosek,
Jolene Garriock, Hyden Mathys and
Matthew Greenhalgh*

This chapter follows a number of students through their school day, illustrating the degree to which young people live out their own individual lives in the classroom, sometimes engaged with what the teacher is doing, sometimes disengaged, floating off into a world of their inner thoughts. Their motivation is sometimes down to the skill of the teacher in engaging their interest but sometimes it is their own inner drive that keeps them going while sometimes the teacher actually seems to inhibit their learning, distracting them from their own goals.

The life of individual students in the classroom

We chose to evaluate the motivational influences which are experienced during a day, looking at interaction with teachers and fellow students, the range of learning styles experienced, the length and time of day, the influence of lunch and breaks, the general school atmosphere and ethos.

In order to make this assessment, individual students were shadowed for a period of two days, during which time the researcher made detailed observations of the shadowed student's behaviour and experiences. The 'shadowee' was asked at regular intervals to complete a spot-check to gain insights at a given moment about their level of motivation. Finally, we recorded comments and information from an interview with the shadowed student.

The assessment involved three stages:

* plotting motivation over the course of the day;
* plotting learning;
* examining learning and motivation.

Two days in Gitta's educational life

Figures 16.1, 16.2 and 16.3 from Learning School 2 illustrate the ups and downs of motivation for Gitta over the course of one day and then, in Figure 16.2, the ups and down in learning, each rated on a 4. point scale (4 high, 1 low). Figure 16.3 shows these two together and raises provocative questions about

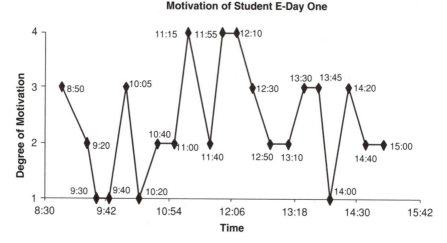

Figure 16.1 Motivation of Student E – day 1

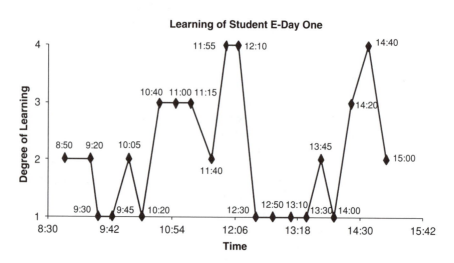

Figure 16.2 Learning of Student E – day 1

their inter-relationship. Can you learn when you're not motivated? Can you be highly motivated but not learn?

In these short extracts from two school days in the life of Gitta, a 16-year-old German student we see a rollercoaster pattern of motivation and productivity following results of tests and in anticipation of tests to come. Particularly striking is the explanation of rises and falls in motivation which do not have anything to do with the present but with the anticipated future. Gitta's motivation is high in a boring lesson because she is looking forward to what is coming next and low in an interesting lesson because of the dread of a forthcoming test. The

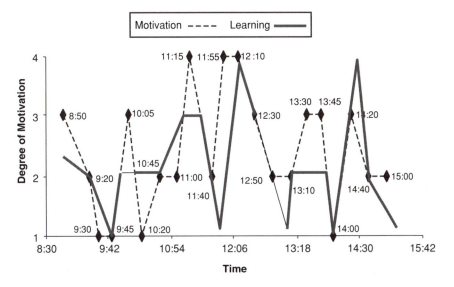

Figure 16.3 Motivation and learning

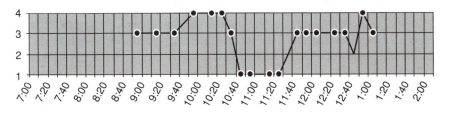

Figure 16.4 Gitta: day 3 motivation

influence of her peers and teacher on her self-confidence is also evident in these extracts.

Gitta Day 3

Figure 16.4 shows Gitta's motivation on day 3.

Chemistry (08.50–09.35)

The teacher began the lesson by demonstrating an experiment. Gitta took notes and during this time her productivity rose. It began to decrease during the break while she talked with her classmates but her motivation remained high in anticipation of her next class which was English – her favourite subject. Gitta said this was a very motivating factor for her.

English (09.45–10.30)

Gitta was active for the first 30 minutes, during which time she answered many of the teacher's questions. Both her motivation and productivity were high during this time. However, as the teacher's questions began to get more difficult towards the end of the class and Gitta could not answer them, her productivity and motivation began to drop.

Her motivation decreased rapidly at end of the lesson because she said she did not have a good feeling about the Maths test that they were about to receive in the next class. She did not expect good results. However, according to the graph, her productivity rose during the break as she felt that she was enjoying her conversation with her friends.

Maths (10.40–11.25)

Gitta's productivity dropped again when she received the marked test and was awarded no points. Her motivation continued to be low throughout the lesson. She later explained that she was longing for the next class because Geography was one of her favourite subjects and this accounted for a rise in her motivation.

Geography (11.35–12.25)

In the Geography class, she maintained high motivation and productivity throughout the lesson. This was observable from her behaviour such as asking the teacher many questions and taking notes.

However, in the break time, her productivity fell again because she was tired which, she said, was caused by a lack of sleep the night before. But her motivation rose because she was looking forward to receiving the results of a test in the next class which she thought she had done well in, at least much better than the results from the Maths test.

Politics (12.20–13.00)

The teacher just talked at the beginning of the Politics class, causing Gitta's motivation to decrease. However, her productivity rose because she tried to listen to her classmate's secret discussion. In the middle of the class, her motivation rose suddenly because she got twice as many points in this test as in the previous Politics test. When the teacher changed the topic from the test to current political events, her motivation decreased.

Day 4

Figure 16.5 shows Gitta's motivation on day 4.

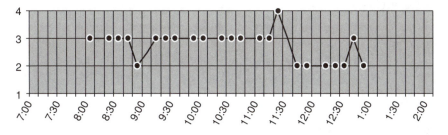

Figure 16.5 Gitta: day 4 motivation

French (08.00–08.45)

During the French class, Gitta's motivation and productivity stayed the same because the teaching style did not change. In the break, she noticed that she had forgotten her homework. This shocked her and caused a drop in her motivation.

English (08.55–09.40)

In English however, both her motivation and productivity rose again. The teacher told Gitta her final grade, which she was satisfied with. Later in the interview, she said that the teacher was very nice to her even though she was very strict and that helped her to maintain concentration. She said that this was the reason for her high motivation and productivity during the class.

Politics (09.45–10.30)

In the beginning of the Politics class, Gitta was told her final grade by the teacher. She was satisfied with the result and both her motivation and productivity increased again.

German (10.40–11.25)

In the German class, Gitta's motivation and productivity reached a peak. Prior to this lesson, the class had been translating old German texts to contemporary German but in this lesson the teacher made the classroom atmosphere friendlier and Gitta enjoyed and laughed at the humorous answers of other students.

However, in the break between classes both her motivation and productivity decreased considerably because she was not looking forward to the next class, which was her least favourite.

Religion (11.30–12.15)

Gitta's motivation remained very low during the first Religion class. At the beginning of the class, she had received a very bad grade and she said that she did not feel like studying at all because of this. This bad feeling carried on through the break because she said that she was going to have Religion again for another lesson.

Religion (12.20–13.00)

In the second Religion class, her motivation rose at one point because of the light relief provided by one student who had said something funny to make Gitta laugh. This student's contribution provided a brief light relief for Gitta and revived her motivation for a short time. When this student stopped talking, however, her motivation fell again.

Comment

Understanding what was happening in these classes, from Gitta's viewpoint, proved to be an important factor in explaining her motivation to learn. Even in her favourite subject, her motivation decreased when she could not answer the teacher's questions. We also noticed that her physical condition had an effect on her motivation and productivity. When she was tired, it was difficult to concentrate on the lesson.

Her motivation and productivity rose whenever she received good grades from her teachers. In the interview she explained that getting good grades was the most important motivational factor for her, although other people also proved to be important in motivating her. She said that she felt the expectations from the teacher, sometimes from her parents, and from herself. This meant she was conscious of what others thought of her and this made her anxious at times, thus causing her motivation to decrease. This also happened when she could not answer the teacher's questions and when she forgot her homework in her favourite English class.

We can say that 'refreshment' such as the humour of the teacher or a classmate helped to increase both her motivation and productivity even in her least favourite subject. With regard to the refreshment in the break time, she said that she liked it because she could release her stress by talking with her friends. The high rating for productivity (shown in the spot checks during the breaks) was, she said, because she felt energised and productive even though she wasn't learning anything to do with school work.

It is interesting to note that her productivity was closely related to being active. When she experienced a passive learning style, her productivity dropped. During periods of active learning, such as raising her hand, her productivity and motivation were high.

A life in the day of Naomi
Matthew Greenhalgh

In this report I will focus on Naomi's specific feelings expressed in parts one and three of the 'How Are You?' sheet and see how these feelings affect how one student learns over the course of a whole day – the 19th of April 2000. I will also investigate what factors in a lesson affect these feelings and the reasons behind them. All the three categories – mood for learning, amount learned and amount of chatting – can be marked between 1 and 5, 1 being when there is very little (or low level) and 5 when there is a lot, or very high level.

Periods 1 and 2 Home Economics

Naomi's first lesson of the day was a double period of Home Economics. At the beginning of this lesson Naomi marked a 4 for her mood for learning, which is quite high but we noted that, although she felt happy, she also felt tired and lethargic. When asked about this, she said that she had long evening classes three times a week, which left her very tired for the next day. She also said that because she learns so much in these night classes the benefits far outweigh her feeling tired in the morning.

During the lesson

The next step was then to look at the lesson structure and the learning styles within to see what effect these had on the student. The first point is that students worked on their own projects and at their own pace so as a result the pace was quite slow and the atmosphere relaxed. Second, there were only one or two learning styles available, consisting of listening to the teacher then researching and working on a project. Naomi worked on hers individually so the work was, for her, quite monotonous. Third, the lesson was a double period so Naomi was working on the same thing for a very long time. The combination of these three factors plus Naomi's initial lethargy, from the 'How Are You?' sheet, made Naomi feel negative. The spot check in the middle of the lesson showed that she was bored, wishing to be somewhere else, drowsy, had little energy, not willing to participate, finding it difficult to concentrate and that time was passing slowly. From this we can see that the structure, pace and nature of the task had quite a negative effect for Naomi and that it did not drive her to work to her full potential.

The amount the student interacts with other students during the lesson, whether it is chatting or discussion, is also another factor that can help explain the student's feelings and reactions. In her Home Economics class Naomi felt that she hadn't chatted very much even though in general it was a very sociable lesson. This helps us understand a bit more about her character and suggests that Naomi is not a student who is not much interested in chatting. She likes interacting with her friends when it is concerned with the task in hand but she wants to learn and likes to concentrate on class work.

At the end of the lesson

After the lesson Naomi said that she had not learned a great deal, giving a rating of 3, a smaller mark than her mood for learning. Whether or not the lesson was productive depends on the relation between the mood for learning and the amount learned. If the mood for learning is higher than the amount learned, then it suggests that the lesson did not maximise the student's potential motivation. If the mood for learning is below the amount learned, then we can see that, although the student was not initially motivated, the lesson managed to stimulate the student to learn and thus was very productive. In this case Naomi felt that she learned a little less than she was in the mood for, so as a preliminary indicator we conclude that the lesson was not very productive.

Period 3 Japanese Classics

Beginning of the lesson

Japanese Classics is a subject that Naomi says she finds very interesting, much more so than Home Economics. Yet she again marks a 4 for the mood for learning, the same as for Home Economics, even though Japanese Classics is a lesson that she should really be looking forward to more. So, as a result of Naomi's feeling of negativity created in the Home Economics lesson she was not as positive as expected for Japanese Classics. The lesson starts at 10.35 but although it is well into the morning Naomi marked that she still felt tired and lethargic. Because she found Home Economics so boring and monotonous it left her feeling less motivated to work in her following lesson, she was later to explain. She had also started to feel hungry, which could also have proved to be a distraction.

During the lesson

Naomi again felt negative because the isolated nature of the lesson made her feel lonely and inactive so the lethargy and boredom continued. This is one of the negative points about this style of lesson. It needs the students to concentrate for long periods of time and gives them little incentive, apart from their own interest in the subject or sheer determination, to sustain their interest. Naomi marked very low, a 2, for the amount she interacted with others in the class. This suggests that the lack of interaction may have been a factor in explaining her negativity in the class.

At the end of the lesson

After the lesson ended she marked a 3 for the amount she learned, which is again both quite low and less than her mood for learning, suggesting that this was not a very productive lesson either.

The Japanese Classics lesson is fairly typical of the way in which students learn in NWUSS. The lesson was at a very fast pace. Throughout the lesson there were few different learning styles and these consisted mainly of listening to the teacher and taking notes. Naomi and a number of other shadowed students said that they found this type of lesson to be very effective for their learning but not one that they usually enjoyed. The reason she and others gave was that the lecture style meant that the students received a lot of facts and information that needed to be remembered and the sheer weight of information made the students feel that they had learned a lot. However, to learn it properly, students need to go over the work in their own time to make sure that they remember it, giving them extra-curricular pressures. This learning style is seen as acceptable in terms of giving out a lot of information but does leave a lot of work for the students and relies on students taking responsibility to learn it properly.

Period 4 Geology

Beginning of the lesson

So far the day has proved quite negative for Naomi and at the beginning of the Geology lesson she was still feeling lethargic, tired and hungry but also happy. Why was she so happy? When asked, she said that the reason for her continued happiness was because she enjoyed the time in between lessons when she could meet and socialise with her friends. Her negativity in the class came more from a lack of motivation as a result of an emotionally unsatisfying morning, although she has, in her judgement, been learning.

Naomi said in her interview that her Geology teacher was her favourite because he made the work interesting with his enthusiasm for the subject and humour. As a result she was really looking forward to this lesson, shown by the fact that she marked a maximum 5 for her mood for learning and that she was excited about the lesson.

During the lesson

This lesson was more productive than her first two lessons of the day so let's look at the differences and discuss why. One point was the class structure in the other lessons in which there was just one or two different learning styles but in this lesson there were many changes throughout the lesson so it was more varied and engaging. Naomi's liking of the teacher is also a factor, as she was more willing to listen to him and do what he asked. The seating arrangement had her sitting in a group so she could help, and get help from, friends. This created a more relaxed atmosphere, something that Naomi said she liked in a lesson and that helped her understanding. She also gave a 4 for the amount that she interacted and this opportunity to talk with her friends made the lesson more fun. She also had some participation in the lesson in the form of working on rock samples and because she was doing something active, she had had a greater zest for the work. In Geology she marked that she felt relaxed, wishing to be there, happy, excited and cheerful. So not only did Naomi feel that she had learned more but she enjoyed it too. All of the students said that they found Japanese Classics a more interesting subject than Geology but this class succeeded in engaging their interest despite its lack of intrinsic interest to many of them.

What was it about the teacher that made the lesson more fun? Obviously his personality is the most significant factor. Naomi said that she found him funny; he used humour to ease the tension in the class but more importantly he came across as being very animated about what he was teaching so the students found it interesting. Although he was eager to impart knowledge, he was thorough and helpful so that students did not have to struggle or be afraid to ask for help.

At the end of the lesson

At the end of the lesson she marked her highest mark for the day so far for her learning – a 4. It is still lower than her mood for learning so the lesson was not a complete success but as she marked a 4 for amount learned it may be seen as productive. Considering that Naomi had felt lethargic and tired from her previous lessons, and given that it was the last lesson before lunch, it was a good result.

Period 5 World History

Beginning of the lesson

World History was just after the lunchtime break so Naomi no longer felt hungry although she still felt tired but happy. She was tired for the whole day, not an optimum state for maintaining her concentration. On a more positive note she had managed to shake off her lethargy. There are two possible reasons, one was that it was after lunch so the time with her friends had livened her up, the other was that the active and productive nature of her previous lesson had created interest to counter her lethargy. However, she only marked a 3 for her mood for learning, the lowest for the whole day because she had just been with her friends and wanted to go on chatting to them. Also, with the lesson being near the end of the day she may have been looking forward to finishing school for the day.

During the lesson

During the lesson Naomi completed her spot check stating that she was finding it difficult to concentrate and that she was feeling drowsy. This may have been affected by the fact that some others in her class were sleeping. After lunch can also be a low point in the day in terms of energy and she did enter the class with a fairly low motivation. Throughout the lesson the students had to listen to the teacher and take notes on worksheets and occasionally answer a question verbally. While there wasn't much variety the random questioning by the teacher did seem to keep Naomi and most of the others students from drifting off task. She was also kept alert by not wanting to make a mistake because, she said, students felt embarrassed if they made mistakes in front of their friends.

At the end of the lesson

At the end of the lesson she marked a 3 for the amount she learned, the same as her mood for learning so her learning seemed to match her mood. Naomi marked a 4 for the amount of interaction with others in the class, a factor which may have contributed to the relatively productive nature of the lesson.

Kotoro's school day from 9.40 to 14.05

Japanese (9.40–10.30)

Kotoro indicated in the first spot check in this class that he was motivated to learn 'quite hard' which he explained was because of his own interest. He said his motivation was lower than in the later two spot checks because it was still only the beginning of the period. When Kotoro answered in his spot checks that he was motivated to study 'really hard', the teacher was on both occasions explaining the lesson from the blackboard and making a lot of notes for them to copy. He commented that his motivation had risen to this level because he not only found Japanese interesting but also had to study it to achieve good grades and because the teacher made things clear it helped to sustain his existing interest. The spot check graph which showed his level of learning as always lower than that of motivation he explained as being due the fact that there were lots of things spoken about that he did not have to learn. His learning level rose when the teacher made more notes on the blackboard.

Music (10.35–11.20)

The teacher began the class by greeting the students and handing out a sheet of music. The teacher then played recorded classical music to the students. Kotoro became quiet and started listening to the music. His spot check shows that at this point he was really motivated. He later explained that this was because of his own interest as he played contrabass and piano at home and loved music. He added that this was also the reason for his motivation throughout the whole lesson. His learning was low at the beginning because they were 'just listening to music'. His learning increased in the middle of the period because the teacher explained the music they were listening to. The student was learning 'a lot' towards the end of the lesson because he really had to think about it.

Chinese Classics (11.25–12.15)

Kotoro felt really motivated at the beginning of the lesson but also felt that he was not learning anything at all. The teacher lectured the class for the whole lesson and wrote occasionally on the blackboard. At the beginning of the class the teacher handed out new books, which Kotoro spent the first half of the lesson reading. He said later in the interview that the teacher was telling them how to behave, which bored him, so he read his new book instead. His motivation dropped and he fidgeted a lot, and later said that he would usually start to fidget when he felt bored. His motivation picked up again towards the end of the lesson, at which point he was looking at and laughing with the teacher who was visually explaining something to the class. He explained in the interview that the reason he learned was that he was really motivated by the subject which he found interesting. It was, in fact, was one of his favourite subjects and he did not put his motivation down to the influence of the teacher at all.

Kotoro them went to lunch.

Home economics I (13.20–14.05)

After organising the seating arrangements Kotoro sat down and joked and laughed with his friends. The teacher started the lesson five minutes later. There was a relaxed atmosphere in the class and the teacher had lively discussions with the students. However, Kotoro indicated in the spot check that he was motivated only 'a bit'. He explained later that this was because he was tired and in 'break mood'. He said he was not learning at all because they did not have anything to do (such as taking notes or a task) because it was an introductory class.

Each student spoke briefly in the middle of the period and most students laughed or smiled. Kotoro felt relaxed but, he said, this had no effect on his motivation either way. According to him, his motivation rose during the lesson because he 'woke up' after the break and became involved. However, he was not learning at all, he said, because they did not have to take notes or anything else, just listen. The students were given a handout, which they were to fill in towards the end. Kotoro started working on it immediately and he talked with his neighbours while he did it. His motivation was high at that time because he had to think about the questions, however, he still rated his learning as only 'a bit' because it was too easy.

Maths (14.05–15.00)

After the greeting, the teacher started with an explanation at the blackboard, while asking students questions. Kotoro answered in a spot check that he had been motivated to learn 'a little' but was actually learning 'a lot'. He later explained that it was only the beginning of the class and he was still in 'break mood' but he began learning a lot because the teacher was explaining and asking questions. The teacher used the same approach during most of the lesson, giving the class a lecture from the blackboard while asking questions from time to time. He set two individual tasks towards the end. Kotoro's motivation was at a maximum because, he said, the teacher frequently asked challenging questions. Likewise, his learning was high all the time because he had to answer these questions either verbally or on paper.

Conclusion

In summary, we can see from the classroom lives of these three students that whatever the timetable and whatever the curriculum to be got through students have their own ebbs and flows of interest and engagement. How they judge their own motivation and their learning provides a complex equation. Sometimes motivation is high and learning relatively low. Sometimes learning exceeds their expectations. The matrix in Figure 16.6 attempts to illustrate what the relationship is between high and low motivation, high and low learning.

When we evaluate either motivation or learning we discover that it is not simply related to that particular classroom or that particular teacher but to what went before and what may come later in the day. And what we are reminded of

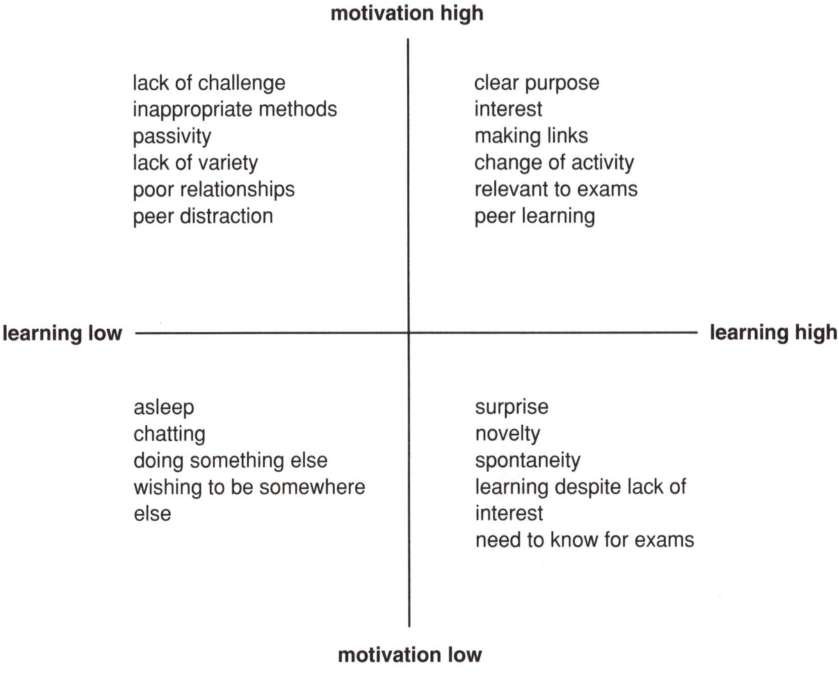

motivation high

lack of challenge	clear purpose
inappropriate methods	interest
passivity	making links
lack of variety	change of activity
poor relationships	relevant to exams
peer distraction	peer learning

learning low ———————————————— **learning high**

asleep	surprise
chatting	novelty
doing something else	spontaneity
wishing to be somewhere else	learning despite lack of interest
	need to know for exams

motivation low

Figure 16.6 The motivation and learning matrix

again is the importance of the social environment and how, for many students, this is the chief motivator of their learning. We also see evidence that 'learning' often seems to be measured in quantitative terms – the weight of their notes or the sheer amount of information covered. It prompts the question 'what is learning?' and what teachers might do to pursue that issue with their students.

17 No two the same

How students react differently to the same lessons

Jeremy Barnett and Matthew Greenhalgh

The same class, the same teacher, but a different response from two students who sit beside each other and are good friends. These three examples from Japan and Sweden illustrate a more general truth about learning and teaching. These examples raise the question of how aware teachers can be of what is going on in young people's minds as they sit, head down taking notes, or apparently listening and how teachers accommodate to the very different expectations that young people have of their teachers, classmates and the pace of teaching.

The first example, from Japan, follows Takayo and Kaori of 5B, while the second example follows another pair of students from 5C. The third example, from Sweden, follows Fredrik and Elin, boy and girl, again living out separate and distinct lives in the same school and classroom.

Takayo and Kaori

During my first shadowing in Japan I spent two days with class 5B and observed the same teaching approach that was predominant for the majority of the time. The response to this from students was different in the case of the two students, Takayo and Kaori, whom I was shadowing.

At the beginning of every lesson the class would take quite a long time to settle down. I noticed that it was only a small group of students who caused the unsettling atmosphere. On a number of occasions this would last for the majority of the lesson and would result in the teacher having to stop the lesson to speak to the disruptive students. Sometimes the teacher would direct a random question to one of the boys, which would stop the socialising for a little while. When the teacher selected the students to answer questions, many of them didn't seem too confident. During my shadowing in Japan I was told by some students that they do not feel confident expressing their views in front of their classmates as they are worried about making mistakes. This may be a very important cultural factor contributing to our understanding of what is going on in this classroom.

Takayo's response to this style of teaching was similar to that of the majority of students in the class. She was well focused and concentrated for the duration of the lesson. I noted that she spent a large percentage of each lesson with her head down writing, even when the rest of the students in the class were watching the teacher and listening. I asked her about this in the interview and she told me that on a number of occasions she completes her homework for other subjects during school time as she does not really study a lot at home. But she also said that when she hears something she doesn't understand, a new word in English, for example, she will write the word down and then and seek an explanation later. She explained to me that this is why more often than not she was writing something in her book.

Takayo's focus lasted for the duration of the lessons and she undertook practically no student interaction with her classmates, only very occasionally speaking to Kaori about the work that they were doing. I asked Takayo what she thought about this teaching style being so prevalent and she told me that she didn't mind it. She said that although it was whole class teaching, students tended to work individually and could write their own notes in the way they wanted to, which lends some individuality to the work that they do. She also told me that this teaching style is OK as long as a teacher can be easily understood. They sometimes find new teachers with different teaching styles difficult to relate to and this causes a problem until they become used to the teacher. Takayo's spot checks throughout most lessons were very similar, showing her to be generally quite positive. In Maths on the first day she felt she was concentrating (3), alert (3), quite sociable (2) and quite motivated (2). During the second lesson of Maths on the second day she felt she was concentrating (3), quite sociable (2), productive (3) and motivated (3).

I also asked Kaori what she thought about this class work and she told me that it was not her preferred way of learning. She said that she sometimes gets confused on a particular point and found it difficult to ask questions as she didn't want to speak in front of the class as a whole. Kaori would much rather work individually and if she has a problem with her work she can go up to the teacher and get individual help and attention. She also occasionally enjoys the chance to work in a pair with another of her classmates as this gives her the opportunity to interact with another student and get a view other than her own. Although this is the case, I observed that Kaori responded when the teacher called on her and her motivation picked up when she got the chance to work with a classmate or when she looked for help from the teacher and was able to clarify her understanding of what was she was expected to learn.

Boys and girls: Miki and Gregor – learning alone, or with your friends?

Miki likes to work on her own. She prefers silence but she is also greatly affected by her peers and how she judges their ability. Gregor, on the other hand, likes to work with his friends and sees them as a resource for his own learning.

Miki said that her friends motivated her because of a virtual competition among them. She said that because she saw how good her friends were, she wanted to get on to the same level and therefore she studied hard. At the very end of the interview she was asked to comment on the silence in the classroom. There was no discussion going on and the students were sitting quietly the whole time carrying out their tasks. She said that this was good for her motivation because she preferred a silent class, as it was better for her concentration.

She felt that her peers had a very positive influence on her because she thought most of them were quite clever, something which she thought caused her to work hard in order to keep up with them. She did not speak to anyone during the class, but was grateful to those students who questioned the teacher during the lesson because it assisted or benefited her as well.

Gregor

Although there was a relaxed atmosphere in the class, most of the students paid attention to the teacher and were involved in discussions. However, Gregor is easily distracted and seems to rely heavily on social interaction for his learning. He was seen speaking to his neighbours many times during the lesson. He said in the interview afterwards that these conversations were work related. He said that his peers had a positive influence on him because they served as a resource when he was unsure about certain issues.

He spent his breaktime in the classroom with his friends, although he wanted to study Maths but was distracted by his friends talking to him during the break. While he felt highly motivated throughout the break, he felt that that he was not learning at all. He ate his lunch and talked with his friends for most of the time.

Elin and Fredrik

Elin and Fredrik are in the same class. Both hope to go on to university from this, their final year. Both share some common interests and ways of working. Both respond in similar ways to their teachers and their friends but there are also differences, some which seem gender-related, others which are explained by their different personalities and expectations of school and learning.

English

The day started with the English teacher returning work that she had corrected. During this time students were left to their own devices and chatted sociably in a very relaxed atmosphere. They were then given a questionnaire to complete individually, this taking half an hour and then were told to read love poems in English out loud to the class. The students listened intently throughout the explanation as it gave them a chance to improve their marks. The final task for the lesson was for the students to speak to one another in English. They started a bit hesitantly and most started to speak in Swedish but after a while they all started to speak in English. This seemed to us a very good way of getting the students to practise their English because they could choose any topic so they usually just spoke to one another about their social lives. As they talk about the same things that they talk about in Swedish, they find it more interesting and fun. Students feel they learn the language more easily when they practise using everyday conversational English.

Elin's spot check was quite positive but as she is always positive, this is a typical response. It shows that she is alert, relaxed, happy, sociable, cheerful and willing to participate. These are all factors that relate to social interaction. As English is one of Elin's favourite subjects, she said in her post-lesson interview that one reason for this was that she enjoyed speaking in English and using English in a social situation with her friends and classmates. She also said her previous teacher, Mr Hagman, was another reason why she liked the subject, so it was interesting to see if she would enjoy the lesson as much with the new teacher. The fact she did may suggest a greater interest for the subject than simply a particular teacher. Despite this, she marked on her spot check that the time is passing very slowly. This may have been as a result of it being first thing on a Monday morning as she was tired and not yet ready to focus fully on her work after the weekend.

Elin read her poems out very confidently and showed a lot of interest in the lesson when she spoke about the poems with her friend instead of more 'off task' chatting like others in the class. She thrived on the opportunity to speak freely in English. She thoroughly enjoyed it as it didn't feel like work to her. It gave her the freedom to talk about what she wanted, so it was interesting and fun for her. At times, with no restraint from the teacher, she took advantage of her freedom and spoke in Swedish.

Fredrik's spot check was slightly more negative than Elin's but it was about average for Fredrik. His spot check showed he was alert, relaxed, happy, sociable and willing to participate. This was not because he enjoyed the work, he said, but because there was little for him to do and it left him a lot of time to socialise with his friends. Fredrik sits in a group of six boys who seem to be good friends and they like to chat amongst themselves. He seems to draw confidence from the group and they all spent a lot of their time chatting with one another. When the class was asked to speak in English he was the first to start speaking which suggests that he must have confidence in his English when he is feeling comfortable and does not have to worry about being wrong. But when he had to speak individually in his small group he did not have that same assurance and seemed to be a little nervous. Was he able to be more confident in the whole class, with a mixture of girls and boys? Was he more inhibited in his all-boys peer group in which there was a different norm and set of expectations?

Fredrik read well from his group report to the class but then did not listen to the others when they read, perhaps because there was such a large gap before it was his turn to speak again that his mind had wandered. He was one of the least interested students when the teacher was explaining about British and American English. This may have been because he hadn't built up the same respect for this teacher as he had for the previous English teacher and thus was less inclined to pay attention. At one point the teacher told the whole class off – telling them to listen to those who were reading aloud. Fredrik responded at first but then started to speak with his friends almost immediately afterwards. His lack of concentration could have also been because it was nearing the end of the one and a half-hour lesson so he was finding it difficult and his attention had wandered. He said he wasn't in the mood for anything else at that point and he was finding that the time was passing very slowly, that he was also bored and lacking energy. Perhaps this was because the lesson was so long or perhaps because he and the rest of his group spent so little time participating.

While both Elin and Fredrik responded in the same way to interactive aspects of the lesson, Fredrik was much more apt to lose concentration, chat to his friends and enter a downward spiral of demotivation.

Modern Studies

The class was split into two groups to provide two different learning environments. Fredrik was in the smaller of the two groups. The teacher started in this group and left the other group with Elin in it to work on their own. I observed Elin's group first as they worked on their own. They had more opinions and ideas to work with but there was a greater problem for all of them staying focused. It wasn't long before they started to chat and the work was only being done by a few in each group. Elin was one of the students who found the responsibility of working without supervision near her friends too much and was soon chatting and laughing. As there was no change or variety in the work, students became increasingly unproductive.

When the teacher came into the class there was a mad panic by the students who hadn't been working so they began to copy from their friends so as not to get into trouble. As a result, most of them missed what the teacher was saying to them. Maybe the teacher saw that they were not concentrating well so he gave them a ten-minute break, which was enthusiastically welcomed by everyone in the class. The monotony of the group work had made them all restless.

When I went to the other group of boys with Fredrik in it I found that they had been locked in and so I didn't get in until the teacher went in to teach them. All the boys that were in Fredrik's group, including Fredrik himself, were working really well individually and in absolute silence. There were two boys who were not working and were lying on the sofas quietly so they were not acting as a distraction. The teacher had already set up this quiet working environment and was content to be in the background and just help those that asked for it. There was some chat but it was only about the work.

This seemed like a bit of a gender reversal so I asked the teacher how she had managed to get these boys to work so well where others had struggled. She said that they had the choice of working or leaving and as there was an assessment to be given to them at the end of the lesson they all chose to work. I think that another reason was that there was no one to show off to as they were all working in the other room. Perhaps by separating them from the girls, one less important distraction was removed.

The boys were then given a ten-minute break which took twenty minutes. When they came back the rest of the class joined them and they immediately went to the sofas and started to chat. Now in their larger group it seemed it was more difficult for the teacher to manage. Or might it have been because the sexes were one again together? Elin and Fredrik were both amongst the noisier ones. Even after they were given the assessment, both continued to talk until the teacher came over to Fredrik and told him to get on with his work. But as they had wasted so much time Fredrik, among others, was left with having to complete it for homework.

Fredrik's spot check was almost totally negative. His only positive element was being alert, relaxed and sociable and all but one of the fourteen categories were marked as a 1. Fredrik claims that when there is no fun this has a negative impact on his concentration, motivation and his ability to learn. Yet, from where we sat, it appeared that Fredrik had been concentrating and working well for much of the lesson, at least until the last quarter. Could it have been that his self-confidence and dignity had been dented by the external motivation forced upon him by the teacher? Could it have been significant that this was also in front of the girls?

Elin's spot check was average for this lesson with the exception of one category. She said that she was feeling drowsy. This is apparently because there was no teacher at the time of the spot check to keep her working and alert so this made it too easy for her to chat. Elin ignored the work and instead chatted for the majority of the time with one friend. Neither of them did much work and fed off each other's unwillingness to work because, as Elin said later, they did not find the work fun or interesting. Elin said that she works at her best if she is interested or enjoying the work. She, however, does not often make the distinction between enjoying the work and the enjoyment of socialising with her friends.

The seating seemed, from our point of view, a significant factor in the amount of work that was done in this lesson. Students were split up from their group and when sitting individually none of them could instigate any distractions so they had nothing to do but work or sit and do nothing. And, with the added pressure of the assessment, they all chose to work. In the interview Fredrik said that he works best on his own but does not enjoy it. This individual way of working could not be sustained because he felt that the irritation and boredom of this learning style would build up to a point where it would no longer be tolerable. Most interestingly, though, was that at the beginning of the lesson Fredrik marked a 1 for his mood for learning but at the end marked 3 for how much he learned. So it would appear that the individual silent work was effective despite everything.

The seating in this main classroom did not seem to us well suited to effective study. The sofas give a too relaxed and homely atmosphere, instead of it being a place to work, it reminds them of the social areas around the school and so they treat it like one. This could be seen when the class started and they all sat on the sofas, they were all loud, noisy, joking and shoving each other about playfully. Here both Elin and Fredrik reacted in the same way. When they changed to individual seating and group work around a table they acted more as though it was a place of work.

Elin's and Fredrik's responses to the lesson were obviously very different due to them being in different rooms and working in very different ways. However, in many respects both had a similar attitude to their work. Both worked well under pressure from the teacher as when Elin had to write down the notes when the teacher arrived and when Fredrik had the teacher over him pressuring him to work.

In many respects both Elin and Fredrik responded in the same way to the different styles of teaching as well. They were both very positive in terms of interaction and both found themselves with the freedom to speak. They, however, used this freedom in slightly different ways. Fredrik chatted with his friends and Elin discussed her work. This is a result, I think, of peer pressure. They are both prominent members of social groups and tended to fit in with the norms of the boy and the girl group whatever they are at the moment in that subject and with that teacher. Both groups give priority to a need for enjoyment but overall the boys were more likely to distract each other whereas the group of girls tended to use their time more productively and although they appeared to chat just as much, it was often more 'on task'.

The French lesson

French was the final lesson on the second day of shadowing. Throughout the lesson the teacher tried to speak only in French to the students in order to get them accustomed to hearing the language. In the long run this would hopefully lead to faster language acquisition. These students are at a level where they can pick up quite a lot of what she says and are less engaged when it's too easy for them. The first task that the students had to do was to listen to the teacher and follow her instructions. For example, put the pen on top of the book, under the book, next to the book, and so on. Everyone in the class seemed to respond to this really well, even if they didn't quite understand what they had to do, they could just copy their friends and remember the words for next time. The teacher would tell them to do the actions again so the students who worked out the words first time could see if they were right. The students liked this because it was simple and fun, more like a game than work. Elin especially enjoyed this task as it had all the hallmarks of her favoured learning style. She said that she likes to work in a group with the freedom to speak to her friends. She also said that she learns best if she finds the work fun, which this was for her. The task with the book and the pen was both visual as well as listening to the teacher so it was easier for the students to learn as they had the image as well as the word to remember.

This first task made all the students quite lively and maybe more receptive to their next task which was a French speaking exercise in pairs to transfer information from one partner's sheet to the other. Elin was almost on a high, laughing and chatting with her partner. She did settle down but did take slightly longer than the rest of the class. Elin then started to sort out her folders while the others in the class worked in groups to make up a sentence to write on the blackboard. Because the lesson had been so productively sociable, the students were comfortable and confident and the resulting teamwork was excellent. Elin too worked well in her group when she took part and then settled down to take notes when the teacher was telling them about what would happen in future lessons. There was a positive response from the whole class, possibly because the lesson only lasted for fifty minutes and as they were interested they had no problems maintaining concentration.

I could see that Elin really had enjoyed that lesson. In her spot check she marked twelve out of the fifteen categories a 3 (top score). The three other categories were marked as 2s. Most interesting from this spot check is that she not only marked her usual social categories high but also the good work as 4s too. She marked the 'How are you?' sheet a 4 for in the mood for learning at the beginning of the lesson, at the end of the lesson she marked a 4 for how much she felt she had learned. This suggests that her potential for learning in this lesson was well used.

A good thing about this lesson from Elin's point of view was that the different learning styles only lasted about ten minutes at a time, so she was always trying new things which worked to keep her and the rest of the class interested. In the interview Elin often said that she liked to try new things and that she got bored very easily. There was also a variety in who she worked with, about 30 per cent class work, 10 per cent group work and 35 per cent pair work. In her interview she said that she preferred to work in a group or a pair and so she felt very comfortable and therefore was very productive throughout this lesson.

Mathematics

As Fredrik had forgotten his kit for Physical Education I was unable to shadow him, again leaving me with only one student to shadow. A radio reporter was in school to follow me while I shadowed my students in History. Both students felt uncomfortable with her presence in the classroom, a reaction I had not anticipated, and left the room after ten minutes, thus ending my shadowing for that lesson. Mathematics was loud and boisterous with the teacher having little control over the students in the class, including both shadowed students. I was told by some of the students that the reason for this was that although the teacher has a lot of knowledge about the subject he doesn't have the ability to explain what he is trying to teach. This left the students feeling irritable with a sense of hopelessness at not being able to complete the work so they became easily distracted and disruptive. After twenty minutes of mathematics the students left the classroom to watch a choir in the school hall. Interestingly one of the students I was shadowing never made it to the hall.

18 Talking about learning

Students as self-evaluators

Duane Henry and Mary Lee

How good are students at evaluating their own learning? This was the focus of Learning School 3's inquiry, unearthing some penetrating and disturbing insights. What became very clear from both the quantitative data and the qualitative data from student interviews is that students can reflect on their learning but have often never been given the opportunity to do so, and have never engaged in a conversation about their learning, or rarely if ever been asked to think about the internal and external influences on their motivation. Confirmation for this comes from teachers who were also interviewed and agreed that their students were not good self-evaluators, admitting that often the pressures of time and assessment produced a collusion to just 'get through'. It is a reminder of Entwistle's work on surface and deep learning and what he called 'strategic' (or tactical) learning designed for examination purposes and not for life after school.

In this chapter the focus is on a German school because this was the first from which a complete data set was available at the time of writing. But the issues which emerge here are, according to the two LS3 research teams, representative of what was emerging consistently in other countries, in Hong Kong, Sweden, Scotland and South Africa.

The following questions attempt to ascertain whether students reflect on their learning or not.

1   When you have finished some study, do you think about whether you have understood it?

This question attempts to explore whether students' reflection is important to self-evaluation, as it involves students thinking about whether or not they are satisfied with what they have done. A student can learn a new fact, but may not fully understand it. As Figure 18.1 shows, only 1 in 5 do this on a regular basis but 65 per cent say they do it often. A small minority say they rarely or never try to understand their work.

2   Do you think about the process of your learning?

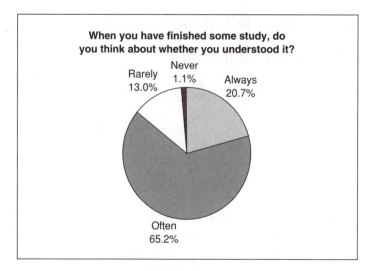

Figure 18.1 Do you think about whether you have understood or not?

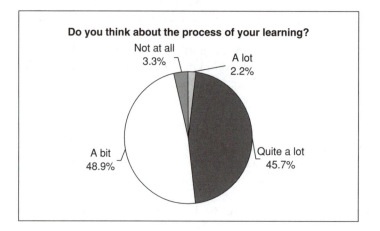

Figure 18.2 Do you think about the process of your learning?

The second question probes a little deeper and finds a less positive answer than question one. The largest group (nearly half) say they do this 'a bit' while only 2 per cent say this is something they do a lot (see Figure 18.2).

3   Can you identify the strengths and weaknesses in the way you learn?

A very positive answer is given to this question. It suggests that students have some implicit or intuitive understanding of what motivates and demotivates them and know when they are learning most effectively and when their learning is at a low ebb (see Figure 18.3).

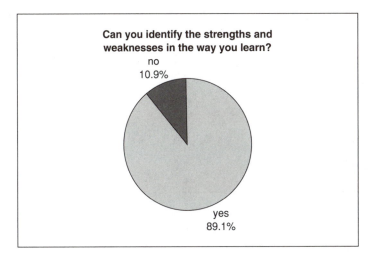

Figure 18.3 Can you identify the strengths and weaknesses in the way you learn?

Table 18.1 Identify one strength

Strength	(%)
Good memory	16.0
Understanding	12.3
Notes	3.7
Logical thinking	2.5
Persistence	8.6
Concentration	3.7
Learning fast	16.0
Making use of interest	7.4
Connections	12.3
Time management	3.7
Aural learning	1.2
Learning by writing	1.2
Visual learning	3.7
Learning by reading	2.5
Good studying technique	4.9

More light is thrown on this by the next question which asks them to identify one of their strengths. As can be seen from Table 18.1, the perceived strengths cover a very wide range of strategies and capabilities. It is significant that 'good memory' figures so highly, suggesting that much of school work and homework is about memorisation. 'Learning fast' is given equal priority, perhaps suggesting that learning is something to be got over quickly, or more positively that being a speedy learner means being able to absorb new ideas quickly. Understanding and making connections are the two next largest categories, very important for self-evaluation and for effective learning. It is perhaps very significant that aural

Table 18.2 Identify one weakness

Weakness	(%)
Laziness	36.0
Memorisation	11.0
Easily disturbed	5.0
Time management	9.0
Concentration	17.0
Takes long time	3.0
Learning by reading	7.0
Aural/Visual learning	1.0
Dependency on others	3.0
Motivation	8.0

learning is given the lowest rating of all given that so much of what students are expected to do in school is to listen.

When it comes to identifying weaknesses the largest category is 'laziness' (see Table 18.2). This has a ring of truth about it, suggesting a pretty high level of student self-knowledge. Memorisation is again given emphasis, followed by difficulties in concentrating, something that runs as a theme throughout much of the observation of students in classrooms. Managing time is also one of the problems that student often struggle with and is chosen as a priority by one in ten.

4   Do you try to make use of your strength?

This question aims to discover the extent to which those strengths are used. While 63 per cent say they do use their strengths 'often', only 17 per cent say they do so consistently (see Figure 18.4). And what happens to the 15 per cent who rarely or never use their strengths?

5   Do you try to overcome your weaknesses?

A quite different, and perhaps worrying, picture emerges from this question. It appears that more than half of students rarely if ever try to overcome their weaknesses (see Figure 18.5). And only 3 per cent say they always try to do this. It leaves a big question as to what students do and might do to be better learners.

6   Do you recognise how your environment affects your study?

This question was intended to discover how conscious students were of where they did their study or homework on the assumption that a self-evaluating learner would reflect on the environment that was most and least conducive to learning and then do something actively to create a more congenial place of work. As the data in Figure 18.6 show, nearly half of these students said they

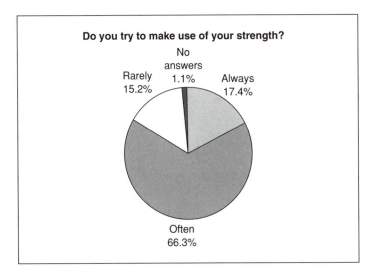

Figure 18.4 Do you try to make use of your strength?

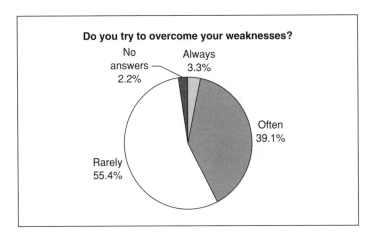

Figure 18.5 Do you try to overcome your weaknesses?

rarely or never thought about it. Only 12 per cent seemed to take it systematically and continuously into account.

7   Do you think about your study goals?

When asked about their study goals most students (three-quarters) said they did keep them in mind, leaving another quarter not very committed on this issue (see Figure 18.7). This may be seen as a worrying statistic if it means that many

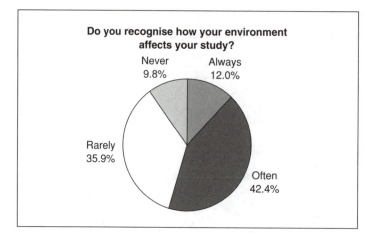

Figure 18.6 Do you recognise how your environment affects your study?

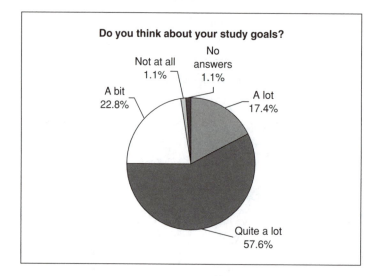

Figure 18.7 Do you think about your study goals?

students go through a routine without a clear thought-through purpose, priorities and ambition to achieve.

8   How much does your class atmosphere affect your learning?

When we turn our attention to the classroom environment, students showed a higher level of awareness than when asked about their home study. One in five said atmosphere was very significant with nearly half saying 'quite a lot'. What is perhaps most surprising is that as many as 32 per cent did not say it had a

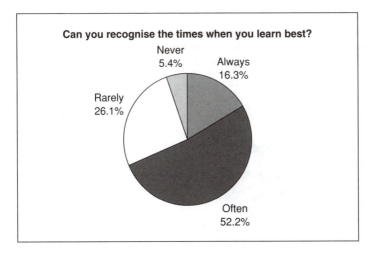

Figure 18.8 Can you recognise the times when you learn best?

great effect, as in conversation most students express a high degree of awareness of the classroom context. Another inference we may draw from these data is that many students who do think about their environment for learning have not transferred this knowledge from the classroom context to the home context.

9   Can you recognise the times when you learn best?

Related to this is student awareness of their own body clock and their own preferred times for studying or learning more generally. As the data in Figure 18.8 suggest, one-third of all students tend not to think about this. Looking at it positively, the fact that 70 per cent do take this into account is an important statistic although this does not tell how they then use that knowledge to most advantage.

10 In a school day, do you think about why your motivation has either increased or decreased?

In response to this question, 58 per cent of students said this was something that they consciously thought about (see Figure 18.9). Certainly in formal interview or conversation students could articulate what made them interested and uninterested, bored or excited. That 12 per cent never think about their motivation is perhaps the most surprising statistic.

When asked to describe the most important sources of their motivation (see Table 18.3), students came up with a range of incentives. Once again 'interest' tops the list, perhaps the single most consistent theme from the three Learning School studies. When coupled with understanding, this accounts for one-third of all students. Grades, teachers and future jobs follow closely behind while

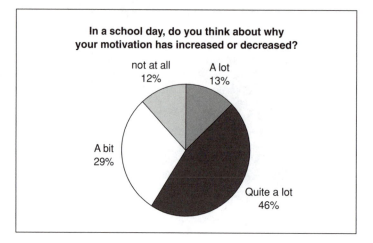

Figure 18.9 In a school day, do you think about why your motivation has increased or decreased?

Table 18.3 Most important sources of your motivation

Most important source of motivation	(%)
Interest	17.1
Teachers	12.3
Personal condition	7.3
Understanding	5.6
Grades	16.2
Competition	2.8
Fun	3.4
Environment	3.4
Social environment	11.7
Personal development	2.8
Social success	2.8
Future job	14.5

'social environment' is mentioned by 1 in 8 of all students – a reminder of the earlier question about classroom atmosphere. It is significant that competition is mentioned by so few.

11   When you have the opportunity, do you ask questions?

We should perhaps not be surprised by the answers to this question as in many classrooms it is teachers who ask the questions not the students, but the admission from more than half of the student body that they rarely or never ask questions is quite a dramatic commentary on the process of learning and teaching (see Figure 18.10).

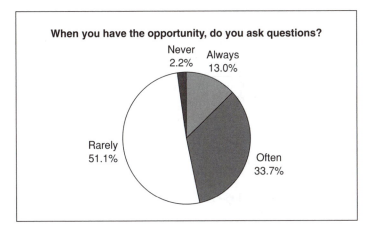

Figure 18.10 When you have the opportunity, do you ask questions?

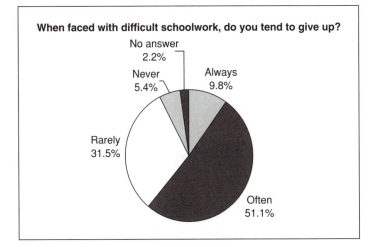

Figure 18.11 When faced with difficult schoolwork, do you tend to give up?

12 When faced with difficult schoolwork, do you tend to give up?

Possibly the most alarming of statistics is that in answer to this question (see Figure 18.11). The question is perhaps the severest of all tests of the effective and self-evaluating learner but reveals that 1 in 10 always give up when things get difficult and a massive 51 per cent admit to doing this often.

What do we conclude from these data? There are mixed messages from these figures, suggesting that students may think more about their learning than we might have thought at first sight but when we put more specific and challenging questions, it is less clear that students are able to use their intuitive knowledge to critically review their learning and improve its effectiveness. The data leave us with many questions unanswered or half-answered and we therefore need to probe deeper through interviews with students and with their teachers.

Probing further into each shadowed student's capacity was carried out through a major interview, the final research tool. It serves as the most detailed documentation of each shadowee's thoughts on his or her ability to reflect on their learning. It took the form of a confidential, focused and lengthy discussion between the shadowee and researcher.

Marga

Marga (not her real name) has developed her own criteria for her learning and makes use of it to improve herself. She also has a strong desire to improve herself as a person through how she learns. She has found it difficult, however, to achieve this in the system.

'Interest' plays a most influential part in her learning. She is aware just how, and by how much, interest can influence her learning and she focuses on interest when deciding what is necessary knowledge for her. She insisted frequently that 'learners should follow their interest' and she is resolute in following this dictum. Shadowing and spot-check results corroborate this, showing that her interest level influenced her learning level, and influenced her attitude towards a class, both positively and negatively. On the other hand, she knows that this has a negative side too occasionally, but did not give evidence of making much effort to control it, nor did she even regard it as a weakness that she feels the need to overcome. Studying strongly following her interest clearly results in Marga being unable to achieve in subjects in which she has little interest. Based on evidence, we can say that, while she can recognise and make the best use of her interest as positive motivation, she has not been able to control her interest when it works negatively. She admits to building on her strengths but ignoring her weaknesses.

Another criterion in her learning is 'the efficacy and necessity in her future life' which Marga feels about a topic 'instinctively'. She said in the major interview that she is motivated when she 'intuitively' feels that she can make use of a topic in her future and she trusts this intuition a lot in her learning. She regards the school as a place where she can find out what is necessary and unnecessary for her future by gaining different kinds of information. She has her own clear personal criteria derived from an understanding of herself and her learning so far, and appears to make use of them in her learning. We can also see these two criteria, interest and her future goal, as inter-related.

Concerning external influences from her environment, she continuously stated: 'It can influence my learning, however, not so much because I take all responsibilities for myself and can overcome external influences.' She claimed in the major interview that this is because nobody can influence what she wants to do, nor can anybody else influence her final decisions. In addition, we can say that, although she knows her friends and family can support her in emotional aspects, and her classmates and teachers can help academic aspects through interaction with them, she seems to focus on negative external influences more than positive ones.

While Marga understands that external factors are related to her learning, she seems not to have thought very critically about this and perhaps overstates her own influence on her decisions. An example from her major interview – when she jumped from the eighth grade to the tenth grade, her teacher first of all suggested this jump and her parents supported it. So she took the tests for this promotion and was able to pass them. While there is no doubt that these external decisions played an important role in her development, Marga asserts that she made the final decision and everything depended on her. By focusing only on the final decision point she seems to have overlooked the process through which that decision came about and, we might conclude that, by misreading the process she has not appreciated the wider context of her own decision-making.

Overall, she can understand her ways of learning – finding and making connections among topics based on 'a topic's whole context and detailed parts'. She explained that just to acquire and recall knowledge does not make sense on its own. She also said it is important to ask questions and consider ideas for herself in order to understand perfectly. She also makes her own individual study plan based on what she see as her recognition of her strengths.

Marga maintains that the school system does not teach students the importance of different ways of thinking about the learning process. She says the school system just encourages students to get good grades and teaches too much standard knowledge, including 'unnecessary' knowledge for her. She knows that she must study for herself, but does not practise it. She usually studies only for tests and said she does not have any motivation to study for school at home except for homework. The data from the home spot check and daily interview support this. She believes that 'an ideal school should care about and cater to learners' interior development, and that teachers should take more responsibility to give students both "necessary" knowledge based on students' individual needs and enough opportunities to discuss and exchange their own opinion'. Marga has been unable to find out her personal aims and reasons to go to school presently, because she believes her school does not fulfil such individual needs nor does it motivate her. She realises, however, that she has no choice and she must do her duty to study for tests, so she does not know how she can change the present situation even though she is not satisfied with it.

Marga thinks that it is most important for learners to develop their own thoughts and opinions which exist 'inside of individuals themselves'. She feels that the development of her learning must be about 'learning for life' which is her biggest goal. She believes that discussion with her peers can lead her to achieve such a development. She thinks 'the most exciting thing about her school is the discussion in class and it is the one and only way which she can learn for her life in the school system'.

Conclusion

Marga has many self-evaluative qualities, meaning she can recognise her learning and herself and establish her own criteria in her learning, and make use of that. She also sets her own criteria for achievement in tests apart from the external assessments. She has, however, stopped improving her approach to learning at present even though she told us she wants to improve it. This seems to be a clear contradiction but she says that her present way is enough for now simply 'to achieve tests'. She claims to have suspended what she really wants to do in order to just get through, as if she could not apply effective learning techniques to achieve that tactical goal. She does tend to overestimate her own self-direction and seems to be unaware of external factors in her motivation and learning. Her peers, for example, are apparently an important source of her motivation. We conclude she has the potential to be a strong self-evaluator if she simply finds a way to take a broader and more critical view of herself and is ready to address her weaknesses as well as building on her strengths.

Helga

Introduction

Helga appears to practise a medium level of self-evaluation. She can often recognise and understand the influences upon her learning. She has, however, not used this awareness to improve her learning, as she has not reflected or discussed her learning before in the context of self-evaluation and learning improvement. She shows a capacity to self-evaluate, but has not yet used this because she was not aware she possessed this ability.

Analysis

Helga can easily recognise how her environment affects her. She can also sometimes distinguish the reasons behind this, which points to a fair understanding of these influences. She said that she has not reflected upon this to any great extent and so is unable to use this knowledge to influence her learning improvement. For example, she said that a noisy class atmosphere disturbs her learning, and this was why, according to the spot checks, she was not concentrating in biology class. She sits close to her friends and talks with them and as other students in the classroom often do this as well, it makes the atmosphere rather noisy. But, she said, she had never reflected on this before, and had not seen it as in her power to change anything.

Helga appears to have mainly intrinsic motivation, which she can differentiate from school assessment. She said that she is learning because she wants to 'learn about how the world works, why people behave in certain ways, how everything functions, and also to become a good human and social being'.

While she does have grades in mind while studying, this is not the main motivational factor. This shows that she possesses a good understanding of learning as a lifelong process but that this is not something which she thinks of regularly, and she had never experienced a school discussion about learning in this way. It was observed that she could speak more freely and in detail about her learning at the end of the research period than in the beginning.

Helga can clearly recognise her strengths and weaknesses in her learning but appears to fail to use her strengths to a very great extent. She also said that her attempts to overcome her weaknesses did not satisfy her. Once again, the reason for this is because she was not very aware of what her particular strengths and weaknesses were in relation to her learning.

Helga feels that she knows herself 'quite well' in relation to her learning, and also feels that she takes responsibility for her studying. Her questionnaire showed that she 'never' has problems with meeting deadlines. She is satisfied with the amount that she learns in some subjects, and she thinks that one way that self-evaluation could help her is to make her more aware of which subjects she has to study harder in, and how to 'learn in more interesting ways'.

Teaching style and the influence of her friends are important for Helga. Her interest level is raised if she likes the teacher, and if it accords with her idea of a good teacher, which is someone able to explain ideas clearly. If her friends are interested in a subject, then her own interest is accordingly raised.

Conclusion

When asked, Helga can explain certain behaviour and influences related to her learning. She has not, however, by her own admission, reflected upon them by herself and has therefore been unable to make the most of this awareness. The reason why she has never discussed self-evaluation is because she did not know anything about the concept of learning-improvement or anything similar. She does take responsibility for her studying and shows clear self-evaluative capabilities, so if given the opportunity and necessary tools, she would probably be able to self-evaluate well.

Petra

Petra is a moderate self-evaluator, based on the evidence that she understands many of her learning capabilities and skills, while she is able to make only limited application in the context of learning improvement. On a deeper level, Petra thinks she knows herself quite well and is satisfied with her learning development. This report will show, however, that this may be partly due to her often superficial reflections and lack of deep analysis of herself and her learning development. As a result, external factors rather than internal factors influenced Petra more heavily.

Analysis

Petra sees learning as a 'duty', and therefore learning turns her off. This may be because she thinks that her school cannot prepare her for the future. She explained that her school cannot provide the subjects which could enable her to study to be a social worker, and she feels most of the subjects are unnecessary for her to learn. Having little interest in learning could also come from the fact that she does not recognise learning as a lifelong process, but only as a means to get a good job. On the other hand, Petra explained that she also feels 'learning is an opportunity' for her to achieve her future goals – career goals.

The dilemma between wanting to learn but feeling turned-off to learning in school suggests that Petra is feeling lost in her learning and she reveals that she has had a sense of losing control in recent years, having got her worst results at this time. She knows it is a consequence of her 'laziness', and says she tried hard to regain control by 'trying not to watch TV' and 'trying to study more for tests'. But despite this positive action, she is frustrated and her efforts are based on a limited and superficial recognition of the problem.

Petra said that she had never had the occasion to discuss her learning before, and no one ever 'told' her about the meaning of learning. This may suggest that her limited understanding is, at least in part, a result of the lack of opportunity.

Strong external influences

Given Petra's inability to reflect deeply on internal conditions in her learning, it seems to follow that she is influenced a lot by external factors and this is confirmed by her own story. She thinks that her parents are the main source of her motivation and play an important role in her learning. They support her learning through her successes and failures alike. Petra realises she is also affected deeply by teaching style. We find from the shadowing reports and her spot-check results that her motivation rises and falls according to teaching styles and she is unable to overcome the negative influences of weaker teachers, or teachers she does not relate to. She also consciously evaluates her own learning by comparing her learning methods with her friends. Together they have designed a competition to motivate their learning.

Although Petra can talk at length about the external influences of people such as parents, teachers and friends, she is unable to speak in the same way about internal influences that motivate her. She is clear about her own strengths and weaknesses. She thinks she is good at summing up texts in books and practises making her own summary or notes, also recording them on cassette tapes and sometimes listening to them the whole day so as to memorise the material. She realises that one of her major weaknesses is she cannot concentrate on things in which she has little interest, while her related weakness is laziness.

Petra does recognise the importance of the environment, as she explained that she cannot concentrate if it is noisy or temperatures are extreme. But she does try to compensate by having discussions outside noisy classrooms and studies in her room at home where she can control the environment. It can be concluded that she understands the importance of her learning environment and knows her ideal learning environment well. She additionally makes use of this understanding and changes the environment when she can.

Petra also makes use of the best times for her to learn – the afternoons – and during weekends and she usually studies on Sunday night because she cannot finish her work earlier, which she acknowledges as bad time management. She said she usually plans her study in order of importance and the time she needs to study the subject. She does think that self-evaluation is important and she does notice that she has taken a step from just memorising facts to engaging with and understanding what she is learning.

Conclusion

Petra has a limited understanding of learning. She does not fully recognise learning as a lifelong and continuous process. This leads to her recognition of learning as a duty more than an opportunity. Although she feels that she has lost control of her learning, she attributes this only to laziness but has failed to realise that there may be other, deeper factors related to her lack of internal motivation. These include lack of deep knowledge of herself, a lack of honest self-reflection on her failures in school and that she does not understand how she might use the school system better as an avenue to achieve her career goals.

Petra does have an ability to deal with her environment and make thoughtful use of her understanding of external motivations to improve the conditions for her learning. She is capable of self-evaluating, as she is willing to improve her learning and have good understanding about her external influences and changing needs.

Teacher interviews

We interviewed eight teachers from Graf Friedrich Schule, asking each for their views on self-evaluation and what role the school could or should play in providing students with opportunities and tools for self-evaluation.

There was a remarkable degree of consensus among them about the value of self-evaluation as well as the obstacles to embedding it in everyday practice. Some are more optimistic than others about how this might be achieved within the timetable and pressures of assessment and students' attitudes to learning and simply getting through. Some general issues emerging from the eight teachers were:

- the pressure of assessments means that less attention is given to self-evaluation;
- teachers do, nonetheless, encourage students to think about their learning;

- there are difficulties in individualising learning and teaching;
- greater priority should be given students' individual development.

The following are four examples from those interviews.

Teacher A

Teacher A does the following:

- thinks students should understand the importance of lifelong learning;
- tries to pay much attention to students' individual development;
- recognises it is difficult to teach students self-evaluation in the present school system.

Teacher A believes that student self-evaluation is important for learners. She thinks, however, that most students do not self-evaluate and do not understand the concept of lifelong learning at present. She indicated that students should think about how to pay attention to their own learning and understand how to learn. Such processes could lead a learner to improve their understanding and use of learning skills. She added that most students do not practise such processes in their learning, however, and react only to demands of assessment, which means they attempt to achieve good grades because it equates success for them in the present school system. She also thinks students have been unable to grasp that learning that is not assessed is also important and that they should not be motivated only by immediate results.

Teacher A tries to give her students opportunities to discuss and exchange their own opinions, and collect students' wrong answers. She also thinks if students like subjects or topics, they can develop that field more. Therefore, she wants to support her students by making them aware of various sources of information and a range of possibilities.

Teacher A thinks teachers try to advise their students on how to think about their learning but it has not been very effective, the reason being that teachers do not have enough time and materials to improve the situation. She said the school system requires students to achieve average levels and treats everyone similarly. Teacher A thinks that, regardless of understanding the importance of lifelong learning and learning improvement, a student can still be considered 'a good student' if they meet the school's assessment criteria.

This teacher thinks that the school should pay greater attention to students' individual development, not only by teaching general skills but also by talking about learning based on interest and how students can do best. She points out the German school system's lack of oversight of such students' individual development. She mentions that the issue for teachers is how and by how much they can move within a system that has a traditional framework.

We may conclude that teacher A is very concerned about students' individual needs in her teaching but finds it difficult to support students' individual development within the present school system. Even though she also is aware of issues concerning students' situation or attitudes and the reasons behind them, she has not been able to come up with solutions for them. She sees it is as difficult to teach students self-evaluation without modifying the present school system.

Teacher B

Teacher B thinks the following:

- Student self-evaluation is very important.
- Students can only practise self-evaluation when 'guided' and taught by teachers.
- There are students in GFS who do self-evaluate.
- The teachers from each subject should consider and think about how self-evaluation can be 'taught' in their subject.

Teacher B says that:

- Further professional training for teachers is offered and that many teachers do take this up.
- It is impossible for teachers to know the individual way of learning of each of their students, still, she said that she tries her best.
- She tries very hard to make the students reflect on their learning.

Teacher B considers self-evaluation to be very important and thinks that it is possible for students in GFS to practise it. In her opinion, however, they need to be 'taken charge of' since they cannot do it on their own.

Teacher B thinks that there are students in GFS who practise self-evaluation to a certain extent. She also believes that self-evaluation can hardly take place in the lower grades but only from approximately grade ten or eleven on, while in the last two years it could be quite frequent. Another obstacle is time pressure. For example, students have to give back their textbooks after each school year and therefore have almost no opportunity to study outside the curriculum. This could be considered a traditional approach – textbook schooling – and overlooks other opportunities for students to learn inside and outside the curriculum.

With reference to the teachers' role in student self-evaluation, teacher B said that since she has approximately 150 students to teach, it was impossible for her (and her colleagues) to know every student's individual way of learning. The only thing she could do (and, according to her, actually does) is to offer as many different learning tools and methods as possible, for example, the opportunity for students to learn by visual or acoustic aids, depending on their preferences.

Teacher B added that if she notices any striking features about the learning of a certain student, she would naturally make an attempt to get to know that student better and try to help. She also said that she tries to make the students reflect on their learning by discussing class material as well as learning itself, although she did not offer any evidence to support this point.

In teacher B's opinion, teachers have more opportunity to engender self-evaluation in the humanities more than in the sciences. But teachers from each subject should, she argued, gather and discuss ideas on how to promote self-evaluation in school.

Teacher B seems to have thought about self-evaluation before. She wants her students to reflect upon their learning and to improve it. As she did not give any suggestions as to how it could be realised in practice, it does suggest that there is a gap between what is seen as desirable and the tools and strategies to make it happen. Although she herself is clearly in favour of student self-evaluation it seems that its has not been explored to a great extent within the school.

Teacher C

Teacher C thinks that it is very important for students to self-evaluate. This is because it makes the students think about their own learning processes and not make other people responsible for their successes or failures. She thinks this requires the students, however, to be honest with themselves.

Teacher C says that she tries to make students self-evaluate in her lessons. She has even constructed her own questionnaire about students' learning with questions such as 'What exactly did you learn today' or 'Do you think the teacher was patient?' She said that this not only helps the students but also helps her to reflect on her work. In this way she can find out if her opinions about the lesson are the same as the students. She uses this questionnaire exercise regularly. She says that she is always surprised to find so many thorough answers to her questions, but still she thinks that at most 50 per cent of students in GFS self-evaluate – something we see as an optimistic estimate.

Teacher C said that the role of school is to discuss learning with students and to help them find their own criteria and reasons for learning. She thinks that the biggest obstacle to student self-evaluation in schools is that students usually do not know how to think about their learning and how to self-evaluate. Teacher C suggested that teachers should discuss with students why they are learning, how they learn and how their learning could be improved. She realised, however, that an obstacle to this is time. She also believes that many other teachers do not see the importance of self-evaluation and do not believe that students would be really interested or able to take part in such discussions on learning. She added that some of her colleagues could be afraid of students' self-reflection, because it is not always pleasant to read students' opinions about their (teachers') work.

Teacher C seems to be very interested in self-evaluation and tries practically to help students self-evaluate. She also practises self-reflection to better understand her performance as a teacher. She seems to be very sure about what self-evaluation is and how to practise it. She take pains to define circumstances in which self-evaluation can occur. She is aware of the need to set personal criteria for learning and considers that it is the school's job to help students to find their own criteria and understand them in learning discussion.

Teacher D

Teacher D believes that a student's ability to reflect on or adapt their learning decreases with time. She thinks that a teacher's lack of time can damage the positive development of students. She stresses that maturity and the attitudes of students towards their work affect their development.

Teacher D took time to explain the learning ethos of GFS students, as she sees it. Teacher D believes that teachers' ability to support the learning development of their students is severely inhibited by the students' attitudes towards teachers and learning, as well as the lack of time teachers have to communicate effectively with students.

Teacher D said that if students have not 'learned to learn' by the 12th or 13th grade, then there was not much she felt she could do to change this. She added that, 'in the lower grades the students feel they know best' and are therefore less likely to take heed of information given to them. Teacher D feels students' 'bad learning habits' need to be caught by teachers when they are young because it is 'impossible' to change them in later years. In combination with Teacher D's explanation of the limited role of the school, it would seem that she feels there is very little that can be done to help students to 'learn how to learn'.

To elaborate further her thoughts on student's limited willingness to learn, Teacher D used an expression which she felt applied to most students: 'putting pieces of information in the drawer'. 'Once a student feels they have studied', she said, 'they tell themselves they know it, so they move on to the next thing.' They 'put the information away', with the result that they are more likely to forget the information, as it is 'not in the forefront of their minds'. She identified two main reasons for the lack of communication between teachers and students. First, she talked about the time pressure put on teachers, which affects the amount of time teachers can spend talking individually with students. Second, students' attitudes towards school, learning and teachers at a young age make it difficult for teachers to help them improve their learning. She is also of the opinion that the lack of communication between teacher and pupil could account for students not being able to identify their strengths and weaknesses in learning.

Teacher D often referred to the need for students to 'learn to learn'. When asked to explain this phrase, she referred to students revising and studying information continuously rather than reflecting on the process of learning.

Teacher D talked mainly about the adaptation and development of study skills, in terms of 'fixing bad learning habits', while mentioning only briefly the process of student self-reflection. Clearly, Teacher D recognises a role for the school in teaching younger students how to learn, and supporting their development as learners but blames students' arrogant attitudes for their failure to be better learners. Teacher D is pessimistic about any practical role for teachers or for the school.

In summary we find a rich vein of information on students' capacity as self-evaluators, the interviews with teachers and students confirming and filling out what emerged from the quantitative data. However, we are still left facing the big questions on student self-evaluation.

19 Learning out of school

Jimmy Karttunen, Robert Janícek and Saeko Yoshida

No matter what country you are in, it seems that homework is greeted with little enthusiasm by students and is not always welcomed by teachers or parents. Yet all seem to agree that it is a necessary adjunct to learning in school. The much bigger question is what students do when they are in their own time, how long they spend on homework and how productive it is and how it relates to work done in the classroom. Figure 19.6 shows data from the recent OECD PISA study (OECD, 2001) comparing hours of homework from different countries. This major international study is perhaps as surprising as the data here and is interesting to set alongside the Learning School inquiry.

What homework is

By homework we mean all school-related tasks that a student studies out of school, not only tasks distributed by a teacher. Homework is generally seen as important for the development of knowledge in any subject. We considered that there are three main kinds of study out of school, these being:

- an assigned task from a teacher;
- supplementary study by a student for a deeper understanding of the subject;
- preparation and revision for tests/examinations.

In each of the schools in Learning School 1 we asked some common questions but also took a different tack as we progressed and as our own understanding developed. So in the following figures not all the countries are included. Figure 19.1 compares four countries on time spent on homework. The pattern is quite similar but there are marked differences between Sweden at one extreme and Japan at the other.

The second question asks about how students feel about their homework (see Figure 19.2). The Czech Republic stands out here with the largest percentage of students feeling homework is too much. Only in Japan do students complain about too little homework (although Scotland does have one renegade student in this category).

The next question is 'When do you do your homework?' comparing three countries, with only South Africa having students who say they don't do it,

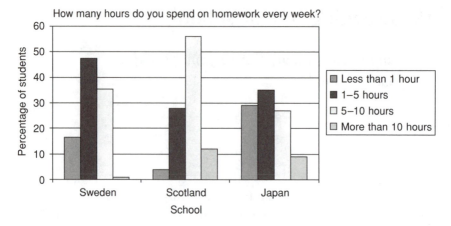

Figure 19.1 Hours of homework in three countries

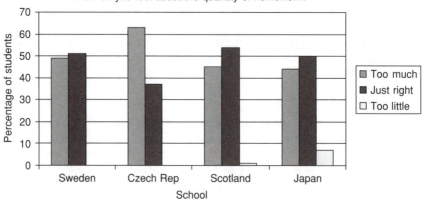

Figure 19.2 Comparison between four countries on the quantity of homework

with the Czech Republic having the largest group admitting to it being last minute (see Figure 19.3).

Where do students study? As Figure 19.4 shows, the context for homework is predominantly the home. This figure does not show, however, other out-of-school learning and study centres such as the *juku* (intensive tuition and study centres) in Japan which is attended by a very substantial number of young people. Many Japanese students also go to extra English lessons either in the *juku* for examination purposes or English conversation school in order to improve their communication skills.

And finally the question 'How do you feel more comfortable studying?' Comparing two very different countries – Sweden and the Czech Republic – we find strong similarities (see Figure 19.5). Homework and home study are primarily seen as an individual activity. Is this why so many students find it boring and

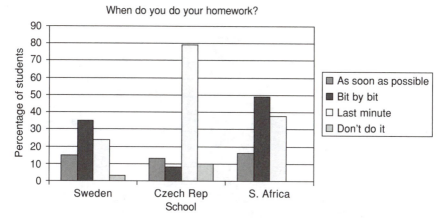

Figure 19.3 Comparison between three countries on time for homework

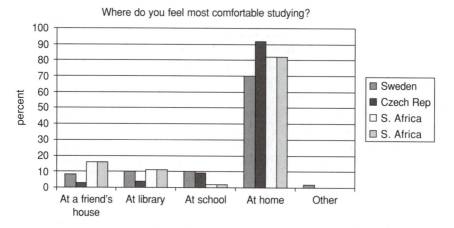

Figure 19.4 Comparison between four countries on places for homework and study

difficult to manage when so much learning is social? Would homework be more congenial and more effective if students were encouraged to work more closely with friends and classmates?

A closer look at one school, in the Czech Republic, helps to fill out the picture.

The Czech Republic School

Over a two-week period, six members of the Learning School students interviewed their hosts. All of the hosts were third-year students in Gymnázium Zlín apart from one girl who was in second year. By focusing on the homework activities of these six students, the Learning School members could gain a valuable insight into the quantity and quality of homework done by representatives of

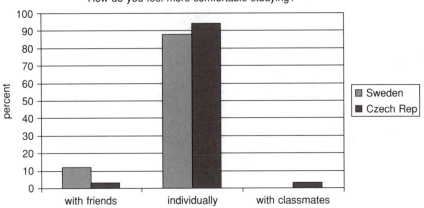

Figure 19.5 Comparison between two countries on how students like to work

the school. The group members were able to observe for themselves how much homework their hosts did, and could see where the students worked, when they worked and could see the how effective their homework study was. They could feel the atmosphere of the students' home working conditions and were able to discuss the topic very naturally and easily with them.

From the student researchers' interviews and by having daily chats with the students, it became clear that certainly they do their homework and take it seriously. All hosts made the comment that 'Homework is very important.' Generally the students spend a lot of time doing study in the evenings unless they are sick, tired or for some reason arrive home late in the evening and have no time. Most of the students said they should do homework for 2–3 hours every day. The following are some of the reasons they said why they study out of school:

- personal interest in the subject or it is required for future study or career;
- catching up on work they have fallen behind on;
- have to make a presentation in the next lesson, so have to prepare;
- don't want to get bad mark in tests, so study for the tests;
- I don't want to see the teacher's face if I didn't do homework.

There are many tests at Gymnázium Zlín depending on the subject. Some subjects have 5–7 small tests per week and students spend a lot of time doing revision for the tests. Students are under pressure due to the tests and at the same time they get motivation from them. There were some tests during the time they were hosting members of our group so we could see them preparing for these tests. On the other hand students weighed up the importance of the test and if they felt it was not a high priority they didn't bother studying for it. Too much unproductive homework could also have a negative effect.

More than half the students commented that they usually studied more for those subjects in which they are interested. If they are interested in the subject or require it for the future, for example, students who have specific subject requirements for higher education institutions say they study for those subjects more easily. They do not feel as much pressure for these subjects since they have a natural interest in them. They also can enjoy doing homework and feel like they are learning for themselves and learning it more effectively.

But sometimes they have to do homework which they are not interested in at all. For example, this may be a task which has a deadline given by a teacher or having to present something in front of the class. These are tasks which perhaps students feel pressure to do but are often not interested in. Also, some teachers, they told us, are very strict and some have told them that a student only has three chances to forget, or not do, their homework. If an individual fails to submit homework a fourth time, their total result is marked as the lowest possible, in this school that is a 5.50. So, in general, students feel pressure to hand in assignments given by the teacher, otherwise their overall performance for that subject will suffer.

South African School

We asked the nine groups in the South African School about the quantity of homework which students are expected to do. Mostly students answered that they get too much to do. Of course it is different each day and each week but generally they feel it to be too much. All groups except one get Maths homework. They said that out of all their subjects they get most homework for Maths and next comes Accounting. Usually some homework is given for every subject.

How long students take to do their homework differed a lot and did, of course, depend on the individual. The shortest time was five minutes every day while one student answered that he did three hours of homework every day, which was the highest we found.

We asked the question, 'Do you find your homework useful?' Only one group answered that it was very useful for their learning. But the other eight groups all said that they found the homework not to be so useful. Some students said that they tended to prioritise their subjects and, depending on which subjects they considered to be important, that dictates the amount of homework they do. Some students tend not to do homework for the subjects they consider to be less important. If they think the subject is important, they will spend more time doing homework and will also do some extra work to help them fully understand all aspects of the subject.

Tests

The issue of tests and testing was then introduced. Generally students agreed that the quantity of tests given depended very much on the subject. The average number of tests, however, is two or three per week. Some students mentioned that some weeks they can do up to one test per day. This is not a usual week but can happen sometimes. The students tended to do some revision for these class tests and spent a lot of time revising for their final exams. Many students commented that they would spend one or two hours revising the night before a small test. Some groups agreed that they do not usually do any revision for these, especially if they consider the test to be unimportant. When revising for these, the majority said that they could not concentrate in the homeroom class because of the many distractions around them so they tended to do most of their revision at home.

All students said that they found the thought of the final exams stressful and so had many positive things to say about continuous assessment. They felt that this spread the pressure over the full year and made sure that they understood each part of the course as they did it. The students want to do well therefore they feel pressure, with an additional source of pressure coming from their parents.

In summary, we find responses to homework to be very similar no matter what country we are in, something done individually, after school, often in preparation for tests and with sanctions for not doing it. It is fair to conclude that homework is not a favourite past-time and that the pressure does not make students see it as an enjoyable activity. Students do enjoy study, though, when it is interesting and chosen by them.

Postscript

Data from the recent OECD PISA study (OECD, 2001) provides an interesting point of comparison with the Learning School data (see Figure 19.6).

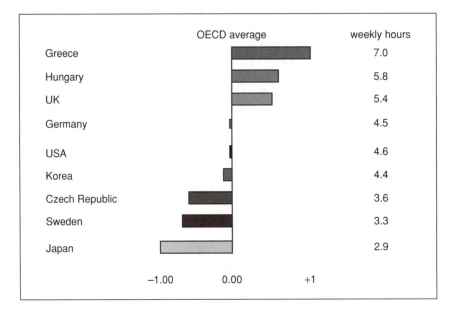

Figure 19.6 OECD data on hours spent per week on homework
Source: OECD (2001)

20 Students and their parents

Jan Balac and Kazuyo Mori

This chapter helps to get behind the somewhat surprising statistics in Chapter 12. Who has most influence on your learning? Clearly it is parents, who encourage, cajole, nag, set high expectations or more unobtrusively, provide an environment in which you are allowed to grow for yourself.

In the first three extracts we see three different kinds of relationships between students and their parents. In their own ways all illustrate the power of parental expectations and support. Ulf, driven to achieve more than his parents, recognises this and acknowledges his debt to their continuing interest, despite the background – they are both too busy. Ironically they do not see themselves as influential. Hans' parents, by contrast, see themselves as important in his motivation but Hans himself is more ambivalent. He relies on his parents at times of trouble but wants to be his own person. Gaby wants an even more hands-off relationship, finding her parents at times too intrusive and irritating. But in the sub-text there is a clear acknowledgement of their importance.

The four accounts from Japanese parents and their children that follow illustrate some of the same tensions despite the quite different cultural setting. The same themes are there, universal themes of parent and child relationship. Parental ambition for their children comes through very powerfully, confirming some of our preconceptions about Japanese cultures, although we can easily recognise these scenarios as applying in our experience or in our own context. A surprising insight comes from the case of two of the students whose parents encourage them *not* to go to *juku* because it gives them a false sense of achievement.

We find at one level a recognition by students of parental influence and a gratitude for their concern but this is overlaid by a frustration and irritation that is seen as nagging. These young people resent the 'benchmarking' of their achievements against those of their brothers or sisters and want to be treated as individuals and allowed to develop in their own way. In Rie's case the decision to leave the *juku*, promoted by her parents, leads her to find a new motivation and a learning style which suits her best.

This is a very important chapter in its unravelling of one of the complexities of parental 'involvement' which tends to be treated so superficially by policy-makers and politicians.

Three German students

Ulf

Role model

Ulf's parents said that while they tried to motivate their son, they certainly had no influence on his grades. Ulf said that his parents did indeed have an effect on his motivation. He thought that they had expectations of him and he did not want to let them down.

Homework

Ulf's parents wrote that their son was old enough to work alone on his homework. Ulf said that he did his homework because if he did not do it he would not achieve all his goals. When asked whether he would like his parents to participate in his homework, he said that it would probably be very good but he knew that his parents had no time for this because they both worked so hard and he understood and respected that and made allowance for it.

Special support

This was the first case in which money occurred as a possible motivational factor. The parents answered in the questionnaire that they rewarded their son for achieving good grades. While Ulf commented that this was a motivational factor for him too, it was definitely not the major one. He said that it was not necessary and that he would work equally hard without that incentive.

Conversations

The parents said that they try to talk to their son regularly and Ulf said that he found this very helpful. He said that his parents' support was beneficial and that he appreciated it a lot.

Pressure

Ulf's parents did not think that pressure was necessary for their son to achieve. However, Ulf did mention in the interview that he felt a bit of pressure from his parents although this was not a negative thing. He said that this did not have so much influence on him because he worked for his own sake.

Decisions

The parents wrote that they would respect all their son's decisions as long as they were the same as his interests.

Expectations and goals

Ulf's parents had very modest expectations. They said that they wanted their son to achieve his best. Ulf himself, in his interview, was much clearer about his goals and what he wanted for himself. He wanted to complete high school then to go to university to study further. He thought that those were quite high goals but he had enough courage to achieve them. He said again that his parents were a big motivational factor for him. He mentioned that they were not very wealthy and he wanted to achieve more than they did. His parents wanted the best for him and he did not want to disappoint them.

Conclusion

Ulf was very concerned about the family situation. He saw how important it was to study hard and to achieve a high level of education in order to have a secure future. His parents' ambitions for him were to be the best he could be, which for him was to achieve more than they had done by going on to university and further study. We see Ulf as very self-driven with high goals for himself but attributing these to the influence and support of his mother and father.

Hans

Role model

Hans' parents said that they were an important influence on their son's motivation and grades. However, Hans said that his parents had very little influence on either his motivation or grades.

Homework

Hans' parents mentioned in the questionnaire that they still had to tell their son to do his homework. While Hans confirmed this, he could not say if it was good or not for him. He commented that sometimes it was useful but sometimes it became annoying. He did add, though, that he found it good when his parents helped him with difficult homework.

Conversations

Hans' parents said that they always spoke with their son when it was needed or when he wanted to discuss something. Hans fully confirmed his parents' comments. He said that they spoke at home when problems arose that needed to be discussed. He did not find this particularly motivating. It was just 'natural.'

Pressure

Hans' parents thought there was enough pressure put on their son to achieve success. Hans did not perceive it as 'pressure'. He knew that his parents had certain expectations but would not call it pressure. To meet these expectations was, for him, one among other motivational factors.

Decisions

Hans' parents wrote that their son was old enough to make his own decisions. Hans added that he usually asked his parents for advice and that they would give him both the positive and negative sides of the story. Then it was just up to him to decide.

Expectations and goals

Hans' parents wanted their son to achieve everything he could as long as his motivation and abilities were sufficient. They would support their son to achieve this by building trust in one another. Hans had more concrete goals, saying that he would like to continue studying and maintain good grades. He thought that his goals were in line with his parents' expectations.

Conclusion

Hans stated that his parents gave him very little motivation and that he did everything for himself but it is evident that his parents gave him a lot of space to make his own decisions and go his own way. They discussed problems only when required. They gave him advice and showed him both sides of a problem when he was about to make a decision. Hans appreciated this and it is clearly a factor in his confidence and motivation to reach his goals.

Gaby

Role model

In this case the student disagreed with her parents. The parents answered in the questionnaire that they had a great influence on their daughter, both on her grades and motivation whereas Gaby stated that her parents had no effect on her motivation or grades. She explained that she had her own life and that she did not think parents should interfere too much.

Homework

The parents wrote in the questionnaire that they did not force their daughter to do her homework and that their daughter knew what she had to do. Gaby agreed with this and added that she did her homework alone, without being told. The motivation to do it came naturally, according to her.

Conversations

Gaby's parents mentioned that they tried to talk to their daughter daily after school, if possible. Gaby confirmed this but was not sure if it was either useful or positive for her. She said that it often became annoying, negative and de-motivating.

Pressure

The parents clearly stated that they did not agree with putting any pressure on their daughter and that it was not the right way to success. Gaby obviously resented being under control or pressure. She did not like too much discussion with her parents and she also said that she had her own life and nobody should interfere.

Decisions

Gaby's parents answered in the questionnaire that they would support their daughter's decisions as long as they considered the decision was well thought through and reasonable. Gaby said there had not been any disagreement so far and that her parents respected all her decisions.

Expectations and goals

Both the parents' expectations and the student's goals were the same: to pass the final exams then build a career. According to the parents, this was their daughter's decision which they respected and helped her to achieve.

Conclusion

This student decided what she wanted to do in her career and everything she did was aimed towards this goal. Her parents were not a motivating factor for her, as she liked going her own way without anybody interfering, despite the fact that her parents thought of themselves as motivating. The fact that her parents supported her and gave her a high degree of autonomy may be seen as laying the groundwork for Gaby's motivation.

Japanese students

Kayo

Kayo's parents responded that their son's motivation to learn was not affected by them at all now. In the interview, Kayo also admitted that his parents did not directly affect his motivation to learn. He mentioned that what made him want to learn was just what he felt would be interesting and enjoyable. However, we also found out that his parents' subtle daily comments could significantly motivate him to learn, at least temporarily.

Homework and grades

Kayo's parents mentioned that his mother checked whether he did his homework or not because she thought that establishing the habit or practice of completing all school work would be advantageous in various aspects of later life. However, Kayo commented that it depended on how you asked, 'how could he be motivated to do his homework?' If his mother repeatedly asked and nagged him to do his homework, he lost motivation and did not feel like learning. On the other hand, if his mother reminded him a little, it encouraged his motivation because he could listen rationally and appreciate her advice.

This was also the case with school grades. Kayo explained that if his parents encouraged him slightly to make an effort in the subject in which he got a bad marks, he felt that he had to. But too much energetic encouragement did not work, because even without it, he realised that he had to improve in the subject, and such nagging did not actually increase his motivation.

Expectation and pressure

It could be seen from the questionnaire that his parents thought that they did not put any pressure on their son. On the other hand, Kayo commented that they sometimes compared him to his sister who got better grades than he did. This worked on him in a negative way, and he did not feel like learning at all. However, his parents did not normally compare them, because they had the policy of 'one was one'. So, he ignored the pressure because he regarded his learning as his own business.

With regard to their expectations of Kayo, his parents said that they expected him to have a dream and look for a favourite thing that he would be absorbed in doing. They explained that setting goals and enjoying the process of reaching them would ensure effort was put in. He was not actually aware of these expectations, but as mentioned above, his opinion that what made him want to learn in the final analysis was just what he felt interesting and enjoyable, and it corresponded with his family's expectations.

Respect

In the questionnaire, Kayo's parents answered that they respected his education and future decisions. They regarded his ability to make decisions as useful in enabling him to overcome problems when he faced them in future. He in turn felt comfortable with their attitude, which was to tell him to do what he wanted, and doing what he himself wanted was the best environment for him to learn.

Miki

Pressure and expectation

In the questionnaire, Miki's parents responded that they did not put any pressure on their child. However, Miki answered that she did feel quite a lot of pressure from her parents as they compared her with her brothers. Her brother who was not as good as her at studies was involved in entrance examinations for university. Her mother often told her that she should be aiming to go to a more prestigious university than her brother.

The questionnaire also revealed that Miki's parents expected her to get into a high profile university, as they believed that by being educated at as high a level as possible she would develop herself to the full. Miki knew of this expectation because her mother did tell her to aim for a high level of university education.

Miki mentioned that she worked hard because she did not want to disappoint her mother by not studying. She was not really happy with that feeling but she did not dislike it either.

Homework and grades

Miki's parents thought that they affected Miki's grades. However, she denied this and said that they did not affect her performance. She felt irritated when her parents complained about her grades because she felt the way they complained sounded angry. She wondered why her mother wanted to interfere with her grades when this was her own problem.

Respect

Miki's parents indicated that they respected her decisions but they still regarded her as immature and so advised her about university and work in the future. With regard to this advice, Miki mentioned that sometimes her mother criticised the job she was interested in. This was mainly because her mother objected to her only receiving a small salary. However, Miki's view was that she would only consider things that she wanted to do irrespective of what her mother said. Therefore she would be content once she had determined what she wanted to do in her future, and her parents would then just have to respect her decision.

Help

Miki was grateful for her parents' help in her studying. This ranged from helping her to remember vocabulary for her exams to paying for *juku*. She felt it was very helpful but felt some guilt that she had to make an effort to try and achieve good results but in a way she could not fully understand why or how she got there.

Rie

Homework and grades

Rie said that her mother told her to study (including doing homework) at home every day. However, she did not feel like doing her homework, especially when her mother told her to.

With regard to her grades, her parents said that they influenced her grades. However, Rie denied this in the interview. When she got bad grades, her parents repeatedly encouraged her, by saying for example, 'Get a better mark next time'. This did motivate her to study for a better grade, but her motivation was often short term.

Pressure and expectation

In the questionnaire, the parents said that they put pressure on her. However, Rie answered that they used to put pressure on her, but not now. She explained that when she was young and got good marks, she felt pressure from her parents. However, as her marks dropped, as she got older, her parents started to complain. But then, as she explained, they grew tired of complaining as her grades did not rise, no matter how hard they pressured her. So they gave up applying pressure.

Comparison

In the interview with Rie we found that her parents often compared her with her friends with regard to how much she studied at home. She felt uncomfortable with this and said she hated being compared. Rie's mother had her own standard, which was that her daughter had to go to a prestigious university. This standard, or value sense, was different from Rie's aspiration. Because of this difference Rie did not listen to her parents and in her view her parents had no effect on her motivation to learn. On the other hand, she said that her standards might, in fact, be affected by her mother and though she did not want to admit it there was perhaps an unconscious effect.

Respect

With regard to education and future decisions, Rie's parents said that they wanted to respect her decisions if she examined them and thought about them deeply. However, they expected her to make choices about her future, which would afford her feelings of achievement and fulfilment. Rie said that her parents were very curious about which university she wanted to go to, and often asked about it. They usually told her to go to a prestigious national university, or into employment, but not to go to a low prestige university. However, for herself she was not interested in university and had not decided on any goals or plans for her future. Therefore, no matter how hard her parents insisted on her attending university, it did not affect her motivation to learn at all, because she had no intention of going to university and the discussion was a futile one.

Suggestion

In the interview, Rie she said she had just quit the *juku*. This was because her parents continued to tell her to quit because going to *juku* gave her a false sense of satisfaction, from simply studying very hard. After she changed her learning style from the *juku* cramming to learning by herself, she realised that she now felt more motivated to learn than she had before.

Saki

Homework and grades

Saki's parents said that they often told Saki to do homework because they thought she did not study very much and they wanted her to do this at least. Saki explained this even more definitively. She said she did not make any effort to improve her bad grades when she was in junior high school. Her parents even forced her to quit *juku* because they thought that by attending *juku* she was satisfied that she was studying and learning. She began to study at home but still her parents hassled her to study, even when she was actually doing so. Saki confessed that she would be more relaxed if her parents didn't force her to study. She believed it made no difference to her grades no matter how much her parents told her to do more work.

Pressure and expectation

Saki's parents said that their daughter did not feel any pressure from them. On the contrary, Saki responded that they put a considerable amount of pressure on her by telling her that she could achieve anything she wanted if she did her best. In the beginning she listened to this encouragement, was glad to hear it and felt motivated by it. However, as time passed, she thought it was not effective in motivating her to learn, as they began to ask too often and the encouragement became nagging which she ignored, making her parents' encouragement tactics ineffectual.

Comparison

Saki confessed that her parents were very aware of her friends' grades and asked about them. They used them to compare progress and so decide whether she should be working harder. She said that they expected her to get at least the same grades as her friends. Saki resented these comparisons, making her angry. She believed this was because she felt frustrated at the constant nagging despite her working to the best of her ability. She also commented that she did realise she was not very good at studying at all and knew about her own motivation to learn without her parents nagging and comparing her grades. On the other hand, she admitted that she could not stand it when people teased her about her grades, making her feel mediocre. This made her mad and it made her motivation increase because she wanted to be better than them.

Future plans

Saki's parents answered in the questionnaire that they had suggested various ideas to their daughter about her future because she had not come up with any concrete idea herself. Saki said, however, that she *had* decided what she wanted to do in the future but had not told her parents this. She said she had not done so because she would be embarrassed if they undermined her idea by saying that it would be impossible to achieve it. She was interested in music and wished to go to a music university but she did not tell her parents or expect their support because they did not know much about music university. Therefore it was not in her interests to tell them, especially because she was afraid of a negative response.

Conclusion

In summary, we see some very common features across all the studies telling us something about the child–parent relationship wherever you are, as well as how differently it is seen from different perspectives. Above all, it reminds us of just how important parents are.

21 Lifelong learning

How teachers and students saw it

Carla Soudien

As these two examples show, the concept of lifelong learning is one to which people bring their own interpretations and preconceptions. Does lifelong learning only begin when students have left school or is school an integral part of learning which starts at birth and continues into adulthood? Or is there a gap in learning for life? As these extracts show, it is not only seen differently from a student and teacher perspective but also in different cultural contexts. Provision for learning beyond schooling is illustrated through an example from Japan where learning is seen as permeating the community and for young and old alike.

Japan

This chapter looks at lifelong learning in a Japanese city from three perspectives: that of the students, the teacher and from a community perspective, describing the provision that is available for people to go on learning throughout their lives.

What students said about their learning

Most students interviewed said that they were positively influenced by what they learned in school. These students mentioned skills and situations that would, in some way or another, benefit them. Subjects like languages and social sciences were listed as being advantageous. Students felt that they picked up skills such as common sense and clear thinking and teamwork during their school careers, which they saw as vital for success in the 'real world'. Entrance exams and study skills were also highlighted as motivational factors at high school. Some students felt that learning how to study and getting good results were important too.

Those students who felt that school did not benefit them mostly mentioned subjects that they thought were irrelevant for their lives. One or two students also mentioned the fact that they had no plans to go to university and this therefore affected their judgement of what was worth learning.

When we started our research at Nara Women's University Secondary School we became aware that many students at the school took part in club activities.

These club activities seem to form a large part of the students' learning and are seen as crucial for most of them. Lots of time is spent taking part in these club activities and we therefore wanted to find out how and how much students learned from these. Many students mentioned the teamwork that was a feature of what they did in clubs. They said that this sort of cooperation among students would benefit them in the future. They highlighted the social aspect of club activities that they enjoyed as well as its contribution to the improvement of their communication skills.

We asked students about their views of the job market and what they thought they needed to succeed in the commercial world. Most felt it was necessary to have extra qualifications and get further experience when applying for a job. They thought that a part-time job or reading and research would contribute to their experience and ability to function in different environments. Computer literacy was highlighted as an important deciding factor when people are being selected for the majority of jobs. A few students listed confidence and clear and broad thinking skills as attributes of someone who would be likely to be hired by employers.

When the subject of lifelong learning was brought up, various students mentioned that they either had very little time for lifelong learning or they had found it too troublesome or time-consuming to pursue. Students typically thought that lifelong learning meant learning life skills. Students have very busy schedules that include club activities and, in my opinion, while these club activities do make for valuable life skills, these students perhaps just do not appreciate this yet.

At the end of the interview we asked students what extra things they would like to learn at school that would benefit them in later life. Quite a few students said that they valued the languages that they learned and that they would like to learn more in this line. Some students said they would appreciate more practical things like home economics, for example. One student mentioned that he would appreciate learning how to research and collect information.

Teacher interviews

Four teachers were interviewed at Nara Women's University Secondary School as to their personal views on lifelong learning. We also asked them how much lifelong learning was actually taking place in their opinion. The four teachers interviewed teach a very broad range of subjects and hopefully this allowed us to look at a range of different views and approaches to the concept as well as seeing if there was consensus on other issues. These teachers possibly see the same students but might see different aspects of these same students in their particular lessons or subject.

We asked teachers various questions that covered a range of issues including independence and also skills that students need and receive at school. In order to assess how *much* and what kind of lifelong learning was taking place within the school it was important for us to be as knowledgeable as possible, through observation, spot checks, listening and interviewing in order to arrive at some valid conclusions.

Does school prepare students for what life throws at them? We put this question to teachers whose reply was that it did in fact prepare students for life. They all felt that NWUSS provides students with a very good grounding, a good set of basics that they need for life. Students acquire knowledge, learn how to collect information and problem-solve, all skills which, they said, form the basis of day-to-day life. Teachers felt that students who graduate from NWUSS were generally very independent, which is very encouraging news in a cultural context where many young people in Japan remain dependent on their parents until they have graduated from university. Although many students from NWUSS do, in fact, follow this route, teachers felt that their students were at least equipped with the necessary skills, which may not be the case with many other institutions within the country.

We discussed which skills teachers thought students acquired at school and a list was provided. The most common skills mentioned by teachers were the ability to develop clear and logical thinking, discussion and communication skills and creativity. A few teachers also mentioned that they thought students should learn more of life skills as well the ability to apply a critical appreciation of what they are learning.

The job market was also brought up and teachers were asked to mention skills that students acquire at NWUSS that would prepare them for the job market. For this question I received a relatively surprising answer from one of the teachers who said that students do not consider career opportunities, but concentrate solely on their university entrance exams. While it was said that NWUSS does equip students for the job market, most students do not know how and when to use the relevant skills appropriately. Almost every student in the school is computer literate which is, of course, a vital skill for the job market as it is. Teachers also mentioned that this situation might be different from the rest of Japan.

In every country we visited, lifelong learning is incorporated into lessons in very different ways. Some teachers incorporate it into their lessons consciously, others just a little bit and others not consciously at all. One teacher mentioned that she did not teach lifelong learning consciously but that students learn these skills naturally. This teacher tries to teach her students some discipline, however, using the Japanese principle of *shitsuke*, which involves respect for others and your elders. One teacher said that she encouraged students to learn things by understanding and not by memorising what they are reading and listening to. She would also like to see students gathering more information for themselves and also not being afraid to make mistakes and to be confident about themselves. The Home Economics teacher would like students to learn more practical skills, which she feels are essential. This Home Economics programme might in fact be cut by the government in the near future, which, she thought, was totally unacceptable.

Finally, I asked each teacher about their own personal view of the concept of lifelong learning. Interestingly enough, all four answers for me almost perfectly define the concept:

- people thinking about things for themselves;
- living life to the fullest;
- learning and studying about things which interest you for your whole life.

For these things to happen successfully, said one teacher, this process needs to begin while students are in school and learning, then it will become easier and more engaging. One teacher said that she thought that the only way to solve the problems of the world was for people to learn constantly and the country should therefore provide more opportunities for people to be learning throughout their whole lives.

Lifelong learning in the community

Visits to Shiyakisho and Nara City Life-Long Learning Centre

We visited two places, namely, the Shiyakusho, which is the city public office, and the Nara City Life-Long Learning Centre. At both places people were very willing to help us and offered us a wealth of information which has given us quite a good view of the state of lifelong learning in the Nara City Community.

We visited the Shiyakusho first and there we spoke to somebody about the structure of public learning centres within Nara and how they operate as well as what is available at the office we visited. The building we were visiting is responsible for twenty-one public buildings in Nara and is also responsible for what these buildings are used for. At the Shiyakusho building various courses are available, with the majority of people attending these courses being over 50 years old. Courses like computing are very popular, however, only a limited number of people may attend. For the more popular courses, it is not unusual for the number of applicants to be almost triple the number of places available. The courses offered are free and therefore available to everyone.

Also available in each of the twenty-one buildings is an information computer system, called Nara-otto, which makes information on activities available at the twenty-one buildings as well as within the community. The computer programme can pinpoint places that 'will be suitable for any particular need' as well as provide a detailed list of courses or programmes available. Contact details are also provided. The programme is easy to use and I am sure has proven useful for many people seeking advice on particular interests.

The second place we visited was the Nara City Life-Long Learning Centre, which was opened in November 1999 and established by the Japanese Ministry of Education. The centre works in cooperation with influential institutions and makes joint plans and programmes regarding lifelong learning with them. The centre is only five months old and is therefore in perfect condition and is extremely well equipped. This centre holds the server computer for Nara-otto and is therefore the base of lifelong learning and what is available in the Nara community. This centre also runs courses and makes its facilities available to groups needing a venue for various things as well.

The centre operates on the principle of providing courses that are appropriate for real-life circumstances and also provides specialists of various kinds. One of its main aims is to ensure that the demand for learning is met and that research can be carried out. Besides being very new, this place is also unbelievably well equipped and is perfect for the promotion of lifelong learning in various forms. This centre is used extensively by people over 50, but is also used by younger people including school students making use of the remarkable facilities. Some twenty-three rooms are available for use by everyone and may be used free.

There are more than seventy-six courses available at the centre, ranging from basic computing to classical ballet lessons and cooking for men, with the most popular being basic computing. The person we spoke to at the centre said that this computing course is very popular with people over 50 who are eager to become computer literate. At the moment, only forty computer lessons take place a year, but the centre has plans to introduce more courses since they are so popular. A similar situation has arisen at the Life-long Learning Centre as at the Shiyakusho, where the number of applicants far exceeds the places available for various popular courses.

Besides the courses available, the centre also makes its facilities available to groups who would like to practise, do some crafts or have seminars. A fully equipped pottery studio is available for use.

Conclusion

When looking at lifelong learning within Nara Women's University Secondary School and within the Nara City Community, we found that learning in general is very important for people. At NWUSS it is almost assumed that most students will go on to university and will be successful in what they do, and all the necessary measures are in place to ensure that students make informed choices in this respect. The University Guidance Room and the homeroom teachers jointly provide students with a good idea of what is available to them in terms of universities and courses available at the various institutions. Students are very motivated to succeed and spend a great amount of time studying and doing homework. When asked what their opinion of lifelong learning was, both students and teachers said success at university and then continuing formal study for the rest of your life.

An important and interesting aspect of my research was my visit to the Nara City Life-long Learning Centre. There I found a facility which is extremely accessible to a large section of the community and which offers a remarkable set of opportunities for people, free of charge. People can pick up skills and do things that they find interesting, and are learning constantly; this to me epitomises the concept of lifelong learning.

At Nara Women's University Secondary School, club activities form a large part of many students' day. Some students spend up to three or four hours a day taking part in these club activities and value the time spent doing them. For me, this is an important aspect of lifelong learning as well, especially within the Japanese cultural context. Students are given the opportunity to socialise with their peers while picking up skills, both practical and social. Very few lifelong learning daily skills are, however, incorporated into lessons at NWUSS. Many lessons take place without discussion and because of the large amounts of material needed to be covered, teachers do not have time to cover daily skills as much as necessary. Students are under so much pressure to do well academically that there is little or no time apart from that allocated for club activities to socialise with friends. These activities compensate by offering students with enjoyment as well as providing many different skills that will benefit them greatly in many aspects of later life.

Although many students take part in club activities and also pick up various skills at school, which will gear them for independence, it has become apparent to me that the usual situation in Japan is for young people to be dependent on their parents until they have graduated from university. While young people in many other countries would feel ready to leave home and maybe live on their own, this is not the case in Japan, or not within the Nara Community at least. Another contributory factor would be the number of really good universities in Nara or really close to Nara – Kobe, Osaka or Kyoto.

People in this community are provided with the means to continue learning and it is evident that many people make full use of the opportunities made available to them. People are willing to learn and those who have time, many older people, start courses or hobbies in order to enrich themselves socially and academically. If people want to learn there is very good access to information and facilities, so people just need to make the effort to use them.

South Africa

We interviewed four teachers at Harold Cressy High School. Each interview was short and the teachers all responded quite readily and enthusiastically. We also interviewed ten students, two of whom are in Grade 10, one in Grade 12 and seven in Grade 11. Most students interviewed were quite willing to be interviewed and answered as best they could.

Teacher and student interviews

We asked: 'What do you think when you hear the term lifelong learning?' 'Learning from birth to death' was mentioned by one teacher who also said that people should accept everything they do as a learning experience. 'Learning throughout your life' was mentioned by another member of staff, adding 'continually studying and learning but not necessarily in an institution'. Another teacher said, 'People should be prepared to learn in various ways and pick up little skills which they will carry with them for the rest of their lives, things which they will not necessarily learn in school.'

One teacher seemed to be overwhelmed by the concept and thought that people should take a break in life just to relax. This teacher was obviously under the impression that lifelong learning refers only to formal learning taking place in an institution.

Students gave the following answers to the same question:

> You can never stop learning.
> You learn for the rest of your life.
> Learning and remembering what you learning.
> Never too young to learn . . . to learn things every day.
> To continue learning new things every day.

Do you think what students learn in school prepares them for life after school?

Many of the teachers interviewed indicated that they thought that the subject matter prescribed in school was irrelevant. 'Students are not sufficiently prepared to enter a technologically advanced world because the resources available at school are not up-to-date.' Teachers also said that students are spoon-fed and that they need to do more of their own research and take more initiative more often. Because of the above, they argued that students are not able to meet many of the personal challenges which they are faced with.

A few teachers also mentioned that students find great difficulty linking what they learn in school to what they are faced with later. The curriculum is also not very well geared for this transition. In the curriculum so much emphasis is put on the academic aspect that the life skills aspect is often neglected.

Although teachers did agree that certain subject matters are essential for students at university or during other tertiary study, they were all in agreement that real 'hands on' learning takes place outside of school.

Five students responded positively and five responded negatively to this question. Those that responded positively said that they learned to communicate with other people at school. They felt that they needed subjects for university and also basics which they need to get started. One student indicated that he helped with the sports and drama organisation in the school and this would help him later in life almost as much as the formal lessons.

Many of the students who answered negatively said that the subject matter was irrelevant. Theys said that they were not given enough individual work and that they were spoon-fed at school which would prove to be a disadvantage later. They felt that they were not sufficiently being prepared at school at all.

Skills

We asked the teachers: Which of the following skills do you think students learn in your classes?

Common sense, project work, teamwork, computer literacy, clear thinking, discussion skills, numeracy, problem solving, writing ability, how to present yourself.

The English teacher said that she encouraged critical thinking in her classes, and some of the other teachers also indicated that their classes offered their students some sort of grounding in common sense. Teachers generally said they try to encourage interaction and group research is also used in some teachers' classes. Only one teacher said he taught computer literacy in his class and this was a teacher of a formal computer class which is available to students in the lower grades only.

The History teacher uses debate to encourage logical, reasoned answers and questions, these debates and discussions being designed to improve discussion skills as well. This teacher also felt that these debates offered the opportunity for problem solving.

The English teacher thinks that her students encounter real-life situations in English literature and that students therefore have to sort out these issues, this therefore being a form of problem solving, while her students are also required to formulate their own creative ideas and put those to paper.

Most students said quite definitely that they thought they learned common sense in English classes. Many also said that project teamwork takes place quite often, one student citing his work on a class production. Students said that they learned numeracy in Maths and discussion skills in most of their subjects. Students also believed that that the oral presentations that they did in class also helped in preparing them in presenting themselves.

In which ways do you teach daily skills? Which classroom methods contribute the most to lifelong learning?

The History teacher mentioned that she tried to act as a facilitator and not create a 'teacher-centred' environment. She said that she welcomed students' points of view and encouraged them to provide criticism to her views and prejudices. She hoped that this approach would encourage students to be more open-minded.

Three of the four teachers indicated that they tried to incorporate lifelong learning into all of their lessons and all aspects of the lessons. The Biology and Computer teacher said that he used real-life situations in his lessons to teach life skills. One teacher said that she did not consciously incorporate life skills into her lesson but she did see that these often creep into her subscribed subject matter.

Students once again mentioned the importance of the language lessons which they value because they are able to be creative as well as imaginative during these periods. Some students also mentioned that when classes were smaller, the relationship skills which they pick up, would contribute as a positive factor to their further learning. Most students said that they were computer literate, but these skills they had picked up either at home or private courses and not at school.

Do you think your students are prepared for the job market as it is, where students need: good communication, and to be creative, numerate, computer literate, team players?

Despite their own efforts to incorporate life skills into their lessons, these three teachers answered this question with a definite 'no'. These teachers were very negative on this subject. They said that their students' communication and especially linguistic skills were pathetic. Tolerance levels are very low and students therefore consider peer interaction as problematic. In order for students to develop these skills they would have to become involved in other things after school. They would need to get involved with activities which would supplement the things which they learned in school. One teacher felt that work-shadowing should be introduced and that students should receive more guidance regarding this aspect of their future. It was felt that students should read more but because motivation levels were low, students did not see literature as having any appeal.

Most students said that they did not have a job presently but one or two mentioned holiday jobs which they had had previously. Various important skills which they had picked up were highlighted by these students. They mentioned that they had learned to work with and speak to people and also how to make important choices and decisions. They picked up communication skills, tolerance and also, importantly, to be part of a team and therefore cooperation.

How does the pace of the senior grades affect the amount of lifelong learning taking place?

'We don't spend enough time on daily skills' and 'Disastrous in Maths' were just two of the comments made by teachers in response to this question. It was said that many teachers neglect this aspect because they assume that students are old enough and that enough time has been spent on this aspect of schooling. This, however, has proved to be a false impression. The content load is too great and students are sort of encouraged to draw from all the other things they usually do outside school. However, they are not given enough exposure to real-life situations, said teachers, because their schedule is too academically intense.

When guidance was still incorporated into the timetable, these periods were used by teachers to catch up on work and were seldom used for real guidance.

Are students prepared to leave school and be independent at the end of their high school years?

Two teachers said that this was very individual and varied a great deal from student to student. People tend to like the protection which school provides.

Some students couldn't cope with doing research on their own or managing their own learning. One teacher said that her students were definitely not prepared and do not think open-mindedly enough to survive in the 'real world'. The History teacher indicated that her students wanted to be independent but because of financial issues they could not afford to be completely independent of their parents.

Are there any other things you would like to learn at school that you think would benefit you in later life?

All the students who were interviewed mentioned one or two subjects or courses which they thought would be beneficial to their future. These courses are obviously not available at Cressy due to many restrictions experienced, financial and resource based. Students mentioned politics, management, home economics and computer programming. They also said that they would like the opportunity to learn more foreign languages, French, Italian and Arabic.

22 Postscript

John MacBeath

In June 2002 eighteen students arrived in Cambridge to report on the further adventures of Learning School 3. They arrived from Japan late on Wednesday evening and having presented their findings, left on Thursday afternoon for Zlin in the Czech Republic for the final international meeting of the Global Classroom and the Learning School.

Those who were present at the Cambridge seminar described it variously as 'astonishing', 'ground breaking' and 'deeply moving'. It would have been impossible to have been unmoved by the students' graphic descriptions of life in a South African township, the warmth and generosity of people defined not by what they had (nothing) but what they were (everything). It would have been impossible to be unmoved by their accounts of the juxtaposition of corrugated shacks with the grandeur of the Olympic stadia, travelling daily between the extreme poverty of township people and the affluence of the white and 'coloured' South Africans. They discovered how unique their insights were into these two worlds when they were told by white South Africans that, despite living in Cape Town all their lives, they had never ventured into the townships. As one student said: 'It took us, students, from Shetland and Sweden and Germany to tell them what life was like in their own back yard.'

They found themselves doing an educational job with white and 'coloured' South Africans whose knowledge vacuum was filled with racist stereotypes but often had to admit defeat because, as one student said: 'They still only see what they want to see.'

A German girl spoke powerfully of living with a Korean family who spoke not a word of English or German but, nonetheless, they came to be so close to one another that language and cultural barriers were dissolved. Like LS1 and LS2 students before them, they spoke of how deeply their lives and thinking had been changed by the experience of different cultures, different mores, different expectations, different schools. A Korean student told us how, for the first time in his life, at the age of 17, he had learned how to discuss. In all his school life no teacher had ever promoted discussion and it took him months of living with the Learning School to learn how to express his own view and listen to the views of others. He also described eight hours every day of intensive after-school study, as passionate commitment to achievement with the reflective, critical self-evaluation skills that, he discovered in this project, were the marks of an effective learner. A Hong Kong student said that it was only after this year that she had come to see learning 'not as a duty but as an opportunity'.

The self-evaluating student was the focus of Learning School 3's research and the results they presented would have done credit to the most prestigious of researchers. Their definition, from their final report is concise and instructive:

> Self-evaluation is the process taken by an individual to reflect on learning by looking at a past activity and to look at the (non-)reflecting quality of that process and how it could be improved.

> The basis of self-evaluation is knowing oneself, from which can come an understanding of oneself and one's learning. More specifically, understanding one's personality and capabilities can lead to an understanding of one's strengths, weaknesses and preferences in his/her learning. Placing the knowledge of one's self in the context of learning, however, is not enough for complete self-evaluation. A learner must also be able to use this knowledge to develop.

> Self-evaluation should be differentiated from assessment. The two are commonly confused. In assessment, criteria are set by an external body, such as a government, education department, school, or teacher. In evaluation, criteria are set by the individual based on what one understands about his/her learning. Self-based criteria for learning are important because they enable learners to engage in learning improvement. Learners can do this four main ways. Firstly, it enables ownership and control of their learning. Secondly, creating one's own criteria forces the learner to understand the reasons why they learn. Thirdly, self-based criteria inspire the learner to discover their internal motivation. Lastly, the process of creating one's own learning criteria can lead to a greater sense of learning responsibility.

Through questionnaires, shadowing, spot checks, interviews, their research was able not only to identify the profile of a self-evaluating learner but also to show the extent to which students in different school systems met or fell short of that ideal. In LS3 interviews with school staff they heard the same refrain from teacher after teacher, paraphrased by one student in these words: 'We are too busy teaching to give time to think about learning.' This is less a reflection on teachers than on the system in which they work. From Japan to Scotland all seem to be under the spell of the global agenda, the competitive pressure to achieve. But if we ever needed reminding of the superficiality and ephemeral nature of so much of school learning, the three incarnations of the Learning School have brought that back starkly to our attention. Korea, top of the world league table in the latest OECD study, owing that position to a culture of hard work but conspicuously not smart work. Likewise the other Pacific Tigers,

Hong Kong and Japan, equally with an achievement culture but short on the reflective and evaluative qualities that make for good students, thinking employees and employers, creative global citizens.

After three years of the Learning School, what have we learned about learning? What do we know about self-evaluation that we didn't know before? What have these successive studies taught us about the nature of schooling? About culture and how it shapes perceptions, motivation and achievement?

In a sense what schools experienced was less a 'self' evaluation than an external evaluation by a visiting team. The experience was, in some ways, closer to an HMI visit than the internal self-initiated ongoing process of reflection. However, it is the unique features of this experiment in evaluation that distance it from 'inspection' and offer important lessons to schools embarking on, or enhancing, the process of their own self-evaluation. There are a number of distinctive elements which bridge the gap between internal and external evaluation. These are:

- *Time.* The Learning School teams spent between four and six weeks in each of the schools. This gave an extended period for students to get to know the school, for the school to get to know them, to develop a sense of trust and reciprocity.
- *Collegiality.* Being students themselves it was much easier to get alongside their peers, to hear the unvarnished truth without fear of recrimination or reprisal.
- *Context.* Staying with host families for four or more weeks helped students to gain a feel for the culture, to get an insight into adult–child relationships, to see family and community life at first hand.
- *Checking out.* Students did not rush to conclusions nor produce a definitive grade on the basis of a short observation but talked through their findings, checking out with students and teachers what they were observing, refining their own understanding and judgement.
- *Feedback.* Learning School students fed back their findings, sometimes to the whole staff, sometimes to wider stakeholder groups, not in a spirit of judgement but tentatively in the spirit of arriving at a shared understanding.
- *Tools.* The process and techniques of evaluation used by LS students all provided schools with tools that they could use for themselves. Therefore it became for the participating schools a capacity-building exercise.
- *Learning.* The LS students were not there as inspectors or judges but as learners, not with long years of expertise and self-confidence behind them but as neophytes with no claim to authority except as co-learners.

Most of all perhaps their focus was on the student, on learning and motivation, on self-evaluation as something that occurs in the minds and hearts of students rather than some mechanistic dreary time-consuming bi-annual event. OFSTED has much to learn from these students, from the deep reflective nature of their work. 'Rigorous' is a word beloved of the OFSTED regime and a word that has passed from incumbent to incumbent of that office and been taken up with gusto by the present tenant of that high office.

We have also to thank these students for helping us to gain closer insights into the nature of schooling and the nature of classroom learning. There is much to confirm what we already know but there is as well a strong challenge to so much of conventional wisdom. We may now, hopefully, approach international and national league tables of achievement with a greater degree of healthy scepticism.

The importance of culture shines through every page. The problematic relationship between teaching and learning is a continuous strand. We see how much of learning is individual and how much of it is social. We discover anew how motivation and achievement are shaped by peers, both positively and negatively. And we are reminded of the influence of teachers – neutral, negative and positive – and how different their impact can be for different students. As spot checks, shadowing, questionnaires and interviewing show, perceptions of the same situation can be dramatically different depending on where you stand, or sit. And we are shown again, through their own testimonies, how children's and parents' assessments of their relationship can be so out of step with another.

For inspection, for school improvement, for self-evaluation, for leadership, for the growing industry in student voice there is a rich vein of learning here to be tapped. As Learning School 4 embarks on its world journey with an expanded group of schools eager to be involved, we live in hope that the powers to be will sit up, take notice, and learn something themselves.

Bibliography

Brink, A. (1982) *A Chain of Voices*, London: Faber and Faber.

Claxton, G. (2000) *The Intuitive Practitioner: On the Value of Not Always Knowing What One is Doing*, Milton Keynes: Open University Press.

Csikzentimihalyi, M. (1998) *Talented Teenagers*, Cambridge, UK: Cambridge University Press.

Edmonds, D. and Eidenow, J. (2001) *Wittgenstein's Poker: The Story of a Ten-minute Argument between Two Great Philosophers*, London: Faber.

MacBeath, J. (1999) *Schools Must Speak for Themselves*, London: Routledge.

OECD (2001) *Knowledge and Skills for Life: First Results from PISA 2000*, Paris: OECD.

Perkins, D. (1995) *Smart Schools*, New York: Free Press.

Rudduck, J. Chaplain, R. and Wallace, G. (eds) (1996) *School Improvement: What Can Pupils Tell Us?*, London: David Fulton.

Woodhead, C. (2002) *Class War*, London: Little Brown.

Wragg, E.C., Haynes, G.S., Wragg, C.M. and Chamberlin, R.P. (2000) *Failing Teachers?*, London: RoutledgeFalmer.

Yi, J-T. *et al.* (2000) *On the Reality and Causes of the School Education Crisis*, Seoul: Korea Educational Development Institute.

Zimmerman, B.J., Dale, H. and Schunk, B.J. (1994) *Self-regulation of Learning and Performance: Issues and Educational Applications*, Hillsdale, NJ: Lawrence Erlbaum Associates.

Index